STEP BY STEP

STEP BY STEP

AN INTRODUCTION TO CONDUCTING RESEARCH IN CRIMINOLOGY AND CRIMINAL JUSTICE

FIRST EDITION

Edited by Lindsey Vigesaa, PhD

cognella®

SAN DIEGO

Bassim Hamadeh, CEO and Publisher
Mieka Portier, Senior Acquisitions Editor
Tony Paese, Project Editor
Celeste Paed, Associate Production Editor
Abbie Goveia, Graphic Design Assistant
Greg Isales, Licensing Coordinator
Natalie Piccotti, Director of Marketing
Kassie Graves, Senior Vice President of Editorial
Jamie Giganti, Director of Academic Publishing

cognella® | ACADEMIC PUBLISHING
3970 Sorrento Valley Blvd., Ste. 500, San Diego, CA 92121

CONTENTS

INTRODUCTION

As a student or practitioner completing a degree and/or working in the field, you may feel apprehensive about taking a research methods class or the prospect of engaging in research. I have felt your pain. As an undergraduate student I had similar concerns, which intensified after being informed by upper-level classmates about the extremely difficult research courses required for completing our major. For a couple of years I dreaded the thought of having to take these courses and wondered why students majoring in the social and behavioral sciences were required to learn about research. These types of courses should be reserved for those who aspire to work in laboratories and wear white jackets, right?

After a couple of weeks of being enrolled in my first research methods course, I wondered why there was so much fear surrounding this subject. Although discouraged by the dull, encyclopedia-like textbook my instructor had selected, I spent a lot of time combing through the material and working hard to understand the concepts and apply them in a way that made them interesting. Once applied to a topic I was fascinated with, the research process became very interesting, and even fun! From that point on, I envisioned developing a textbook that would inspire others to enjoy learning more about research, the research process, and the importance of research. It is my hope that this book makes you excited about (or at least able to tolerate the thought of) research.

Research as a subject matter, and the process of conducting research, may be intimidating. The purpose of this book is to provide an introduction to research and the research process within the disciplines of criminology and criminal justice and to provide material, resources, and exercises that will enable readers to become active producers and consumers of research. This book was designed to be a valuable introductory guide and reference for many different audiences, including students, practitioners, and anyone interested in learning more about conducting research. Additional important related topics highlighted include ethical considerations, artificial intelligence–related technological advancements, and partnerships between researchers and practitioners. The content and exercises offered within each chapter build on one another, and when completed will result in a research proposal and/or executed research project.

This book is an anthology, which means that the articles selected for each chapter have been written by different authors. The editor has arranged 9 chapters that contain 19 articles, which were selected and organized to provide readers with a strong foundation for understanding the value and importance of research and the research process from start to finish. Each chapter begins with an introduction to chapter content and ends with a conclusion summarizing the key take-aways from each of the selected articles. The end of each chapter provides a list of reflection questions and an exercise designed to facilitate the application of material. These features are labeled "Building Your Research Proposal" in chapters 1-6, "Executing the Research" in chapters 7–8, and "Writing Your Research Proposal/Paper" in chapter 9. These exercises were purposefully designed to assist readers with the process of building their own research proposal and/or executing a research study. The completion of each of these activities will collectively result in the development of a research proposal (which may become a fully executed research project) that aligns with the reader's personal and professional interests.

Summary of Chapter Content

The introductory chapter (chapter 1) features Withrow's article, "The Research Practice." This selection provides an introduction to the foundational elements of research methods in criminology and criminal justice while addressing several important questions, including (1) What is research? (2) Why do research? (3) Who does research? (4) What are the different types of research? (5) Where is research found? and (6) When is research important? Because research in criminology, victimology, and criminal justice commonly involves gathering information from people or using existing records or information that contain sensitive information to answer research questions, chapter 2 summarizes several vitally important ethical issues that must be considered and addressed to protect human subjects from any potential harm related to the research process. Next, Crookes discusses ethical concerns related to the use of artificial intelligence (AI) as a method to assist with or inform various facets of policing. One of the reflection questions at the end of this chapter invites the reader to conduct some independent research to identify how AI is being used (or may be used) elsewhere in the criminal justice system and invites the reader to identify some ethical concerns associated with these applications.

Chapter 3 provides vital information specific to the process of conducting research. Withrow's "The Research Process" introduces and discusses the research progression, step by step. This process begins with asking a research question and ends with communicating the findings and asking another question. This chapter will provide you with an easy-to-understand overview of the entire research process, while the Building Your Research Proposal exercise provided at the end of this chapter encourages you to explore and identify more concrete topics you may be interested in studying. The second article in this chapter, "The Vocabulary of Research" by Dantzker, Hunter, and Quinn introduces several additional terms/concepts that are discussed throughout this text, including the role of theory within research, conceptualization, operationalization, variables, and qualitative and quantitative research. It is recommended that you refer back to this chapter often as you progress through this text and continue to build your research proposal.

In chapter 4, Tompson, Belur, Morris and Tuffin discuss the value and importance of and present the process for developing relationships between researchers and law enforcement agencies. The formation and establishment of these partnerships hold multiple benefits for both entities. Agencies/organizations may benefit by working with external researchers to utilize existing agency data or produce data that is valuable for informing agency decisions. Researchers benefit by having access to data that may be used to support the development of papers and/or publications in their scholarly areas of interest. Although this chapter is specific to forming relationships between researchers and the police, the editor stresses the value of building mutual relationships between practitioners and researchers across various criminal justice and non-criminal justice–related organizations.

Chapter 5 by Paula Dawidowicz introduces an important step within the research process, conducting a literature review. Reviewing the literature includes locating, reading, summarizing, and meaningfully organizing research and related findings from studies that have already been conducted and published. The results of this work should be used to inform the development of and/or continued revision of your research question or hypothesis. The second article in this chapter, "Structuring the Literature Review," describes the types of information researchers should include within summaries of scholarly articles and provides excerpts of articles included within literature review sections from published scholarly papers.

Chapter 6 introduces research design and measurement. After a researcher has selected a topic, reviewed and summarized the literature, and refined the research question or hypothesis, a research design must be selected. Dantzker, Hunter, and Quinn's present basic elements of experimental and quasi-experimental research designs and summarize the four levels of measurement a variable may represent. The second selection continues this discussion by defining a research design as a "feasible plan" or "blueprint" for a research study, while recognizing that "one of the most important steps is choosing an appropriate research design." The authors identify and describe various research designs, including descriptive, historical, cross-sectional, longitudinal (trend, cohort, and panel) and case study, and discuss factors to consider when choosing the appropriate design for a study. Two additional articles by Jake Harwood within this chapter present examples of research that have been designed to measure a single variable, and one that measures multiple variables. These articles walk the reader through the research process using realistic scenarios. Readers are encouraged to use the information contained within these selections to inform the development of research designs, which may be used in individual research proposals or projects.

Chapter 7 presents various sources of information that may be used to collect data to answer a research question or hypothesis. The first article, "Collecting Primary Data," introduces methods a researcher may use to collect primary data (original data collected by the researcher), including interviews, questionnaires and surveys, observation, focus groups, experience, and experiments. The second article in this chapter by Withrow discusses unobtrusive methods for data collection such as utilizing data which have already been collected for other purposes, obtaining existing content from various sources, and engaging in field research.

After a researcher has gathered quantitative or qualitative data (or a combination of both), they must analyze that data. Chapter 8 presents information about data analysis and related techniques. All of the articles selected for this chapter were written by Lawrence T. Orcher; the first article discusses descriptive statistics, and the next two articles introduce correlational and inferential statistics. The final article in this chapter presents information specific to data analysis for qualitative research.

The final chapter of this book focuses on writing and formatting the final research proposal or report. Bayens and Roberson's "Writing Research Reports" provides information and suggestions for preparing to write a research report and introduces the "separate and distinct chapters of the research report," including the introduction, literature review, methodology, findings or results, and discussion sections.

Understanding that there is a lot of information contained within the nine chapters of this book, my challenge to you is this: Approach this text/course with optimism. Read each chapter carefully, highlight and take thoughtful notes, identify a topic for study that you are passionate about, and commit to completing the reflection questions and exercises at the end of each chapter. Think of the research process as a series of steps, like those of a staircase. It is important that you do not become overwhelmed by all of the steps that lie ahead, but that you focus on each step in front of you, one at a time. The completion of each step on the research proposal/project checklist moves you one step closer to the top of the staircase (completion of a research proposal or project). Be creative and excited about the possibilities that lie ahead!

Building Your Research Proposal/Project Checklist*

(Many steps are consistent with Withrow's "The Research Process" diagram).
___ Evaluate research interests (chapter 1)
___ Assess ethical considerations of research (chapter 2; this is an ongoing process)
___ Consider theoretical connections (chapter 3)**
___ Ask a research question (chapter 3)

___ Consider and explore researcher-agency partnerships (chapter 4)**
___ Conduct a literature review (chapter 5)
___ Refine the research question (chapter 5)
___ Define the concepts (chapter 6)
___ Create the measures (chapter 6)
___ Design a method (chapter 6; proposal ends here)
___ Collect the data (chapter 7; executing the research starts here)
___ Analyze the data (chapter 8)
___ Interpret the results (chapter 8)
___ Communicate the findings (chapter 9)
___ Ask another question (chapter 9)

*The *USC Libraries Research Guide* is an excellent source of supplemental information that will help guide you through the research process (https://libguides.usc.edu/writingguide).
**May occur earlier in the process.

An Introduction to Research Methods in Criminology and Criminal Justice

Introduction

Did you know that you are a researcher? You routinely gather information to inform decisions big and small. Is that new cell phone on the market worth the expense? Conduct an internet search to learn about phone features, read online reviews, and talk to others who have purchased that model to inform your decision. What nearby restaurant has the best pizza? Acquire online restaurant menus and customer reviews. How did you decide where to obtain a degree? Did you (1) access the webpages of various schools or programs, (2) visit campuses in person or virtually, (3) search online student reviews, (4) attend presentations led by campus representatives and/or current and former students or professors, (5) ask follow-up questions, and (6) evaluate pros and cons of attending each institution? You are a researcher! You conducted research to inform these decisions. In chapter 1, Withrow notes, "We all do research every day. We just do not call it research."

Research is important to the fields/disciplines of criminology and criminal justice for many reasons. Well-designed and executed research studies may test criminological theories, aid in the development of new theories of crime, and assess practices, policies, and programs within policing, courts, victimology, and corrections to determine whether they are effective or "work." These studies produce outcomes that may inform important decisions within the field. This chapter provides an introduction to research while addressing each of the following questions: *What* is research? *Why* do research? *Who* does research? *What* are the different types of research? *Where* is research found? *When* is research important?

The Research Practice

Brian L. Withrow

S o here you are in a research methods class. Hopefully, the email at the start of the book convinced you that this course will be valuable to you as a criminal justice practitioner or even just an everyday consumer of information. But what are research methods exactly? **Research methods** are basically the tools, techniques, and procedures that researchers use to ask and answer questions. In this book, we will focus on questions that relate to criminal justice. Some of these questions are routine:

- *How many police officers are there in the United States?*
- *How much do we spend annually on prisons?*

Other questions are more complicated:

- *What causes a person to become a serial murderer?*
- *Can a violent offender be rehabilitated?*

[Y]ou will learn how these questions are asked and answered. For now, we will spend some time learning about the practice of research in general. What exactly do we mean by 'research'? And why is it so important?

> **Getting to the Point 1.1.1**—Research methods are the tools, techniques, and procedures that researchers use to ask and answer questions.

What Is Research?

What do people mean when they say, "I did a little research, and ..." or "The research indicates ..."? The term **research** actually has two meanings. First, research is a verb.

To research means to follow a logical process that uses concepts, principles, and techniques to produce knowledge. We do research every day to inform important decisions. For example, when looking to buy a new car, you may want to research the car's safety record, gas mileage, resale value, and so on. By carefully finding and evaluating this information, you can make an informed buying decision.

In the field of criminal justice, research is often more complicated. For example, a study analyzing the effectiveness of various offender rehabilitation programs might require more forethought and rigor. What do we mean by 'rehabilitation'? Do we mean that offenders do not re-offend or that they are rehabilitated in some other way? What types of offenders are we talking about? Are we talking about sex offenders or armed burglars? How will we know if the rehabilitation program actually works? Should it be considered effective if 50 percent of the offenders are rehabilitated? Or should we measure effectiveness in some other way? These are all questions we would have to consider before we even started to research this issue.

Research is also a noun. In this case, research refers to a collection of information that represents what we know about a particular topic. Research that informs everyday decisions can be found in newspapers and magazines, on the television, and through other forms of media like the Internet. A segment on NBC *Today*, for example, might feature an expert talking about a new study on effective parenting techniques. This information can be supplemented with information from books and magazines to form a body of information that a person draws upon when making decisions about how to raise his or her children. Academic research is usually found in academic journals, academic books, and formal reports. Information in these sources is usually more technical and may involve contributions from multiple academic disciplines. Research on domestic violence, for example, spans many disciplines (e.g. law, psychology, criminology, sociology, etc.) and constitutes an enormous literature.

> **Getting to the Point 1.1.2—**As a verb, 'research' means to follow a logical process that uses concepts, principles, and techniques to produce knowledge. As a noun, 'research' is a collection of information that represents what we know about a particular topic.

Whether used as a verb or noun, the critical element of research is the method or process by which the researcher collects and analyzes information. The research method is especially important in the social sciences because social science topics are often difficult to study. Chemists follow a fairly consistent research process because the standards of measurement are generally agreed upon. Social scientists are not so fortunate; there might be many different ways to measure concepts related to social relations and structure. For example, the popular website e-Harmony. com provides matchmaking services that are based on the potential compatibility between two people. But how should we measure compatibility? Should compatibility be based on hobbies and leisure interests? Political beliefs and core values? Level of education and occupation? There may be many ways of measuring compatibility and thus many ways of interpreting the success of a match between two people. As a result, we need to know how social scientists came to their conclusions. How did they measure their concepts, collect their data, and analyze the results? In the social sciences, *how* you know is as important as *what* you know.

Getting to the Point 1.1.3—Research in the social sciences is more challenging than in the physical sciences because the concepts that social scientists study are more difficult to measure and the findings that social scientists produce are more difficult to interpret.

Why Do Research?

Conducting good research is tedious and time consuming. It is not uncommon for a research project to take months, years, or even decades to complete. Often there are no guarantees that a research project will even produce the information the researcher is seeking. So why bother with research? Certainly, there are other ways of gathering information, which I will discuss below. But as I will suggest, these methods are not as good at producing quality information as the tried and true methods of conducting research.

One of the common alternatives to research methods is to rely on authority. There are a lot of smart and well-informed people in the world, such as parents and professors. We could simply rely on them to tell us the truth. The problem here is that parents and, yes, even professors can be wrong. Science, and therefore knowledge, changes constantly. For example, we used to think that criminal suspects who fled in vehicles were best apprehended by large numbers of police officers in fast cars equipped with bright flashing lights and loud sirens. Eventually, we learned that the only thing worse than one car traveling through a city at high speed is multiple cars traveling at high speed. High-speed chases often result in death, serious injury, and/or property damage. So researchers devised safer, more effective ways to apprehend fleeing criminal suspects.

Instead of doing research, we could also rely on tradition or custom. Most of what we do every day is based on tradition or habit. We hold open doors for people behind us. We eat lunch at noon. We put people in jail because we think the threat of jail will keep people from committing crime. To be sure, some traditions are good. But over-reliance on traditions can be harmful. In 1896, the United States Supreme Court established the 'separate but equal doctrine' in *Plessy v. Ferguson* (163 US 537, 1896), which held that individuals could be segregated by race. For years, this doctrine upheld a tradition of separate facilities for African American and White individuals, including separate seating areas in restaurants, separate school systems, and even separate drinking fountains. At the time, the Court believed that mixing the races in social situations would cause social friction and public conflict. Fifty-eight years later, a unanimous Supreme Court reversed itself and ruled in *Brown v. The Board of Education* (347 US 483, 1954) that separate could not be equal. In delivering the opinion of the Court, Chief Justice Earl Warren cited the research of psychologists and sociologists that showed that racial segregation causes harm to children. In this case, social science research instigated a substantial change in American legal and social tradition.

A third option in lieu of research is to just rely on common sense. Common sense is information that we have learned from our experiences or through our interactions with others. It is what we believe to be true. One of my father's favorite expressions was, "That guy is educated well beyond his level of intelligence." He meant that the person lacked common sense. Common sense can be valuable, but sometimes it does not serve us well. During the 1700s, for example, England faced a substantial increase in crime. In response, the government increased criminal penalties such that even minor criminals, like pickpockets, were executed. The English government was responding to the common-sense notion that increased penalties would deter would be criminals. Did it work? Not really. Crime continued to increase and, in an infamous diary from the time, a pickpocket instructed new pickpockets to focus on victims in public crowds who were paying attention to something else, like the hanging of a convicted pickpocket (Anderson, 2002). So much for common sense.

Finally, we can rely on the media—television, radio, newspapers, and the Internet—to tell us information. Unfortunately, some media sources are biased and/or get the story wrong. And a good portion of media sources do not provide sufficient context. For example, the media has reported that from 2003 to 2009, there were 4,688 American and Allied casualties in the Iraq War. But these sources do not put this figure in context. During the Civil War (1861–1865), 618,000 Americans died. And, on a single day during World War II (D-Day, June 6, 1944), approximately 10,249 American and Allied soldiers died. These comparisons are not intended to diminish the death toll from the Iraq War. But they do suggest that context matters and that the media often miss this point. More often than not, competition between media outlets to 'get the story first' ignores the importance of 'getting the story right.' Below is an example.

MAKING RESEARCH REAL 1.1.1—THE KATRINA CRIME WAVE THAT WASN'T

In August 2005, a powerful hurricane (Katrina) ravaged the Gulf Coast and all but destroyed large sections of New Orleans, Louisiana. Thousands of people found themselves homeless. Many were provided shelter in mobile homes provided by the U.S. Federal Emergency Management Administration. Even more were displaced to cities, large and small, throughout the nation.

During the evacuation period, Houston, Texas saw its population rise 7 percent as it welcomed nearly a quarter of a million former residents of New Orleans. Almost immediately, Houston police and criminal justice officials began reporting sharp increases in crime, particularly homicides, robberies, and automobile theft. Most of these increases were blamed on individuals displaced by Katrina. The perception that the Katrina evacuees were causing an increase in crime became pervasive in the community, in large part due to extensive media coverage.

In 2010, five researchers decided to investigate these media claims. They evaluated official crime statistics from three cities (Houston, San Antonio, and Phoenix), all of which had received large numbers of Katrina evacuees. For each city, they examined pre- and post-Katrina crime trends in six offense categories: murder, robbery, aggravated assault, rape, burglary, and auto theft. The evidence suggested that crime rates for each of the offenses were more or less the same in each city before and after the relocation of Katrina evacuees (Verano et al., 2010). Only in Houston was there a modest increase in murder and robbery after Katrina evacuees arrived.

In the end, we have good reasons for conducting research. Research involves the systematic process of testing our claims and evaluating our knowledge. When those claims or that knowledge is not supported by evidence, they are discarded and new ideas emerge. Research ensures that the policies and procedures we use to address crime and other social problems are effective. In short, there is just no substitute for good research (see Table 1.1.1).

TABLE 1.1.1   Limitations of the Alternatives to Research

Alternatives	Limitations
Authority	Sometimes experts are wrong. Research enables us to be critical of expert opinions and to seek answers for ourselves.
Tradition or custom	Societies change and so do their traditions and customs. Research encourages us to question what we do and why we do it.
Common sense	What makes sense to one person or social group may not make sense to another. Research teaches us to reconsider our assumptions and to reach a consensus on the truth.
Media	Information distributed through the mass media may not be objective, valid, or sensitive to context. Research enables us to identify bias, correct false information, and provide context.

Getting to the Point 1.1.4—Relying on authority, tradition or custom, common sense, and the media for accurate knowledge is risky. There is no substitute for good research in the pursuit of reliable knowledge.

Who Does Research?

Everybody does research, not just university professors and lab scientists. If you listen to the morning traffic report before you leave for school to be sure you will not get stuck in traffic, you are doing research. If you decide which movie to see based on the reviews from the newspaper, you are doing research. If you look a professor up using RateMyProfessors.com, you are doing research. We all do research every day. We just do not call it research.

Some people dedicate their professional life to research. In other words, some people get paid to do research! For example, in addition to their teaching and service responsibilities, university professors conduct a great deal of research. Most have a specific research agenda, or a research topic or question that they are interested in learning more about. And they use their research to inform their teaching, such that their students are exposed to current ideas and findings. A few might even use their research to advance an issue that they are passionate about. Most, however, conduct research to maintain their professional status. A university professor's work performance is evaluated, in part, on the basis of how many research papers he or she publishes in scholarly journals.

Other researchers are independent and do research to produce marketable knowledge. For example, many private companies hire researchers, often referred to as consultants, to conduct research and make recommendations. Marketing researchers use focus groups and surveys to test consumer products. Political pollsters measure the public's attitudes about political candidates and issues. Other pollsters conduct public opinion polls on various social issues. The Gallup Organization, for example, has been doing public opinion polls for decades. Organizations like this may work for corporate clients, political candidates, and/or news organizations. Finally, there are numerous think tanks that conduct research, usually to influence legislation or public policy. For example, the RAND (Research ANd Development) Corporation was created by the Douglas Aircraft Company to provide research and analysis for the United States Armed Forces. Over the years, researchers from the RAND Corporation have done research in many other areas, including criminal justice.

By far, the most prolific sponsor of research is the United States Government. Through various research agencies, the federal government provides grants and contracts to researchers to conduct research that informs public policy. Most grants in criminal justice are awarded through the Bureau of Justice Statistics or the Bureau of Justice Assistance, both part of the U.S. Department of Justice. Other government organizations (e.g., the National Science Foundation) provide research grants for thousands of research projects each year. In most cases, researchers are required to produce a final report outlining the results of their research and a copy of the data they collect. These data are cataloged and provided to other researchers interested in similar topics. In addition to funding outside researchers, the United States Government conducts its own research. For example, every 10 years the Bureau of the Census conducts a census of the nation. These data are used to make many important decisions about federal funding and congressional representation. And the Government Accountability Office analyzes how the government spends taxpayer dollars and provides objective, nonpartisan information to Congress.

> **Getting to the Point 1.1.5**—All sorts of people conduct research. Some people and organizations conduct research for a living. Anyone who follows a methodological process to produce knowledge is conducting research.

What Are the Different Types of Research?

Most research projects can be classified into one of three categories. It is also common for a research project to progress from one category to another over time.

- **Exploratory research** is often necessary when we know very little about a new social trend. In exploratory research, the objective is to find out what is happening. For example, there appears to be an emerging crime trend called human trafficking. Exploratory researchers might ask, "What is human trafficking?" They may devise a working definition of this emerging trend, such as: "Human trafficking is the illegal trade of human beings for the purposes of reproductive slavery, commercial sexual exploitation, forced labor, or a modern-day form of slavery."

- **Descriptive research** documents social conditions or trends. In short, it describes social phenomena. There is little attempt to explain what causes the phenomena. Descriptive research is only interested in what is happening now or what happened in the past. Using the previous example, a descriptive researcher might conduct a survey of women who are victims of human trafficking. In doing so, the researcher might want to know who these women are and how they became victims of this crime. The descriptive researcher might also want to learn where these women are from or when they were placed in captivity.

- **Explanatory research** attempts to find a cause for social trends and phenomena. It goes beyond mere description to pinpoint a cause and effect. Using the previous example, explanatory research might attempt to determine the risk factors associated with becoming a victim of human trafficking. A researcher might ask, "What factors predict whether someone will become a victim of human trafficking?" In answering this question, we might be able to prevent this crime or, at the very least, educate potential victims about it.

In a way, researchers are like journalists. Both professionals gather information in an attempt to arrive at the truth and then report what they have found to a larger audience. Journalists learn that each story should contain the answers to six basic questions—who, what, when, where, why, and how. Researchers ask the same questions, but they seldom answer them in a single research project. Exploratory research always asks *what* but seldom asks *why*. Descriptive research always asks *who*, *when*, *where*, and *how*, but seldom asks *why*. Explanatory research asks *why* but seldom asks *what* because this question has usually been answered previously by researchers (see Table 1.1.2). Again, these are not hard and fast rules. Variation exists and it is not uncommon to encounter a research project that fits into more than one category.

TABLE 1.1.2   Questions Asked by Different Types of Research

Purpose	Who?	What?	When?	Where?	Why?	How?
Exploratory	Occasionally	Always	Occasionally	Occasionally	Seldom	Occasionally
Descriptive	Always	Occasionally	Always	Always	Seldom	Always
Explanatory	Occasionally	Seldom	Occasionally	Occasionally	Always	Occasionally

Getting to the Point 1.6—Research can be classified into three different categories. Exploratory research is often necessary in order to learn about social trends and phenomena that we know very little about. Descriptive research describes social trends and phenomena. Explanatory research attempts to explain or find a cause for social trends and phenomena. Sometimes a research project can have more than one purpose.

Research can also be defined in terms of how the researcher intends for the research to be used. University professors conduct research primarily to expand the body of knowledge about a particular subject or to develop theories about social behavior. Typically, this research is published in scholarly journals and read by other scholars interested in the same topics. We generally refer to this type of research as **pure research**. The purpose of pure research is primarily to expand knowledge of a topic.

Other researchers, like practitioners, consultants, and even some academics conduct research to address and solve a particular social problem. This research is often done for a client, who intends to use the knowledge gained from the research to address a specific issue. Typically, this research is published in reports consumed internally within organizations. We generally refer to this type of research as **applied research**. Although applied researchers often produce knowledge, their primary intent is to address a specific issue or solve a current problem. We'll discuss applied research in more detail in a later chapter.

Some researchers also distinguish between applied research and **action research**. Action research is similar to applied research in that it is focused on problem solving. But action research is distinct in that it involves practitioners (e.g., the police) in research design, implementation, and evaluation. And its purpose is to improve some aspect of practice (e.g., combating gang violence). In action research, a problem is diagnosed; an intervention or strategy is devised; and data is collected to fine tune the intervention strategy.

Note that these are not mutually exclusive categories. The knowledge gained from pure research can later be used to solve a social problem. Likewise, the knowledge gained from applied or action research can later be used to develop new theories. The following hypothetical examples illustrate this point.

MAKING RESEARCH REAL 1.1.2—THE 'APPLICATION' OF PURE RESEARCH

Dr. Joe Smith from Central State University is one of the nation's leading experts on robbery. One afternoon, he hears that a convenience store near his home has been robbed for the fourth time this year. He wonders why that particular convenience store is frequently robbed while another store less than a mile away never seems to have any problems at all. To answer his question, he goes to the state prison and gets permission from the warden to interview convicted convenience store robbers. His research reveals a list of factors that convicted convenience store robbers consider when deciding which stores to rob. This list includes things like store lighting, advertisements on front windows that obscure the view into the store, and the visible presence of security cameras. He publishes his findings in a respected academic journal in an article titled "Factors Affecting the Decision to Rob."

Several years later, the owner of a chain of convenience stores happens to be surfing on the Internet and comes across a copy of Dr. Smith's article. He reads it and sends a copy to the vice president in charge of store security. The vice president thinks the findings have merit and contacts Dr. Smith for further information. Using this pure research, which was originally intended for the academic community, the vice president develops a comprehensive program to protect his convenience stores from being robbed.

MAKING RESEARCH REAL 1.1.3—THE 'PURIFICATION' OF APPLIED RESEARCH

Captain Ann James was assigned to the Research and Planning Unit of the Metropolitan Police Department. One afternoon, one of the police officers was injured during a high-speed vehicle pursuit. The chief asked Captain James to evaluate the department's vehicle pursuit policy to see if it needed to be revised. As part of her research, Captain James decided to interview the person that was being chased. During the interview, she asked the person why he ran from the police and why he eventually decided to stop. The driver told her that he ran because he knew a warrant had been issued for his arrest on another matter. He told her that he stopped only because he thought he had gotten away. When she asked the driver why he thought he had gotten away, the driver said "Because I didn't see any police cars or hear any sirens."

Captain James wondered whether this comment could be the basis of a new low-speed pursuit policy. She conducted additional interviews with other drivers who had run from the police and got essentially the same answers. Eventually, these findings became the focus of considerable attention among policing scholars who study vehicular pursuits. One of these scholars used Captain James' research to develop a theory he called "The Calculus of the Decision to Run from the Police."

Getting to the Point 1.1.7—Research may also be classified in terms of how the researcher intends to use the research. Pure research is conducted primarily to advance theory and to expand the body of knowledge. Applied or action research is conducted primarily to address a specific issue or solve a particular problem. These forms of research are not mutually exclusive. Findings from pure research can be used to solve problems; findings from applied or action research can be used to advance theory.

Where Is Research Found?

When you conduct research, you look for information in various places. For example, most of you probably use the Internet and get a lot of information online through sources like Google, Yahoo!News, or Wikipedia. Other popular sources of information include the television, newspapers, and family and friends. Scientists are a little more selective about where they get their information. Academic or **scholarly journals** are probably the most prominent sources of information in the sciences. Journals are used as publishing outlets by university professors and other scholars to communicate their research findings to other researchers. Most are published quarterly or semi-annually. Nearly every academic discipline has its own journal and most have several. Journals like *Criminology*, *Justice Quarterly*, and the *Journal of Criminal Justice* publish research articles on a broad range of criminal justice and criminology issues. Some journals are a bit more specialized. For example, *Police Quarterly* publishes research on policing issues; *Corrections Today* publishes research on correctional issues; and *The Journal of Criminal Justice Education* publishes articles on teaching methods for criminal justice professors.

Most of the articles in scholarly journals are between 20 and 40 pages long and almost all undergo a process known as **peer review**. In the peer review process, research findings are reviewed by experts prior to their publication. Researchers first submit potential articles to a journal's editor. If the subject of the research is consistent with the journal's focus, the editor will send the manuscript to two to five scholars who are knowledgeable about the subject. After one to two months, the reviewers will return the manuscript to the editor with their comments and recommendations. The reviewers are not aware of the author's identity; and the author is not aware of the reviewers' identities. This double blind evaluation process is intended to produce frank comments from reviewers. Based on these comments, the editor will reject the manuscript outright, ask the author to revise and resubmit the article, or accept the article for publication as is. If the manuscript is rejected outright, the author must go through the same process again with another journal. Or, he or she may simply decide not to publish the research. If the author revises and resubmits the manuscript, the original reviewers will have another opportunity to review the revised manuscript. This can take another two months. The process, from original submission to actual publication, can take up to a year or more! Although onerous and time-consuming, the peer review process improves the quality of research and ensures that only good research makes it into the body of knowledge.

> **Getting to the Point 1.1.8—**Peer review is a collaborative process whereby researchers who are knowledgeable about a particular subject are asked to review and comment on another researcher's work and recommend whether it should be published.

Research on broader topics may be presented in a research **monograph**, or book. Research monographs are often published by academic publishing companies. Many universities maintain academic publishing programs to provide scholars a means to distribute their research in a longer format than would be allowed by an academic journal. Like scholarly articles, monographs report research findings from a single research project and are subjected to a peer review process. You may have been assigned to read a research monograph for one of your classes. Or you may have seen them in your school's library. Government agencies also publish monographs on research they sponsor through grants and contracts. Monographs published by government agencies, like the U.S. Department of Justice, may be presented in paper bound booklet form. These are typically found in the government documents section of the library. Textbooks are also an excellent source of research, particularly for individuals who know very little about a topic.

Publishing in scholarly venues is essential to the careers of research scholars and university professors. 'Publish or perish' means to publish research in peer-reviewed journals and monographs or risk being denied tenure or promotion; more on that later. Scholarly venues have the most rigorous review process and are generally regarded as the gold standard of scientific research. But scholarly journals and monographs are not widely read. Indeed, the readership for most scholarly journals is generally quite small. For researchers who want to share findings with a wider audience, newspapers, magazines, and trade publications may offer a better publishing outlet. Here is an example from my own personal experience.

MAKING RESEARCH REAL 1.1.4—MEETING GEORGE KELLING

On a regular basis, the College of Criminal Justice at Sam Houston State University invites prominent criminologists to campus to participate in the Beto Lecture Series. This lecture series is named for the late George Beto, who was the Director of the Texas Department of Corrections and a former Dean of the College. While on campus, invited scholars deliver formal and informal lectures and conduct symposia with students and faculty.

The logistics of getting a scholar to the Sam Houston campus in Huntsville, Texas (90 miles north of Houston) are a bit tricky. The closest airport of any size is George H.W. Bush Intercontinental Airport in Houston. Often the Dean will ask one of the Ph.D. students to be scholars' drivers throughout the three days of their campus visit. This includes picking them up at the airport, driving them to the many events on their agenda, and then returning them to Bush International at the appropriate time. As one of those Ph.D. students I always was quick to volunteer because I recognized this as an excellent way to have several hours of uninterrupted time with some of the most important criminal justice scholars. After all, these were the people I had spent many years reading about and I was anxious to put a name with a face.

In April of 1994, the College invited George Kelling. At the time, Dr. Kelling was a Research Fellow at Harvard University. His article, "Broken Windows," which he co-authored with James Q. Wilson, was groundbreaking in criminal justice research. The article suggested that police should focus on small incivilities in order to deter major crime. Given my interest in his work and his prominence, I volunteered to be his driver for the lecture series. On the way back to the airport, I asked Dr. Kelling why he and his co-author chose to publish their article in *The Atlantic*, a magazine, rather than an academic journal. I'll never forget Dr. Kelling's response. "Because at this point in my career I could [care less] about publishing an article in a journal that is read by less than a thousand people. James and I wanted to start a national conversation and share our ideas about policing with a broad audience," he explained.

Dr. Kelling's comment had a major impact on my own publishing outlets. Over the years since, I have looked for opportunities to publish research in magazines, trade publications, and newsletters that are regularly read by policing practitioners. Sometimes I will publish an article in a scholarly journal and then rewrite it for a practitioner audience. The difference in response is remarkable. Sometimes it can take years for another scholar to respond to the version of the research that is published in a scholarly journal. The practitioners respond almost immediately through emails and telephone calls. The greater impact from publishing in more popular sources is clear.

Private corporations also publish research information. Some of this is intended for members of the corporation, but some of it may be widely disseminated. When reading this information, it is important to remember that corporations have a vested interest in the outcome of their research. Corporations are not likely to disseminate a research report that casts the goods it produces or the services it provides in a negative way. Likewise, corporations are quick to disseminate information that makes their products or services look good. Hence, research sponsored by private corporations should be evaluated carefully.

Finally, research can reside hidden away in legislative actions and policy decisions. For example, in 2005, the Kansas Legislature passed a law requiring individuals who are convicted of animal abuse to submit a blood sample to the state's repository of DNA information. Research suggests that many adult serial offenders have a history of animal abuse. Supporters of the law argued that gathering DNA information on animal abusers might help the police identify adult serial murderers or rapists in the future. Criminologists, psychologists, and other scholars familiar with the developmental histories of adult serial offenders testified before Kansas Legislature in support of this bill. Their testimony, documented in the form of written transcripts, can be considered a valuable source of information on research.

In the 'old days,' researchers had to visit libraries, comb through dusty volumes that indexed articles, or leaf through card catalogs to find the information they needed. Not so today, when a quick search through an academic database on the Internet can produce a copy of the article on your computer screen within seconds! One of the most popular websites for criminal justice research is the National Criminal Justice Reference Service, or NCJRS (https://www.ncjrs.gov/). This website is administered by the Department of Justice through its Office of Justice Programs. It is essentially a database of criminal justice research and a great place to begin a literature review. The research contained in the NCJRS tends to be more applied and includes a lot of studies conducted by practitioners and criminal justice agencies. Criminal Justice Abstracts (http://www.ebscohost.com/academic/criminal-justice-abstracts) is another great source of information. Like the NCJRS, it is a database of criminal justice research. But most of the studies in this database are published in academic or scholarly journals. Both databases offer links to full text articles that are likely free through your university's library. Table 1.1.3 summarizes these common sources of information on criminal justice research.

TABLE 1.1.3   Where to Find Research

Source	Comment
Academic and scholarly journals	Research is reported in 20–40-page articles. Because research is peer reviewed, other researchers can be reasonably sure that the findings have been rigorously evaluated by experts.
Research monographs	Research is reported in the form of a short book. Often the research is peer reviewed and published by a university publishing house.
Textbooks	Research is presented to a broad audience that does not know a great deal about a particular topic. The research topic is given broad coverage.
Newspapers and magazines	Research is provided in short articles written for a broad audience. Information is up to date and timely, but coverage is typically not in depth due to space limitations. Research is not subjected to peer review.
Trade publications	Research is reported in articles in newsletters and magazines read by criminal justice practitioners. Articles focus on emerging trends in crime and criminal justice practice. Articles are not peer reviewed.

Corporate research reports	Research is presented in reports intended for internal use in the corpora tion. Information usually pertains to research on new products and services. Typically only research that sheds a positive light on the corporation and its products and services are shared with the public.
Legislative actions and policy decisions	Research is presented in the form of comments and testimony made by policy makers, experts, and the public. This information can be difficult to find, but can provide insight into particular topics.
Databases	Individual research studies are indexed and referenced in online databases. Researchers use search terms to look for research on particular topics using these databases. Searches provide a list of citations, abstracts, and/or full-text articles.

Getting to the Point 1.1.9—Research can be found in academic journals, books, newspapers, magazines, legislative actions, policy decisions, and databases. Some of this information is more objective and accurate than others.

How Is Research Used?

Our goal as researchers is to constantly contribute to a body of knowledge that evolves over time. So one of the primary uses of research is to understand and contribute to the body of knowledge. The existing body of knowledge is often described in a literature review, which is basically a summary of what is known about a particular research topic. Researchers write literature reviews to review the work of previous researchers, develop an understanding of a topic, and identify opportunities for further study. Ideally, they will add findings from their own research to this 'conversation' or body of knowledge. Again, research that is conducted to contribute to the body of knowledge is known as pure research.

When it takes the form of pure research, research helps to establish a scholar's professional credentials. Newly hired assistant professors typically have four to six years to establish their teaching qualifications, perform service to the university and publish their research in peer-reviewed journals and books. At the end of this time, their work is reviewed by a tenure and promotion committee, which evaluates the professor's work and decides whether he or she should be granted tenure and/or promoted to the rank of associate professor. If the professor is granted tenure, he or she can be reasonably assured of continued employment at the university. If not, the professor is given one year to find another job and leave the university. If promoted to associate professor, professors spend the next four to five years establishing more teaching, service, and research credentials to be promoted to full professor. In these tenure and promotion evaluations, research is considered a central factor in a professor's professional credentials. Even researchers who are employed by consulting firms will use research to establish their professional stature and as a basis for promotion.

Research is also conducted to decide particular court cases, inform policy decisions, or address social problems. Again, this type of research is generally referred to as applied research. For example, in 1994, State Superior Court Judge Robert Francis (New Jersey) asked Dr. John Lamberth, formerly of Temple University, to conduct a study on traffic stops by the New Jersey State Police. The state police had been accused of racial profiling by a group of African American and Hispanic drivers. Dr. Lamberth's research convinced the court that the state police had in fact targeted African American and Hispanic drivers for stops in an effort to identify drug couriers traveling on Interstate Highway 95. Eventually, the case was settled (*State of New Jersey v. Pedro Soto*, 734 A.2d 350, 1996) and the judge ordered that the routine operations of the New Jersey State Police be supervised by the court for a decade (Lamberth, 1996). Lamberth's study was the first full-scale racial profiling study ever conducted.

Finally, research is often used by organizations to develop new products or services, advance a social or political agenda, and/or to improve some aspect of professional practice. Criminal justice agencies, for example, change their policies and practices in accordance with new research findings. In one such instance, the Texas Department of Public Safety (DPS) issued revolvers to its troopers until the mid-1980s since revolvers were more durable and more reliable than automatic pistols. But when technological improvements in automatic pistols were made, the DPS conducted a study of the relative functionality of revolvers versus automatic pistols. Researchers within the DPS interviewed hundreds of troopers and the manufacturers, conducted numerous functionality and durability tests, evaluated the training requirements for both types of weapons, and completed a cost/benefit analysis. In the end, they recommended that the DPS replace its current .357 revolver with a 9mm, 10mm or .45 caliber automatic pistol manufactured by Sig Sauer (Link, McNelly, and Withrow, 1989). Again, when using evidence to develop a set of 'best practices' for use in a criminal justice setting, practitioners and researchers are engaging in a type of research known as action research.

> **Getting to the Point 1.1.10**—Researchers conduct research to expand the body of knowledge, establish professional credentials, inform legal and policy decisions, address social problems, develop new products or services, advance social or political agendas, and improve professional practice.

When Is Research Important?

If you ask a university professor, "When is research important?" he or she will likely tell you that research is always important. To a university professor, research is the foundation upon which we create additional knowledge. Without this foundation, we would be forced to recreate the same knowledge over and over and we would never expand the body of knowledge. There are, however, times when research becomes *critically* important. For example, during the 1990s, methamphetamine use spread throughout the American West and Midwest. Rural areas with limited policing resources and unfettered access to the chemicals needed for methamphetamine production encouraged this trend. Police departments began to meet and confer regularly to share their experience and knowledge about this growing trend. They developed specialized units to detect and seize clandestine meth labs and they encouraged many states to pass legislation restricting the sale of over-the-counter drugs used in methamphetamine production. In this case, police officers and policing leaders were researchers; they recognized a new trend, shared information about the problem, and developed effective strategies in response.

Research is also critically important when resources are few and demands are many. Policy makers have limited funding for social and economic programs and they want to be sure to get the most out of every dollar they have available. The most effective way to make use of limited resources is to conduct research and make sure those resources are being put to good use. For example, what is the most effective strategy for reducing drunk driving? Should we spend more money on sobriety checkpoints, treatment programs, or educational campaigns? Each program is effective in its own way, but which of these is the *most* effective? Only a competent research project can determine this. Collecting evidence and conducting cost–benefit analyses can help determine which strategies and programs actually work.

Finally, research is critical during times of political instability and conflict. Ideally, policy decisions should not be swayed by political interests or ideologies. Unfortunately, in criminal justice, they often are. Research can cut through the political ideologies and help policy makers make informed decisions. For example, the trend in politics is to 'get tough on crime.' Political candidates who appear tough on crime win political points and boost their ratings. But how effective are 'tough' crime measures? For example, do three strikes laws really reduce crime or do they just fill up prisons? During times of intense political pressure, responsible criminal justice administrators rely on independent research to temper political debate and make decisions without the distracting burdens of political grandstanding.

> **Getting to the Point 1.1.11—**Research is the foundation upon which we expand the body of knowledge. Research is also important when we want to respond to critical social problems, allocate limited resources wisely, and base policy decisions on evidence rather than ideology.

Final Thoughts

You might think that after more than a century of research, we would know why people commit crime and what to do about it. For sure, we know more now than we have ever known. But there are still far more questions than answers. As a criminal justice professional with a Bachelor's degree, you may find yourself in a position to answer some of these questions using the skills and concepts introduced in this book. Thirty years ago, I was in your shoes, reading about crime in the abstract. And suddenly, there I was, in a professional policing career, being asked to evaluate policing programs and to explain how I intended to reduce crime more effectively.

There is for you, more so than there was for me, another reason to learn about research methods. When I started out as a criminal justice practitioner, there were very few computers.

Information gathering was arduous and time consuming. If you wanted to know a suspect's criminal history, you had to request it, via teletype, from another person at a central repository. There were no cell phones, websites, fax machines, or emails. A lot has changed. You have access to a mind-numbing amount of information. Some of this information is useful and accurate, some of it is not. The purpose of this book and this class is to help you develop the skills to do good research, to sift through all that information at your fingertips, and to distinguish the good information from the bad.

Getting to the Point/Chapter Summary

- Research methods are the tools, techniques, and procedures that researchers use to ask and answer questions.
- As a verb, 'research' means to follow a logical process that uses concepts, principles, and techniques to produce knowledge. As a noun, 'research' is a collection of information that represents what we know about a particular topic.
- Research in the social sciences is more challenging than in the physical sciences because the concepts that social scientists study are more difficult to measure and the findings that social scientists produce are more difficult to interpret.
- Relying on authority, tradition or custom, common sense, and the media for accurate knowledge is risky. There is no substitute for good research in the pursuit of reliable knowledge.
- All sorts of people conduct research. Some people and organizations conduct research for a living. Anyone who follows a methodological process to produce knowledge is conducting research.
- Research can be classified into three different categories. Exploratory research is often necessary in order to learn about social trends and phenomena that we know very little about. Descriptive research describes social trends and phenomena. Explanatory research attempts to explain or find a cause for social trends and phenomena. Sometimes a research project can have more than one purpose.
- Research may also be classified in terms of how the researcher intends to use the research. Pure research is conducted primarily to advance theory and to expand the body of knowledge. Applied or action research is conducted primarily to address a specific issue or solve a particular problem. These forms of research are not mutually exclusive. Findings from pure research can be used to solve problems; findings from applied or action research can be used to advance theory.
- Peer review is a collaborative process whereby researchers who are knowledgeable about a particular subject are asked to review and comment on another researcher's work and recommend whether it should be published.

- Research can be found in academic journals, books, newspapers, magazines, legislative actions, policy decisions, and databases. Some of this information is more objective and accurate than others.
- Researchers conduct research to expand the body of knowledge, establish professional credentials, inform legal and policy decisions, address social problems, develop new products or services, advance social or political agendas, and improve professional practice.
- Research is the foundation upon which we expand the body of knowledge. Research is also important when we want to respond to critical social problems, allocate limited resources wisely, and base policy decisions on evidence rather than ideology.

References

Anderson, D.A. (2002). The deterrence hypothesis and picking pockets at the pickpocket's hanging. *American Law and Economics Review, 4*(2), 295–313.

Brown v. The Board of Education, 347 US 483 (1954).

Lamberth, J. (1996). Report of John Lamberth, Ph.D. Washington, DC: American Civil Liberties Union. Retrieved from http://www.clearinghouse.net/chDocs/public/PN-MD-0003-0006.pdf (accessed March 2013).

Link, M., McNelly, J. and Withrow, B. (1989). *A comparative analysis of the 9mm semi-automatic pistol and the .357 revolver.* Austin, TX: Texas Department of Public Safety.

Plessy v. Ferguson, 163 US 537 (1896).

State of New Jersey v. Pedro Soto, 734 A.2d 350 (N.J. Super. CT. Law Div. 1996).

Verano, S.P., Schafer, J.A., Cancino, J.M., Decker, S.H. and Greene, J.R. (2010). A tale of three cities: Crime and displacement after Hurricane Katrina. *Journal of Criminal Justice, 38*(1), 42–50.

Conclusion

In this chapter, you learned that the purpose of conducting research is to produce information that may be used to contribute to a knowledge base about a particular issue or topic, test theories or ideas, and/or inform decision-making in areas such as criminal justice–related programs or policies. Withrow stated that "the critical element of research is the method or process by which the researcher collects and analyzes information," noting that this process may be particularly challenging in the social sciences, where there are several ways that constructs may be interpreted or measured. Research is often categorized as (1) exploratory (addresses the "what"; useful for exploring areas where little research exists); (2) descriptive (addresses the "who, when, where, and how"; useful for describing the characteristics of a population or "what is happening now or in the past"); and (3) explanatory (addresses the "why"; useful for establishing a cause-and-effect relationship between constructs, such as, "what are the predictors of recidivism?").

As a practitioner or professional employed in a criminal justice or social services field, you may be both a consumer and producer of research. As a consumer of research, you may access, read, and summarize existing studies to assist with informing agency activities. For example, you may review outcomes of studies that examine specific challenges your agency works to address, such as truancy or recidivism, and use these findings to help guide decision making and program activities within your organization. As a producer of research, you may track and record information within a database and analyze and use this data to inform agency decisions and/or share your findings with others. In your role as a professional, you may also be asked to contribute to research design and execution by assisting researchers employed by your agency or those external to your agency (such as those from local universities) with evaluating policies or programs within your agency. Whether you aspire to work as a professional/practitioner within the field or work as a researcher, it is vital that you have a strong foundation of research terminology and an understanding of the research process.

Chapter 1 Reflection Questions

1. What is research?
2. List and describe the three different types of research.
3. Where is research found? What resources are available? Visit your university library or its website. Locate an academic journal article that focuses on community policing or prisoner reentry.
4. How is research used, and why is it important? List some examples.
5. Discuss one example of how you have conducted research in everyday life. How did this research inform your decision(s)? Do you feel that the outcomes of your decisions were improved as the result of the information you gathered prior to making this decision? Why or why not?

Building Your Research Proposal

Application Exercise 1: Evaluate your Research Interests
Think about how you become interested in the fields of criminology or criminal justice (or human services–related field). Answer the following questions:

1. What are your career aspirations?
2. Which of the following categories best represents your area(s) of interest (choose one or two)?

☐ Law enforcement/policing ☐ Courts/law ☐ Corrections/reentry ☐ Victimology/victim services
☐ Criminological theory/nature, extent, causes, control of crime ☐ Other _____ (List)

3. List a specific topic of interest within the category(ies) you selected. For example, if you chose the category law enforcement/policing, you may be particularly interested in officer use of force. What would you like to learn more about within the area/areas you identified?

Ethical Considerations for Researchers

Introduction

Have you ever taken an ethics class? If so, you are likely able to identify some ethical issues or dilemmas that may surface within a variety of environments. The research arena is not exempt from these matters. There are many ethical considerations that must be considered throughout the research process, including, first and foremost, those related to the protection of research subjects. McCarthy and King's chapter, "Ethics and Criminal Justice Research," introduces several ethical issues that may arise and should be considered throughout the research process and presents principles for promoting ethical research. Researchers affiliated with institutions are required to obtain Institutional Review Board (IRB) approval prior to collecting any information or data. IRB members are responsible for reviewing research proposals to ensure that ethical concerns have been considered and addressed and that each proposed study poses no more than minimal risk to research subjects. IRBs are made up of faculty and other professionals representing diverse disciplines and backgrounds. If your proposed study involves collecting your own data (primary data) and/or proposes to utilize secondary data that are not publicly available, it is important that you consult with your institution's IRB to determine whether your study requires approval prior to data acquisition.

In the second reading, Crookes describes AI-powered predictive policing as "an attempt to identify the individuals who are the most likely to commit a crime or become a victim in the near future. It uses vast data sets and machine-learning algorithms to assess potential risks."

Proponents of these strategies contend that using existing data (such as information regularly collected by police departments) to develop algorithms to uncover patterns which may be used to "predict" crimes before they take place can result in more efficient and effective crime prevention and public safety strategies, but there are several ethical concerns that have yet to be uncovered; one of the primary fears associated with the use of AI in policing is inaccurate prediction. Crookes states, "[I]naccurate prediction—false positives or negatives ... has raised ethical issues around surveillance and autonomy, as well as the 'potential reversal of the presumption of innocence.'" Further, there is concern that racial and other biases may be exacerbated by the utilization of these technologies as the crime data/records available to inform these models originate from existing suspect and victim incidents, which have been collected from arrest or conviction data. As AI-related technologies are increasingly being used or considered in many different capacities, it is vital that researchers and criminal justice professionals are aware of the associated ethical concerns and implications. An exercise at the end of this chapter invites you to continue to explore how various types of AI are being used or considered for use across the criminal justice system.

Ethics and Criminal Justice Research

Belinda R. McCarthy & Robin J. King

N o area of life or work is free of ethical dilemmas, and the field of research is no exception. In recent years a number of scandals surrounding the professional behavior of academic researchers have made newspaper headlines and stirred government inquiries. Academic researchers have been charged with falsifying data to obtain additional research funding and to falsify publication of results.

Of a different nature, a conflict within a sociology department at Texas A&M University has left faculty choosing sides in a nasty dispute (*Chronicle of Higher Education*, 1999). Three professors have accused each other of plagiarism and theft of data. While no amicable resolutions have been made, the department has suffered a major public relations blow. The incident escalated to a degree requiring investigation by the university, the National Science Foundation, and the American Sociological Association (*Chronicle of Higher Education*, 1999).

> **KEY CONCEPTS:**
>
> codes of ethics
> coercing participation
> confidentiality
> privacy
> randomization
> self-determination
> willingness to participate

A noted criminologist was investigated by the Florida Commission on Ethics when it was disclosed that he had been paid millions of dollars by private corrections firms while simultaneously being paid via a contract as an academic consultant (*Miami Herald*, 1999). The professor admitted that his involvement in both research projects was a conflict of interest (*Miami Herald*, 1999).

The issue of plagiarism in academic publication is an area that deserves much attention in the literature. Published research has the potential to influence the

Belinda R. McCarthy and Robin J. King, "Ethics and Criminal Justice Research," *Justice, Crime and Ethics*, ed. Michael C. Braswell and Bernard J. McCarthy, pp. 393–415. Copyright © 2008 by Taylor & Francis Group. Reprinted with permission.

conduct of practitioners and policy within criminal justice and other social professions (Jones, 1999). Thus, it is imperative that criminal justice researchers are conscious of these potential pressures when disseminating results from research projects.

One might think that scientific endeavors, with their objective and unbiased approach to the world, would create fewer dilemmas than other occupational activities. Although most researchers are not faced with the same kind of corrupting influences confronting street-level criminal justice officials, the pressures of "grantsmanship" and publication provide significant motivations. The dilemmas of working with human subjects in a political environment are equally challenging. Moreover, the goal of scientific purity, of unbiased objectivity, may be corrupting as well, as researchers are tempted to put scientific objectives before their concern for the welfare of others.

In this chapter we will examine the nature of ethical dilemmas confronting the criminal justice researcher. To a large degree these problems are comparable to those difficulties faced by other social scientists. Additional problems arise as a result of the particular focus of research on deviance and law-breaking.

Problems Involving Work with Human Subjects

Stuart Cook (1976) lists the following ethical considerations surrounding research with human subjects:

1. Involving people in research without their knowledge or consent.
2. Coercing people to participate.
3. Withholding from the participant the true nature of the research.
4. Deceiving the research participant.
5. Leading the research participants to commit acts which diminish their self-respect.
6. Violating the right to self-determination: research on behavior control and character change.
7. Exposing the research participant to physical or mental stress.
8. Invading the privacy of the research participant.
9. Withholding benefits from participants in control groups.
10. Failing to treat research participants fairly and to show them consideration and respect (p. 202).

Involving People in Research Without Their Knowledge or Consent

Often the best way to study human behavior is to observe people in a natural setting without their knowledge. Self-reported descriptions of behavior may be unreliable because people forget or are uncertain about their actions. Although most people might tell you that they would attempt to return a lost wallet, a hidden camera focused on a wallet lying on the sidewalk might reveal very different behaviors. People who know they are being watched often act differently, especially when unethical, deviant, or criminal behaviors are involved. For these reasons, studies of deviance often involve direct observation, which involves listening as well as visual observation.

At times, the observer participates to some degree in the activities being studied. Whyte's (1955) study of street-corner society involved just this form of participant observation. Humphreys's (1970) examination of homosexual behavior in public restrooms, Short and Strodtbeck's (1965) study of delinquency in Chicago, and Cohen's (1980) observations of female prostitutes in New York all involved the observation of persons who never consented to become research subjects.

Studies of persons on the other side of the criminal justice process have also been undertaken without the consent of those participating in the research. Meltzer (1953), for example, studied jury deliberations through the use of hidden microphones. The importance of discretion in the criminal justice process and the hidden nature of most decisionmaking support the greater use of such techniques in efforts to understand how police, prosecutors, and correctional personnel carry out their duties.

The ethical dilemma, however, is a complicated one: Is the value of the research such that persons should be turned into study "subjects" without their permission? The conditions of the research are extremely important to this deliberation. If the behaviors being studied would have occurred without the researcher's intervention, the lack of consent seems less troubling. Such studies involve little personal cost to unknowing subjects. Unobtrusive research that involves only behaviors that occur in public view is also less questionable, because the invasion of personal privacy is not at issue.

> "Human subjects have the right to full disclosure of the purposes of the research as early as it is appropriate to the research process, and they have the right to an opportunity to have their questions answered about the purpose and usage of the research" (Academy of Criminal Justice Sciences Code of Ethics, 2000:5).

But what about experiments that create situations to which subjects must react, such as those involving a "lost" wallet? Or a study of witness response to crime that involves an actor or actress screaming and running from an apparent assailant down a crowded street? Observation might be the only method of determining how citizens would really respond, but the personal cost of being studied might be considerable.

Not only may such research be troubling for the persons involved, but when sensitive activities that are normally considered private or confidential are the subject of study, additional problems may arise. Cook (1976) reports that Meltzer encountered such difficulties in his study of jury deliberations:

> Members of Congress reacted to the jury recording as a threat to fundamental institutions. When the news of the study came out, a congressional investigation resulted. Following the investigation legislation was passed establishing a fine of a thousand dollars and imprisonment for a year for whoever might attempt to record the proceedings of any jury in the United States while the jury is deliberating or voting (p. 205).

Although the response might be less severe, one can anticipate similar objections to the taping of discussions involving police, attorneys, judges, correctional officials, and probation and parole authorities.

Coercing People to Participate

You have probably received a questionnaire in the mail at some time that offered you some small incentive for completing the form—perhaps a free pen or a dollar bill. This practice is a common one, reflecting the assumption that people who are compensated for their efforts may be more likely to participate in a research endeavor than those who receive nothing. Similarly, college students are often provided a grade incentive for participation in their instructor's research. When, though, does compensation become coercion? When is the researcher justified to compel participation? The issues here involve the freedom not to participate, and the nature and quantity of the incentives that can be ethically provided without creating an undue influence.

The person receiving the questionnaire in the mail is free to keep the compensation and toss away the form. Students may be similarly free not to participate in their instructor's research, but the instructor's power over the grading process may make students feel quite ill at ease doing so. Thus, the relationship between students and researcher as teacher can be particularly coercive. One example of the coercive nature of this relationship can be seen when researchers, acting as teachers, *require* student participation in a research project as part of their course grade (Moreno, 1998). Again, there is a discernable differential in power that would eliminate the students' ability to refuse to participate in the research project.

It might seem that the easiest way out of this dilemma is to simply rely on volunteers for research subjects. But volunteers are different from others simply by virtue of their willingness to participate. At a minimum they are more highly motivated than nonvolunteers. It is important to obtain a more representative sample of participants, a group that mirrors the actual characteristics of those persons to whom study results will be applied.

This problem becomes especially critical when research subjects are vulnerable to coercion. Although students might be considered a captive population, jail and prison inmates are clearly the most vulnerable of research subjects.

> "Criminologists must not coerce or deceive students into serving as research subjects" (American Society of Criminology Code of Ethics, 1999:6).

The history of inmate involvement in research is not a very proud one. Prisoners have been used as "guinea pigs" by pharmaceutical companies that set up laboratories at correctional institutions. For minimal compensation, or the possibility that participation might assist in gaining parole, inmates have participated in a variety of medical research projects.

In the United States, the first use of correctional subjects for medical experiments took place at the Mississippi state prison in 1914, when researchers attempted to discover the relationship

Criminologists "should inform research participants about aspects of the research that might affect their willingness to participate, such as physical risks, discomfort, and/or unpleasant emotional experiences" (Academy of Criminal Justice Sciences Code of Ethics, 2000:5).

between diet and the disease pellagra. The Governor of Mississippi promised pardons to persons volunteering for the experiment. The situation may be contrasted to a more recent experiment in New York in which eight prisoners were inoculated with a venereal infection in order to test possible cures. In exchange for their voluntary participation, the subjects, in their own words, "got syphilis and a carton of cigarettes" (Geis, 1980:226). Today, prisoners are forbidden to engage in such research efforts, but inmates are frequently required to participate in efforts to evaluate the impact of correctional treatment, work, or education programs.

In the early 1990s, research on prisoners was allowed under federal regulations. In order to pass federal guidelines, research on prisoners had to take one of four forms: (1) studies of treatment or therapies that were implemented with the goal of helping prisoners, (2) low-risk research examining inmate behavior and inmate criminality, (3) studies of correctional institutions, and (4) research that examines inmates as a class or group (Moreno, 1998). Currently, the standards by which prisoner or prison research is determined to be ethical depends on the degree to which the research will ultimately benefit individual prisoners or prisoners as a class or group (Moreno, 1998).

The reason for requiring participation is the same as that stated above. Volunteers are sufficiently different from others that relying on their participation would probably produce more positive outcomes than the intervention alone would warrant. Freedom of choice is highly valued in this society, but how much freedom of choice should prisoners have? Before denying a subject the opportunity to refuse participation, it should be clear that the overall value of the research outweighs the harm of coercion. In this consideration, the nature of the participation must be carefully evaluated—coercion to participate in weekly group therapy is quite different from coercion to participate in eight weeks of paramilitary training. One must also assess whether coercion is the only or best means available to obtain research results. Confronting this dilemma requires a balancing of such matters with a concern for individual rights.

Withholding from the Participant the True Nature of the Research

Informed consent requires that subjects know fully the nature of the research, its possible effects, and the uses to be made of the data collected. However, even in the most benign circumstances, written notification may deter further action. Full and complete notification has the added potential of prejudicing responses. Often more accurate assessments are achieved when the subject believes that one aspect of his or her behavior is the focus when research interest is really on something else.

Researchers are understandably reluctant to provide too much information in this regard, especially in the early stages of a project, when the need to develop rapport and a willingness to cooperate are especially important. From a research perspective, fully disclosing the purpose of the research could severely limit findings of the study. For example, a participant's mindfulness of being observed can seriously alter his or her behaviors. Specifically, research participants are typically less willing and likely to admit to undesirable attitudes

> "Criminologists should not mislead respondents involved in a research project as to the purpose for which that research is being conducted" (American Society of Criminology Code of Ethics, 1999:3).

or behaviors if they know they are being studied (Singleton & Straits, 1988). This *social desirability effect* can produce error in the data collected from the research. Ethically speaking, informed consent should precede involvement in the study, so that individuals are given a meaningful opportunity to decline further participation.

Balancing research interests and respect for human dignity requires that subjects be informed about all aspects of the research that might reasonably influence their willingness to participate. Any risks that the subjects may expect to face should be fully discussed. Geis (1980) recommends that researchers remember the example of Walter Reed, who participated as a subject in his own experiments on yellow fever because he could ask no one to undergo anything that he himself was not willing to suffer.

Deceiving the Research Participant

Perhaps the most flagrant example of deception in criminological research is provided by Humphreys's (1970) study, *Tearoom Trade*. Humphreys assumed the role of lookout in public restrooms so that strangers unaware of his research objective could engage uninterrupted in homosexual activity. He copied down the automobile license tags of the subjects and obtained their addresses. Later, he went to their homes, explaining that he was conducting a health survey. He asked the respondents many

> "Members of the Academy should take culturally appropriate steps to secure informed consent and to avoid invasions of privacy" (Academy of Criminal Justice Sciences Code of Ethics, 1999:3).

personal questions that became part of his research on public homosexual conduct.

The rationale for such deception emphasizes the importance of the research and the difficulties of obtaining accurate information through other means. All deceptive acts are not equal. There are differences between active lying and a conscious failure to provide all available information. Deception may be considered an affront to individual autonomy and self-respect or an occasionally legitimate means to be used in service of a higher value (Cook, 1976).

One alternative to deception is to provide only general information about the research project prior to the experiment and offer full disclosure after the research has been completed. Another technique relies on subjects to role-play their behavior after the nature of the research project has been explained. There is mixed evidence, however, on the effectiveness of this technique (Cook, 1976).

In regard to deception, the researcher must evaluate the nature of the research and weigh its value against the impact of the deception on the integrity of participants. The degree to which privacy is invaded and the sensitivity of the behaviors involved are important considerations. Finally, the possibility of harming the research participant should be considered before attempting to deceive the participant. If the nature of the research is potentially harmful, the research participant should be able to fully assess whether he or she wishes to risk participating in the study.

Leading the Research Participants to Commit Acts that Diminish their Self-Respect

Research subjects have been experimentally induced into states of extreme passivity and extreme aggression. Efforts to provoke subjects to lie, cheat, steal, and harm have proven very effective. Cook (1976) describes a study in which students were recruited to participate in a theft of records from a business firm. The inducements described included an opportunity to perform a patriotic service for a department of federal government. A substantial number of students were significantly encouraged to take part in the theft, although ultimately the burglary was not carried out.

Research by Haney, Banks, and Zimbardo (1973) involved the simulation of prison conditions, with 21 subjects assuming the roles of prisoners and guards. After a very short time, the guards began behaving in an aggressive and physically threatening manner. Their use of power became self-aggrandizing and self-perpetuating. The prisoners quickly experienced a loss of personal identity, exhibiting flattened affect and dependency; eventually they were emotionally emasculated by the encounters.

Because of the extreme nature of the subjects' responses, the project was terminated after only six days. The debriefing sessions that followed the research yielded the following comments:

> Guards:
> "They (the prisoners) seemed to lose touch with the reality of the experiment—they took me so seriously."
> "... I didn't interfere with any of the guards' actions. Usually if what they were doing bothered me, I would walk out and take another duty."
> "... looking back, I am impressed by how little I felt for them ..."
> "They (the prisoners) didn't see it as an experiment. It was real, and they were fighting to keep their identity. But we were always there to show them just who was boss."
> "I was tired of seeing the prisoners in their rags and smelling the strong odors of their bodies that filled the cells. I watched them tear at each other, on orders given by us."
> "... Acting authoritatively can be fun. Power can be a great pleasure."

"... During the inspection, I went to cell 2 to mess up a bed which the prisoner had made and he grabbed me, screaming that he had just made it, and he wasn't going to let me mess it up. He grabbed my throat, and although he was laughing, I was pretty scared. I lashed out with my stick and hit him in the chin (although not very hard), and when I freed myself I became angry."

Prisoners:

"... The way we were made to degrade ourselves really brought us down, and that's why we all sat docile towards the end of the experiment."

"... I realize now (after it's over) that no matter how together I thought I was inside my head, my prison behavior was often less under my control than I realized. No matter how open, friendly and helpful I was with other prisoners I was still operating as an isolated, self-centered person, being rational rather than compassionate."

"... I began to feel I was losing my identity, that the person I call_____, the person who volunteered to get me into this prison (because it was a prison to me, it still is a prison to me, I don't regard it as an experiment or a simulation ...) was distant from me, was remote until finally I wasn't that person; I was 416. I was really my number, and 416 was really going to have to decide what to do."

"I learned that people can easily forget that others are human."

In Milgram's (1974) research, participants showed "blind obedience" to a white-coated "researcher" who ordered them to provide what appeared to be electric shocks of increasing severity to subjects who failed to respond correctly to a series of questions. Although they were emotionally upset, the subjects continued to follow their instructions as the "shocked" subjects screamed in agony.

Follow-up research revealed that Milgram's subjects experienced only minor and temporary disturbances (Ring, Wallston & Corey, 1970). One might argue that the subjects even benefited from the project as a result of their greater self-awareness, but the fact that the educational experience occurred without their initial understanding or consent raises ethical concerns.

To what degree should subjects be asked to unknowingly engage in activities that may damage their self-esteem? Again, the researcher is required to engage in a balancing act, reconciling research objectives and the availability of alternative methods with a concern for the integrity of subjects. At a minimum, such research efforts should provide means to address any possible harm to subjects, including debriefings at the conclusion of the research and follow-up counseling as needed.

Violating the Right to Self-Determination: Research on Behavior Control and Character Change

The film *A Clockwork Orange* provides an excellent illustration of the dilemmas of behavior-modifying research. In the film, a thoroughly violent and irredeemable individual named Alex is subjected to therapy that requires him to observe violent acts on film at the same time that the chemicals he has ingested make him physically ill. After a while, the acts that he has observed make him sick as well, and he is changed from a violent individual to one who avoids violence at all cost, including that required for his own self-defense. At the end of the film, the "powers that be" decide to reverse his treatment for political reasons.

Although there is little possibility of behavior modification being used to exact such effect in the near future, the question remains: To what extent should experimental efforts be made to alter human behavior against the will of the participant? Remembering the vulnerability of the inmate to coercion (in the film, Alex only participated in the violence control project because he thought it would help him gain early release), it becomes clear that the greatest desire to use behavior control strategies will be evident in areas involving those persons most vulnerable to coercion—criminals and persons with problems of substance abuse. Although research on crime prevention and control generally has only the most laudable aims, it should be remembered that it is often well-intentioned actions that pose the greatest threat to individual freedoms.

Exposing the Research Participant to Physical or Mental Stress

How would you evaluate the ethics of the following research project: an evaluation of a treatment program in which persons convicted of drunk driving are required to watch and listen to hours of films depicting gory automobile accidents, followed by horrifying emergency room visits and interviews with grieving relatives? Would it matter whether the actions of the drunk drivers had contributed to similar accidents? If your answer is yes, you are probably considering whether the viewers deserve the "punishment" of what they are forced to observe on film.

This not-so-hypothetical scenario raises a difficult issue. Is it acceptable for a research project to engage in activities that punish and perhaps harm the subject? To test various outcomes, subjects in different settings have been exposed to events provoking feelings of horror, shock, threatened sexual identity, personal failure, fear, and emotional shock (Cook, 1976). The subjects in Haney, Banks, and Zimbardo's research and Milgram's research were clearly stressed by their research experiences. To what extent is it acceptable to engage in these practices for the objective of scientific inquiry?

In most situations, it is impossible to observe human reactions such as those described above in their natural settings, so researchers feel justified in creating experiments that produce these reactions. The extent of possible harm raises ethical dilemmas, however, because theoretically there is no limit to what might be contrived to create a "researchable" reaction. The balancing of research objectives with a respect for human subjects is a delicate undertaking, requiring researchers to scrutinize their objectives and the value of their proposed studies dispassionately.

Invading the Privacy of the Research Participant

The issues of privacy and confidentiality are related concerns. Ethical questions are raised by research that invades an individual's privacy without his or her consent. When information on subjects has been obtained for reasons other than research (e.g., the development of a criminal history file), there are questions about the extent to which data should be released to researchers. Some records are more sensitive than others in this regard, depending on how easily the offender's identity can be obtained, as well as the quantity and nature of the information recorded. Even when consent has been given and the information has been gathered expressly for research purposes, maintaining the confidentiality of responses may be a difficult matter when the responses contain information of a sensitive and/or illegal nature.

Confidentiality

The issue of confidentiality is especially important in the study of crime and deviance. Subjects will generally not agree to provide information in this area unless their responses are to remain confidential. This may be a more difficult task than it appears. Generally, it is important to be able to identify a subject so that his or her responses can be linked to other sources of data on the individual. Institutionalized delinquents might be asked in confidence about their involvement in drug use and other forms of misconduct during confinement. An important part of the research would involve gathering background information from the offender's

> "Subjects of research are entitled to rights of personal confidentiality unless they are waived" (Academy of Criminal Justice Sciences Code of Ethics, 2000:5).

institutional files to determine what types of offenders are most likely to be involved in institutional misconduct. To do this, the individual's confidential responses need to be identifiable; therefore, complete anonymity is unfeasible.

As long as only dispassionate researchers have access to this information, there may be no problem. Difficulties arise when third parties, especially criminal justice authorities, become interested in the research responses. Then the issue becomes one of protecting the data (and the offender) from officials who have the power to invoke the criminal justice process.

One response to this dilemma is to store identifying information in a remote place; some researchers have even recommended sending sensitive information out of the country. Because the relationship between the researcher and his or her informants is not privileged, researchers can be called upon to provide information to the courts.

Lewis Yablonsky, a criminologist/practitioner, while testifying in defense of Gridley White, one of Yablonsky's main informants in his hippie study, was asked by the judge nine times if he had witnessed Gridley smoking marijuana. Yablonsky refused to answer because of the rights guaranteed him in the Fifth Amendment of the U.S. Constitution. Although he was not legally sanctioned, he said the incident was humiliating and suggested that researchers should have guarantees of immunity (Wolfgang, 1982:396).

It is also important that researchers prepare their presentation of research findings in a manner that ensures that the particular responses of an individual cannot be discerned. Presentation of only aggregate findings was especially important for Marvin Wolfgang (1982) when he reinterviewed persons included in his earlier study of delinquency in a birth cohort. His follow-up consisted of hour-long interviews with about 600 youths. The subjects were asked many personal questions, including many about their involvement in delinquency and crime. Four of his respondents admitted committing criminal homicide, and 75 admitted to forcible rape. Many other serious crimes were also described, for which none of the participants had been arrested.

At the time of the research, all of the respondents were orally assured that the results of the research would remain confidential, but Wolfgang raises a number of ethical questions surrounding this practice. Should written consent forms have been provided to the subjects, detailing the nature of the research? Wolfgang concludes that such forms would have raised more questions than they answered. Could a court order impound the records? Could persons attempting to protect the data be prosecuted for their actions? Could the data be successfully concealed?

The general willingness to protect subjects who admit to serious crimes also requires close ethical scrutiny. Wolfgang (1982) takes the traditional scientific stance on this issue, proposing that such information belongs to science. Because the information would have not been discovered without the research effort, its protection neither helps nor hinders police. The ethical judgment here requires a weighing of interests—the importance of scientific research balanced against society's interest in capturing a particular individual.

It should be noted that if researchers began to inform on their subjects routinely, all future research relying on self-reports would be jeopardized. Thus, the issue at hand is not simply that of the value of a particular study, but the value of all research utilizing subject disclosures. Researchers are generally advised not to undertake such research unless they feel comfortable about protecting their sources. This requires that all research involving the use of confidential information provide for controlled access to sensitive data and protect the information from unauthorized searches, inadvertent access, and the compulsory legal process (Cook, 1976).

Withholding Benefits to Participants in Control Groups

The necessity of excluding some potential beneficiaries from initial program participation arises whenever a classical experimental design is to be used to evaluate the program. This research design requires the random assignment of subjects to experimental and control groups. Subjects in the control group are excluded from the program and/or receive "standard" rather than "experimental" treatment.

In a program evaluation, it is important that some subjects receive the benefits of the program while others do not, to ensure that the outcomes observed are the direct result of the experimental intervention and not something else (subject enthusiasm or background characteristics, for example). It is imperative that those who receive the intervention (the experimental group) and those who do not (the control group) be as identical in the aggregate as possible, so that a clear assessment of program impact, untainted by variation in the nature of subjects, can be obtained. Though randomization is important from a methodological point of view, the participants who, by chance, end up in the control group are often denied treatment, or possibly services, that could be of the utmost importance to their lives. The Minneapolis Domestic Violence Experiment is a classic example of how those persons involved the control group were denied potential law enforcement interventions that could have benefited them. Figure 2.1.1 is a description of Sherman and Berk's (1984) study that looked at various responses to domestic violence.

The best way to ensure that experimental and control subjects are identical is randomization. Randomization is to be distinguished from arbitrariness. Randomization requires that every subject have an equal chance to be assigned to either the experimental or control group; arbitrariness involves no such equality of opportunity.

In many ways, randomization may be more fair than standard practice based on good intentions. Geis (1980) reports:

> For most of us, it would be unthinkable that a sample of armed robbers be divided into two groups on the basis of random assignment—one group to spend 10 years in prison, the second to receive a sentence of 2 years on probation. Nonetheless, at a federal judicial conference, after examining an elaborate presentence report concerning a bank robber, 17 judges said they would have imprisoned the man, while 10 indicated they favored probation. Those voting for imprisonment set sentences ranging from 6 months to 15 years (p. 221).

Randomization is also acceptable under law, because its use is reasonably related to a governmental objective, that is, testing the effectiveness of a program intervention (Erez, 1986).

Although randomization is inherently fair, it often appears less so to the subjects involved. Surveys of prisoners have indicated that need, merit, and "first come, first served" are more acceptable criteria than a method that the offenders equated with gambler's luck (Erez, 1986). Consider Morris's (1966) description of "the burglar's nightmare":

> If eighty burglars alike in all relevant particulars were assigned randomly to experimental and control groups, forty each, with the experimentals to be released six months or a year earlier than they ordinarily would be and the control released at their regularly appointed time, how would the burglar assigned to the control group respond? It is unfair, unjust, unethical, he could say, for me to be put into the control group. If people like me, he might complain, are being released early, I too deserve the same treatment (cited in Erez, 1986:394).

Program staff are also frequently unhappy with randomization because it fails to utilize their clinical skills in the selection of appropriate candidates for intervention. Extending this line of thought, consider the likely response of judges requested to sentence burglary offenders randomly to prison or probation. While this might be the best method of determining the effectiveness of these sanctions, the judicial response (and perhaps community response as well) would probably be less than enthusiastic. This is because it is assumed, often without any evidence, that standard practice is achieving some reasonable objective, such as individualizing justice or preventing crime.

Domestic violence was beginning to be recognized as a major public affairs and criminal justice problem. Victim advocates were demanding the automatic arrest for domestic violence offenders. However, there was no empirical research that showed that arresting domestic violence offenders deterred future acts of domestic violence. Thus, Sherman and Berk, sponsored by funding from the National Institute of Justice, designed a randomized experiment that looked at the effects of arrest on domestic violence.

Sherman and Berk enlisted the help of the Minneapolis Police Department. When on misdemeanor domestic violence calls, the police were to respond to the call depending on the random call response they were assigned. There were three responses with which the police could respond to the misdemeanor domestic violence call: arrest, removal of batterer from the premises without an arrest, or counsel the batterer and leave the premises. While the initial findings of this research indicated that arresting domestic violence offenders reduced the incidence of future incidents, the methodology and ethics of this experiment have been heavily scrutinized. The victims of the misdemeanor domestic violence certainly did not consent to the randomized assignment of response to the situation. Thus, not only were potential benefits withheld from the certain women, some victims could have been placed at greater risk as a result of the random treatment. While the benevolent intentions behind this research agenda were admirable, the implementation of the experiment and the variable being randomized (i.e., type of response to domestic violence) should have been further considered before implementation of the research.

FIGURE 2.1.1 The Minneapolis Domestic Violence Experiment
Based on Sherman L.W. & R.A. Berk (1984). "The Specific Deterrent Effects of Arrest for Domestic Assault." *American Sociological Review*, 49(2):261–272.

Randomization does produce winners and losers. Of critical importance in weighing the consequences of randomization are the differences in treatment experienced by the experimental and control groups. Six factors are relevant here:

1. *Significance of the interest affected.* Early release is of much greater consequence than a change of institutional diet.
2. *Extent of difference.* Six months early release is of greater significance than one week's early release.
3. *Comparison of the disparity with standard treatment.* If both experimental and control group treatment is an improvement over standard treatment, then the discrepancy between the experimental and control group is of less concern.
4. *Whether disparity reflects differences in qualifications of subjects.* If the disparity is reasonably related to some characteristic of the subjects, the denial of benefits to the control group is less significant.
5. *Whether the experimental treatment is harmful or beneficial to subjects compared with the treatment they would otherwise receive.* A program that assigns members of the experimental group to six weeks of "boot camp" may be more demanding of inmates than the standard treatment of six months' incarceration.
6. *Whether participation is mandatory or voluntary.* Voluntary participation mitigates the concern of denial of benefit, while coercion exacerbates the dilemma (Federal Judicial Center, 1981:31-40).

Similar to the management of other ethical dilemmas, an effort is required to balance values of human decency and justice with the need for accurate information on intervention effectiveness. Problems arise not in the extreme cases of disparity but in more routine circumstances. Consider the following example: How do we judge a situation in which a foundation grant permits attorneys to be supplied for all cases being heard by a juvenile court in which attorneys have previously appeared only in rare instances? A fundamental study hypothesis may be that the presence of an attorney tends to result in a more favorable disposition for the client. This idea may be tested by comparing dispositions prior to the beginning of the experiment with those ensuing subsequently, though it would be more satisfactory to supply attorneys to a sample of the cases and withhold them from the remainder, in order to calculate in a more experimentally uncontaminated manner the differences between the outcomes in the two situations.

The matter takes on additional complexity if the researchers desire to determine what particular attorney role is the most efficacious in the juvenile court. They may suspect that an attorney who acts as a friend of the court, knowingly taking its viewpoint as *parens patriae,* and attempting to interpret the court's interest to his or her client, will produce more desirable results than one who doggedly challenges the courtroom procedure and the judge's interpretation of fact, picks at the probation report, raises constant objections, and fights for his or her client as he would in a criminal court. But what results are "more desirable" (Geis, 1980:222-223)?

It could be contended that little is really known about how attorney roles influence dispositions and that, without the project, no one would have any kind of representation. Over the long term, all juveniles stand to benefit. On the other hand, it could be argued that it is wrong to deprive anyone of the best judgment of his or her attorney by requiring a particular legal approach. What if there are only enough funds to supply one-half of the juveniles with attorneys anyway? Is randomization more or less fair than trying to decide which cases "need" representation the most?

Randomization imposes a special ethical burden because it purposefully counters efforts to determine the best course of action with the element of chance. The practice is justifiable because the pursuit of knowledge is a desirable objective—as long as the overall benefits outweigh the risks. The balancing of risks and benefits is complicated by the fact that judgments must often be made in a context of ambiguity, attempting to predict the benefits of an intervention that is being tested precisely because its impact is unknown.

The Federal Judicial Center (1981) recommends that program evaluations should only be considered when certain threshold conditions are met:

> First, the status quo warrants substantial improvements or is of doubtful effectiveness.
>
> Second, there must be significant uncertainty about the value or effectiveness of the innovation.
>
> Third, information needed to clarify the uncertainty must be feasibly obtainable by the program experimentation but not readily obtainable by other means.
>
> And fourth, the information sought must pertain directly to the decision whether or not to adopt the proposed innovation on a general, non-experimental basis (p. 7).

Several conditions lessen the ethical burdens of evaluative research. Random assignment is especially acceptable when resources are scarce and demand for the benefit is high. Denying benefits to the control group is quite acceptable when members of the control group can participate at a later date. Finally, discrepancies between the treatment of experimental and control groups are decreased when the groups are geographically separated (Federal Judicial Center, 1981).

Failing to Treat Research Participants Fairly and to Show Them Consideration and Respect

The basic tenets of professionalism require that researchers treat subjects with courtesy and fulfill the variety of commitments they make to subjects. In an effort to obtain cooperation, subjects are often promised a follow-up report on the findings of the research; such reports may be forgotten once the study has been completed. Subjects are often led to believe that they will achieve some personal benefit from the research. This may be one of the more difficult obligations to fulfill.

Researchers need to treat their human subjects with constant recognition of their integrity and their contribution to the research endeavor. This is especially important when subjects are powerless and vulnerable. Although such treatment may be a time-consuming chore, it is the only ethical way to practice scientific research.

Balancing Scientific and Ethical Concerns

This discussion has emphasized the importance of balancing a concern for subjects against the potential benefits of the research. Cook (1976) identifies the following potential benefits of a research project:

1. Advances in scientific theory that contribute to a general understanding of human behavior.
2. Advances in knowledge of practical value to society.
3. Gains for the research participant, such as increased understanding, satisfaction in making a contribution to science or to the solution of social problems, needed money or special privileges, knowledge of social science or of research methods, and so on (p. 235).

The potential costs to subjects are considerable, however, and it is often difficult for the researcher to be objective in assessing the issues. For this reason, many professional associations have established guidelines and procedures for ethical research conduct. Generally, because little active monitoring occurs, the professional is honor-bound to follow these guidelines.

Institutional Review Boards and Setting Ethical Standards

To ensure that their faculty follow acceptable procedures (and to protect themselves from liability), universities have established institutional review boards to scrutinize each research project that involves the use of human subjects. These review boards serve a valuable function in that they review the specifications of each research project prior to implementation. They are generally incapable of providing direct monitoring of projects so, again, the responsibility for ethical conduct falls on the researcher.

How are the ethical standards being set within the criminal justice community, and how and to what degree are ethics being taught in criminology and criminal justice academic settings? McSkimming, Sever, and King (2000) analyzed 11 research methods textbooks that are frequently used in criminal justice and criminology courses. The authors looked at the extent to which ethical issues were addressed within the criminal justice texts and the type of ethical issues that were covered within the texts. The authors found that there was no collective format being utilized in the major criminal justice texts regarding ethics in criminal justice. Furthermore, the significance and positive functions of institutional review boards were rarely mentioned.

Of further concern was the noticeable absence of some important ethical topics in these criminal justice research methods texts. These topic areas concerned ethics related to the dissemination of information into the criminal justice audience. These areas concerned "plagiarism, fabrication of data, Institutional Review Boards, authorship rank, and ethical considerations in journal editing and grant-writing" (p. 58).

Institutional review boards are often the only source for ethical guidance and standards for the criminal justice academic researcher (McSkimming, Sever & King, 2000). It is imperative that graduate students, publishing professors, and other disseminators of information within the criminal justice discipline have some guideline or gauge with which to measure ethical standards.

Ethical Codes

In order to address some of these key ethical considerations, two predominant criminal justice associations have developed and make known a standard or code of ethics. The Academy of Criminal Justice Sciences (ACJS) and the American Society of Criminology (ASC) have each advanced a standard for those persons researching and writing within the criminal justice discipline. The two codes of ethics are similar; they address the ethical standards of conducting social science research as well as the dissemination of information within the criminal justice discipline. Specifically, these codes provide criminologists with ethical standards concerning fair treatment; the use of students in research; objectivity and integrity in the conduct of research; confidentiality, disclosure, and respect for research populations; publication and authorship standards; and employment practices (ACJS Code of Ethics, 2000; ASC Code of Ethics, 1999).

Ethical/Political Considerations

Applied social research, that is, research that examines the effectiveness of social policies and programs, carries with it additional ethical responsibilities. Such research influences the course of human events in a direct fashion—often work, education, future opportunities, and deeply held values and beliefs are affected by the outcomes. Researchers must be prepared to deal with a variety of pressures and demands as they undertake the practice and dissemination of research.

It is generally acknowledged that organizations asked to measure their own effectiveness often produce biased results. Crime statistics provide a notorious example of data that tend to be used to show either an effective police department (falling crime figures) or a need for more resources (rising crime figures). Criminal justice researchers are often asked to study matters that are equally sensitive. A correctional treatment program found to be ineffective may lose its funding. A study that reveals extensive use of plea bargaining may cost a prosecutor his or her election.

Often the truth is complicated. A survey that reveals that drug use is declining in the general population may prove troublesome for those trying to lobby for the establishment of more drug treatment facilities. The survey results may lead the public to believe that there is no problem at the same time that the need for treatment facilities for the indigent is substantial.

Such research has been known to produce unintended consequences. The publication of selected results of a study on the effectiveness of correctional treatment programs (Martinson, 1974) was used by many persons to justify limiting funds for education and treatment programs in correctional institutions. The research revealed that there was little evidence that correctional treatment programs were effective means of reducing recidivism (a finding that has been widely challenged). Rather than stimulating the development of more theoretically sound programs and rigorous evaluations of these efforts, the apparent product of the research was a decrease in the humaneness of conditions of confinement.

Sometimes research results conflict with cherished beliefs. Studies of preventive police patrol (Kelling et al., 1974) and detective investigations (Chaiken, Greenwood & Petersilia, 1977) both revealed that these practices, long assumed to be essential elements of effective law enforcement, were of little value. Researchers can expect findings such as these to meet with considerable resistance.

Researchers may be asked to utilize their skills and their aura of objectivity to provide an organization or agency with what it wants. When the group that pays the bills has a direct interest in the nature of the outcome, the pressures can be considerable. Marvin Wolfgang (1982) reports:

> I was once invited to do research by an organization whose views are almost completely anti-thetical to mine on the issue of gun control. Complete freedom and a considerable amount of money to explore the relationship between gun control legislation and robbery were promised. I would not perform the research under those auspices. But the real clincher in the decision was that if the research produced conclusions opposite from that the organization wanted, the agency would not publish the results nor allow me to publish them. Perhaps their behavior, within their ideological framework, was not unethical. But within my framework, as a scientist who values freedom of publication as well as of scientific inquiry, I would have engaged in an unethical act of prostituting my integrity had I accepted those conditions. (p. 395)

In-house researchers, who are employed by the organization for which the research is being conducted, face special problems in this regard, because they lack the freedom to pick and choose their research topic. These problems must balance their concern for rigorous scientific inquiry with their need for continued employment.

Generally, the issues confronted are subtle and complex. Although researchers may be directly told to conceal or falsify results, more often they are subtly encouraged to design their research with an eye toward the desired results. The greatest barrier to such pressures is the development of a truly independent professional research unit within the organization. Such independence protects the researcher from political pressures and at the same time promotes the credibility of the research being conducted. Without this protection, the individual is left to his or her own devices and standards of ethical conduct.

The Purity of Scientific Research

The ideal of scientific inquiry is the pure, objective examination of the empirical world, untainted by personal prejudice. However, research is carried out by human beings, not automatons, and they have a variety of motivations for undertaking the research that they do. Topics may be selected because of curiosity or a perceived need to address a specific social problem, but the availability of grants in a particular field may also encourage researchers to direct their attention to these areas. This is critical if one is working for a research organization dependent upon "soft" money. The need for university faculty to publish and establish a name for themselves in a particular area may encourage them to seek "hot" topics for their research, or to identify an extremely narrow research focus in which they can become identified as an expert.

There is some evidence that the nature of one's research findings influences the likelihood of publication (*Chronicle of Higher Education*, 1989d). A curious author submitted almost identical articles to a number of journals. The manuscripts differed only in one respect—the nature of the conclusions. One version of the article showed that the experiment had no effect; the other described a positive result. His experiment produced some interesting findings—the article with positive outcomes was more likely to be accepted for publication than the other manuscript.

If research that concludes that "the experiment didn't work" or that "differences between Groups A and B were insignificant" are indeed less likely to see the light of day, then pressures to revise one's research focus or rewrite one's hypotheses to match the results produced can be anticipated.

None of the practices described above involve scandalous violations of ethical conduct. Their presentation should function, however, to remind us that actions justified in the name of scientific inquiry may be motivated by factors far less "pure" than the objective they serve.

Public Policy Pronouncements and Teaching Criminal Justice

When is a researcher speaking from the facts and when is he or she promoting personal ideology? If there were any fully conclusive and definitive studies in the social sciences, this question would not arise. However, research findings are always tentative, and statements describing them invariably require conditional language. On the other hand, researchers have values and beliefs like everyone else, and few of us want to employ the same conditional language required to discuss research when we state our views on matters of public policy and morality. Researchers thus have a special obligation to carefully evaluate their remarks and clearly distinguish between opinion and apparent empirical fact. This is not always an easy task, but it is the only way to safeguard the objectivity that is critically important to scientific inquiry. Furthermore, criminal justice researchers acting as teachers and mentors have a responsibility to their students, due to the influence their position has over the lives of the students (ACJS, 2000). Specifically, a researcher's influence and authority used inappropriately has the potential to mislead and distort the perspectives of their students by disseminating information that was merely personal ideology as opposed to scientific findings.

Conclusion

Conducting scientific research in criminal justice and criminology in an ethical fashion is a difficult task. It requires a constant weighing and balancing of objectives and motivations. It would be nice to conclude that the best research is that which is undertaken in an ethical fashion, but such a statement would skirt the dilemma. This is the exact nature of the problem: those actions required to meet the demands of scientific rigor sometimes run counter to ethical behavior.

Evaluating rather than avoiding ethical dilemmas does provide a learning experience, though, the benefits of which can be expected to spill over into all aspects of human endeavor. Thinking and doing in an ethical fashion requires practice, and conducting research provides considerable opportunity for the development of experience.

References

ACJS (2000). "Academy of Criminal Justice Sciences: Code of Ethics."

ASC (1999). "American Society of Criminology: Code of Ethics."

Chaiken, J., P. Greenwood & J. Petersilia (1977). "The Criminal Investigation Process: A Summary Report." *Policy Analysis* 3:187-217.

Chronicle of Higher Education (1989a), January 25:A44.

Chronicle of Higher Education (1989b), June 14:A44.

Chronicle of Higher Education (1989c), July 19:A4.

Chronicle of Higher Education (1989d), August 2:A5.

Chronicle of Higher Education (1999), November 46:A18.

Cohen, B. (1980). *Deviant Street Networks: Prostitution in New York City*. Cambridge, MA: Lexington Books.

Cook, S.W. (1976). "Ethical Issues in the Conduct of Research in Social Relations." In *Research Methods in Social Relations*, 3rd ed., Claire Sellitz, Lawrence Rightsman & Stuart Cook (eds.). New York: Holt, Rinehart and Winston.

Driscoll, A. (1999). "UF Prof Who Touted Privatized Prisons Admits Firm Paid Him." *Miami Herald*, April 21:A1.

Erez, E. (1986). "Randomized Experiments in Correctional Context: Legal, Ethical and Practical Concerns." *Journal of Criminal Justice*, 14: 389-400.

Federal Judicial Center (1981). *Experimentation in the Law. Report of the Federal Judicial Center Advisory Committee on Experimentation in the Law*. Washington, DC: Federal Judicial Center.

Geis, G. (1980). "Ethical and Legal Issues in Experiments with Offender Populations." In *Criminal Justice Research: Approaches, Problems & Policy*, S. Talarico (ed.). Cincinnati: Anderson.

Haney, C., C. Banks & P. Zimbardo (1973). "Interpersonal Dynamics in a Simulated Prison." *International Journal of Criminology and Penology*, 1:69-97.

Humphreys, L. (1970). *Tearoom Trade: Impersonal Sex in Public Places*. Chicago: Aldine.

Jones, K.D. (1999). "Ethics in Publication." *Counseling and Values*, 43:99-106.

Kelling, G.L., T. Page, D. Dieckman & C.E. Browne (1974). *The Kansas City Preventive Patrol Experiment*. Washington, DC: The Police Foundation.

Martinson, R. (1974). "What Works?—Questions and Answers About Prison Reform." *Public Interest*, 35:25-54.

McSkimming, M.J., B. Sever & R.S. King (2000). "The Coverage of Ethics in Research Methods Textbooks." *Journal of Criminal Justice Education*, 11:51-63.

Meltzer, B.A. (1953). "A Projected Study of the Jury as a Working Institution." *The Annals of the American Academy of Political and Social Sciences*, 287:97-102.

Milgram, S. (1974). *Obedience to Authority: An Experimental View*. New York: Harper and Row.

Moreno, J.D. (1998). "Convenient and Captive Populations." In J.P. Kahn, A.C. Mastroianni & J. Sugarman (eds.), *Beyond Consent: Seeking Justice in Research* (pp. 111–130). New York: Oxford University Press, pp. 111–130.

Morris, N. (1966). "Impediments to Penal Reform." *Chicago Law Review*, 33:646-653.

The New York Times (1983). February 26, 1983: 7.

Ring, K., K. Wallston & M. Corey (1970). "Mode of Debriefing as a Factor Affecting Subjective Reaction to a Milgram Type Obedience Experience: An Ethical Inquiry." *Representative Research in Social Psychology*, 1:67-88.

Sherman, L.W. & R.A. Berk (1984). "The Specific Deterrent Effects of Arrest for Domestic Assault." *American Sociological Review*, 49:261-272.

Short, J.F., Jr. & F. Strodtbeck (1965). *Group Processes and Gang Delinquency*. Chicago: University of Chicago Press.

Singleton, Jr., R.A. & B.C. Straits (1988). *Approaches to Social Research*, 3rd ed. New York: Oxford University Press.

Whyte, W.F. (1955). *Streetcorner Society*. Chicago: University of Chicago Press.

Wolfgang, M. (1982). "Ethics and Research." In *Ethics, Public Policy and Criminal Justice*, F. Elliston & N. Bowie (eds.). Cambridge, MA: Oelgeschlager, Gunn and Hain.

AI Predictive Policing

David Crookes

Could the police target you for crimes you're yet to commit? **David Crookes** looks at how a science-fiction concept has become reality

'Ello, 'ello, 'ello—What's All This Then?

AI-powered predictive policing is an attempt to identify the individuals who are most likely to commit a crime or become a victim in the future. It uses vast data sets and machine-learning algorithms to assess potential risks. The idea is that by alerting police forces, officers can consider the most appropriate action—tackling crime before it even takes place.

How Does It Work?

UK police forces, led by West Midlands Police, are working on a system called the National Data Analytics Solution (NDAS). Based on the records of five million people who have committed crimes or been stopped and searched, it uses artificial intelligence to decipher criminal patterns. So far, it has uncovered 1,400 'predictive indicators'—30 of which are deemed to be particularly strong. There's a possibility individuals will be given a risk score that can determine how likely a person is to offend. Those at the higher end will be flagged.

Who Will Be Flagged by the NDAS?

Iain Donnelly, the project's lead, says the system will pick up on a person's history and social interactions, and this could manifest itself in many ways. Someone with a background of mental-health problems, for instance, may be deemed more likely to be a future violent offender. Likewise, someone who hangs around with other violent offenders, or a person whose behaviour is thought to match that of others who have gone on to commit greater crimes, could be flagged as being of greater risk.

Predictive Policing Will Let the Cops Identify Criminals Before They Commit Crimes

So Far, So *Minority Report*?

The parallels between AI-powered predictive policing and the 2002 Hollywood movie starring Tom Cruise have not gone unnoticed. In the sci-fi film, set in 2054 and based on a short story by Philip K Dick, a police department called PreCrime uses three psychics to foresee murders taking place. But although they enable the murder rate to be cut to zero, there are inevitable flaws. The same is true of the NDAS.

Minority Report Covered the Concept of Predictive Policing and Its Potential Flaws

But What Sort of Crimes Are Being Targeted?

At the moment, the NDAS is looking to predict serious violent crime, which means incidents involving a knife or a gun. It will also seek to identify potential victims of crime or modern slavery, but there's nothing to say that the system will stop there. If the system shows itself to be effective, then there's no telling what other crimes will eventually fall under its radar. The jury is also out on how ethical all of this could prove to be.

Could It Lead to False Arrests?

Not at this stage. West Midlands Police says it will not be arresting anyone based on the information thrown up by the NDAS, and that is also set to be the case with the other eight forces involved in the project (among them, the Metropolitan Police and Greater Manchester Police, which means the country's three largest forces have taken an interest). Instead, local health and social workers will be dispatched to visit flagged people in the hope of nipping possible issues in the bud. Potential offenders will be offered counselling while those at risk of becoming victims will be contacted either to warn them or make them aware of how to deal with problems they may end up facing.

The Alan Turing Institute Is Worried about the Ethics of Using AI Predictive Policing

So What's the Problem?

The Data Ethics Group at the Alan Turing Institute in London (www.turing.ac.uk) has been working with the Independent Digital Ethics Panel for Policing (IDEPP) and has praised attempts to develop an ethically compliant proposal. But it also says the NDAS is "moving law enforcement away from its traditional crime-related role and into wider and deeper aspects of social and public policy". The institute is worried about inaccurate prediction—false positives or negatives—and it has raised ethical issues around surveillance and autonomy, as well as the "potential reversal of the presumption of innocence".

Have the Concerns Been Dismissed?

Chorus Intelligence Cleans Crime Data to Try and Stop Mistakes Being Made

No. West Midlands Police says it will draw on the advice offered by Turing and IDEPP "to help develop their approach to the ethical governance of the project". A prototype is set to be produced by March 2019, so it's likely to fall under greater scrutiny at that point to see if the ethical concerns have been ironed out.

There are worries that certain people are likely to be targeted even if they have never committed an offence, and there is no way that anyone can truly foresee whether or not a person may tread down a slippery path. Young black men, for instance, may be disproportionately stopped and searched by the police, and the datasets would reflect that. Machine learning could pick up on such records and reinforce the bias.

Surely the Data Just Needs 'Cleaning'?

Yes, it does, and there are companies that do this: Chorus Intelligence (chorusintel.com) works with 85% of police departments as well as counter-terrorism and Home Office immigration enforcement units to clean data to evidential standard. But bias tends to find a way through and similar systems in other countries have shown this to be an issue. It points towards the need for ultra-clean data as well as clear training for the police officers recording the information.

So the UK Isn't the Only Country Pursuing This?

Not at all. Predictive policing systems are gathering pace and many companies have sprung up to provide software. Dating-mining company Palantir (www.palantir.com), for example, worked with the New Orleans Police Department and developed a system that analysed social media, traced people's ties to gang members and charted criminal histories in order to identify those affiliated with notorious gangs such as the 3NG and the 39ers. Chicago's police, meanwhile, developed an algorithm-based "heat list" that identified people most likely to be involved in a shooting.

But What About People with No History?

Focusing on people who have already had a brush with the law, or those who are affiliated with someone else who has, is always going to throw up dangers. There's a chance police will come to rely too heavily on AI-powered predictive policing and that people unknown to them will slip through the net. Cash-strapped forces may also reduce their presence or concentrate too heavily on particular locations to the detriment of others. In the case of Chicago, it was found that police used the system to target people for arrest rather than to provide social assistance. What's more, the city's murder rate pretty much remained the same.

Predictive Policing Failed to Reduce the Number of People Shot in Chicago

Could AI-Powered Policing Also Affect Sentencing?

Maybe, although not in the UK for the foreseeable future. In Pennsylvania, there's a proposal for a criminal-justice algorithm that predicts the risk someone poses to public safety. Again, there are worries that it will lead to racial bias since nine times more black people are imprisoned in that particular American state but it could potentially lead to someone receiving a higher sentence based on attributes as wide-ranging as age and employment, as well as criminal record. That said, the idea is to keep lower-risk criminals out of jail to reduce costs

SPOTTING FACES IN A CROWD

As well as investigating technology designed to predict the risk of offending, UK police forces have used facial-recognition tools at high profile public events, including the Notting Hill Carnival, a Six Nations rugby match and the UEFA Champions League final in Cardiff in 2017.

The UK's data commissioner Elizabeth Denham is currently looking into the technology, in particular at the lack of a national governance framework. There is concern that it is intrusive and that the artificial intelligence had a 98% false-positive rate when tested by The Met. Yet despite worries about a lack of transparency and even that the system struggles in low-light conditions and with large crowds, automated facial recognition continues to be used.

Conclusion

This chapter discussed several ethical issues that researchers must consider and address. Any human subject involved in or thinking about becoming involved in a research study must be informed about and protected from potential harms that may occur as an outcome of their participation. Researchers must ensure that consent is obtained from research participants prior to study participation, that a subject's identity (name and/or other potentially identifying information) is kept anonymous or confidential, and that subjects are treated fairly and with respect. Researchers must ensure that they do not deceive subjects about the research, coerce subjects into participating, or "expose the research participant to physical or mental stress." Although it may be tempting for researchers to engage in practices that misrepresent findings when a study produces outcomes that are disappointing, it is vital that researchers present study outcomes honestly. Published study outcomes and findings may influence program and policy recommendations within the jurisdiction being researched and other jurisdictions who review and use study outcomes to inform their efforts. Ethical issues related to the use of AI-predictive policing and sentencing were discussed in the second selection in this chapter. Question 4 invites the reader to conduct some research in the area of AI in the criminal justice field. In what ways are these technologies being used or proposed? What are some ethical concerns associated with the use of these technologies within criminal justice?

Chapter 2 Reflection Questions

1. List and briefly describe five of the ethical considerations surrounding research with human subjects. Why are each of these considerations important for researchers and study participants?

2. Projects that involve research with human subjects and the use of data that are not publicly available must be reviewed and approved by your institution's IRB. What are IRBs? Why are they important? Locate your institution's IRB website. Complete the human subject training, and download and submit your training certificate to your instructor.

3. Imagine that you have been asked to survey community members about experiences with and perceptions of law enforcement within your city. What are some of the ethical considerations you must consider as you prepare to engage in this research? What additional concerns may arise as you gather survey responses and report the findings from your study?

4. Conduct an internet search on applications of AI in the criminal justice system. Discuss some potential applications of the ways in which AI is currently being used or considered and how these applications may be used within the field of criminal justice in the future. What are some of the related ethical concerns? Be sure to provide relevant citations for your findings.

5. Review the Academy of Criminal Justice Sciences Code of Ethics (https://www.acjs.org/page/Code_Of_Ethics?&hhsearchterms=%22ethics+and+code%22). List at least five of the codes under the "Members of the Academy as Researchers" section.

Building Your Research Proposal

Chapter 2: Begin to Assess Ethical Considerations of Research

Recall the general area of interest you identified in the Building Your Research Proposal exercise at the end of chapter 1. Start exploring and thinking about how you could conduct research in this area. What ethical concerns or dilemmas do you anticipate? How can you address these concerns? Do you think that your study will require IRB approval? Why or why not?

The Process of Conducting Research

Introduction

The articles in this chapter introduce the process of conducting research and present several foundational concepts and terms that are vital to this practice. Withrow's article summarizes the research process, or action steps required to produce information or data able to address a research question or hypothesis. This active process begins with step 1: ask a research question and ends with step 11: ask another question. Withrow notes, "Good research raises more questions than it answers." This process involves asking questions, reviewing existing studies, refining questions, defining concepts and creating measures, designing the study, collecting data, analyzing and interpreting data/findings (remember your stats class?), and summarizing research findings in a report.

In the second article, Dantzker, Hunter, and Quinn present the vocabulary or language of research, expanding on many of the foundational concepts presented in Withrow's article. The authors further introduce additional concepts and terms that are vital to the process of conducting research, including unit of analysis, population, sample, validity, reliability, and quantitative versus qualitative research, while highlighting the important role theory plays in the research process. Theoretical components may be used to inform the development of a research question and/or the research process (deductive approach). Research findings/ outcomes/observations may be used to develop new crime theories (inductive approach). This selection contains a lot of important information, so be sure to refer back to it often to ensure that you understand and apply the constructs introduced in this chapter to your research proposal or project.

   Phew. Take a deep breath. Relax. Learning about this process is not as complicated as it sounds, although learning to apply the steps outlined in this chapter to your area of research focus will take some time and practice. As you continue to establish your areas of research interest, be sure to select a topic that you are incredibly interested in and excited about. That is the most important piece of advice I can give you. If you choose to focus on an area you are moderately or mildly interested in, this process will be much more painful. I promise.

The Research Process

Brian L. Withrow

Sometimes, during my office hours, one of my students will point to the badge displayed on the wall and ask, "Do you ever miss being a cop?" I have a standard answer: "I miss the camaraderie among police officers. But I don't miss witnessing the tragedy of crime. In many ways, being a professor isn't all that different from being a police officer. Conducting research is just like conducting a criminal investigation. And I like to think that my research, like my job as a police officer, makes us safer." The similarities underlying research and policing are apparent in the true story below.

MAKING RESEARCH REAL 3.1—THE CLOSEST THING TO SHERLOCK HOLMES

Pierce Brooks joined the Los Angeles Police Department (LAPD) in 1948. Brooks is famous for leading the investigation that eventually became the story line for James Wambaugh's *The Onion Field*, a book and later a film about the kidnapping of two plainclothes LAPD officers and the subsequent murder of Officer Ian James Campbell. But Brooks' contributions to American policing go far beyond his work in the LAPD.

As a homicide detective, Brooks was assigned a case that at first seemed routine. But something about the case led Brooks to believe that the offender had killed before. Shortly thereafter, he was assigned an unrelated case that struck him the same way. He decided to see if he could connect other homicides to these cases. He spent countless hours reading newspaper articles in the Los Angeles Public Library and traveled to other libraries looking for similar cases. This was before the Internet, so his task was difficult. Eventually, he found a connection between one of his cases and another murder. He matched fingerprints from both crime scenes and eventually identified a suspect (Crime Library, 2012).

Roy Hazelwood, who later became a famous criminal profiler, recognized the value of Brooks' investigative technique and suggested the creation of a central repository for unsolved serial crimes. Congressional hearings were conducted wherein experts testified that if local agencies had shared information, lives could have been saved. One of the experts, true crime writer Ann Rule, estimated that a central repository might have saved as many as 15 of the 30 women Ted Bundy murdered in seven states from 1974 to 1978 (Crime Library, 2012).

Eventually, the Federal Bureau of Investigation created a program called the Violent Criminal Apprehension Program (VICAP), which encourages local police agencies to share information about unsolved violent crimes. Brooks was its first director. When a local agency submits a case, the VICAP staff compares features of the case with other violent crimes. If they find similar modus operandi or evidence, they contact the interested departments and encourage them to share investigative information. Today, the staff at VICAP uses the latest computer technology and data mining software to do, in minutes, what it took Brooks months to do when he was a homicide investigator. Brooks passed away in 1998. Dan Browser, a retired LAPD detective who had been Pierce's partner for nearly 20 years said of him, "He was the closest thing I ever saw to Sherlock Holmes" (*San Francisco Chronicle*, 1998).

What is the actual process by which investigators like Brooks and professors like me research particular issues and topics? This chapter provides an overview. Later chapters will provide more information about each step in the research process. Here, I just provide a brief description. Before reviewing each step of the research process, we will discuss the objectives and characteristics of the research process.

Objectives of the Research Process

The research process is a set of specific steps that, when done correctly, produce data. Researchers use data to produce information, what we call findings, to share with other researchers and criminal justice practitioners and policy makers. The research process has four overall objectives. The first is to answer a research question or set of research questions. A research question can be as simple as deciding what restaurant to visit. A simple check of a restaurant's published reviews on the internet provides the information (data) necessary to make this decision. In academic research, research questions tend to be a little more complicated, such as determining the cause of criminal behavior.

The second objective of the research process is to resolve disagreements among researchers. Equally competent researchers may look at the same set of facts and reach very different conclusions. Likewise, equally qualified researchers may measure social phenomena differently. Subsequent researchers may attempt to resolve these differences through additional research. The aim of subsequent researchers is not necessarily to determine who is right. Instead, they attempt to clarify how the differences came about and get us closer to the truth.

The research process also has the objective of filling gaps within the body of knowledge. No single research project produces all the answers. For example, the findings from one research project may shed light on the motivations of adult male serial killers, but not adult female serial killers. Therefore, subsequent research might want to fill this gap by focusing on the motivations of adult female serial killers. Each research project builds off previous research by targeting a different population or a different aspect of the problem.

The fourth and final objective of research is to produce more research questions. This may sound strange. Presumably, the point of research is to answer questions, not ask them. But we cannot hope to explain everything through one study alone. We can only hope to explain bits of things. We rely on other researchers to do the same, such that we all contribute to the body of knowledge. Part of the research process is asking additional questions such that subsequent researchers can help put the pieces of a larger puzzle into place.

> **Getting to the Point 3.1** –The objectives of research are to answer research questions, to resolve disagreements among researchers, to fill gaps within the body of knowledge, and to produce more research questions.

Steps of the Research Process

Figure 3.1.1 depicts the research process as a set of ten steps. As depicted here, it is generally linear. By this, I mean that the steps are usually completed in a certain order. The research process always starts when a researcher asks a research question. Then, the researcher goes to the literature to find out what we already know about the subject. The next five steps culminate in the design of the method used to answer the research question.

Between the literature review (step 2) and the method design (step 6), the research process is internally cyclical. By this, I mean that the steps may be revisited as researchers experiment with different ideas. For example, after the creating measures (step 5), a researcher may determine that the measures do not adequately capture the essence of the researcher's conceptual definitions. In this case, the researcher may need to redefine his or her concepts (step 4) or go all the way back to the literature review (step 2) for guidance.

The research process is also externally cyclical. By this, I mean that the research process is on-going. A particular project may end when the findings are communicated (step 10), but begins again as researchers ask new questions. Good research always produces additional questions and the need for additional research. For example, during the 1930s, Clifford Shaw and Henry McKay conducted sociological studies of Chicago (Shaw and McKay, 1942). Among other things, they identified distinctive zones within the city. One zone was where the factories were located. Another zone was where the men and women that worked in the factories lived. The most important zone to their research was what they called the zone of transition. This zone was where most crime and other social problems existed. Their work led to the creation of a new criminological theory called social disorganization. Following the work of Shaw and McKay, the automobile became more affordable and the interstate highway system expanded. As such, factory workers could live farther away from where they worked. This resulted in a change in how Chicago was socially organized, compelling subsequent researchers to reevaluate

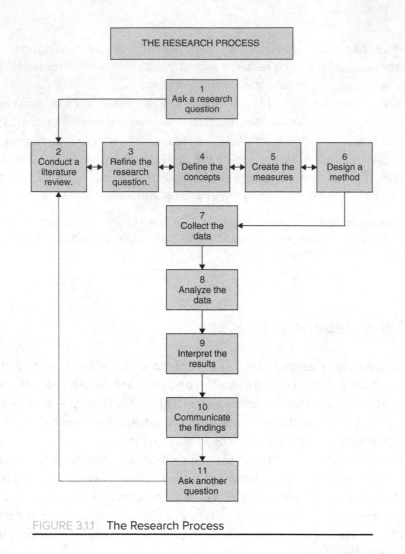

FIGURE 3.1.1   The Research Process

the social disorganization theory (Bursik, 1988). Today, we commonly find that crime patterns happen along major traffic thoroughfares rather than within transition zones.

> **Getting to the Point 3.2**—The research process is characteristically linear in that the steps must be completed in a certain order. However, the process is also internally cyclical, because researchers often have to revisit previous steps, and externally cyclical, because good research leads to additional research questions.

Step 1: Ask a Research Question

The research process begins with a question, but not just any question. **Research questions** are interrogative. This means that they are actual questions that can be answered, not statements that make some claim. For example, the statement, "*The best way to combat crime is to lock up criminals* *and throw away the key!*" is not a question. It is a claim about the best way to combat crime. A better research question might be: "*Do longer prison terms deter people from committing crimes?*"

Research questions often begin with casual observations or mere curiosities. For example, a researcher may observe that most of the individuals that are booked into the county jail are male. From this observation, the researcher may become curious about why males are arrested more frequently than females. Do males commit more crime than females? Are police officers more likely to arrest males than females? Do males commit the kinds of crimes that are most likely to be observed by the police? All of these questions came from a single observation.

> **Getting to the Point 3.3**—Research questions should be actual questions that can be answered rather than statements that make some claim.

Step 2: Conduct a Literature Review

In social science, we *search* for answers. But we do so through a process of *re*-search. The prefix 're-' in the word 'research' communicates the natural repetitiveness of the research process. Finding out what we already know and do not know about a particular research topic is an essential task of the researcher. Hence, the second step of the research process is conducting the **literature review**, which involves locating and understanding what previous researchers have learned about a topic. The literature review reveals gaps in the body of knowledge, areas of disagreement among researchers, and remaining questions that need to be answered. It can also provide tips on effective methods for conducting research. In general, the literature review helps fine tune our research question by ensuring that we are not asking a question that has already been asked and answered.

Generally speaking, there are five sources of information that researchers draw upon during the literature review process. Each source has advantages and disadvantages. Books are great sources if you are unfamiliar with a topic. But because they take years to produce, the information might be outdated. Scholarly articles are timelier, but because editors limit them to 30 or 40 pages, authors do not always have enough room to fully discuss the topic. Newspapers and magazines provide even timelier information, but they often do not contain enough details about how the information was gathered. As such, we cannot assume that the information is objective or reliable. The Internet provides probably the timeliest information, but it is often difficult to determine a website's objectivity and accuracy. Finally, experts are a great source for information, but some experts may have a professional bias. For example, you may see a seemingly objective report on the Internet written by a former chief of police claiming that a particular anti-theft device is "the only effective way to be sure you car does not get stolen." It may appear legitimate but you might also learn that this former chief of police actually works as a paid spokesman for the company that makes these devices. Table 3.1.1 summarizes the advantages and disadvantages of these commonly used sources. Scholars and practitioners generally draw on a combination of all five sources of information when conducting a literature review. **Pyramiding** is an effective technique for locating research and determining when you have enough information. Here is how it works. Say you go to the library and find four good articles or books that are relevant to your topic. You take copies of these sources home with you and glean from them the information you want to include in your literature review. This information may be in the form of quotes, findings, statistics, definitions, or anything else you want to borrow and cite. Then, you look at the bibliographies, reference pages, or footnotes included in your four sources. Chances are you will locate additional sources cited here that are relevant to your research. Even if you only find one additional source in each of the original four articles or books, you have doubled your sources. You may then go back to the library or Internet to locate these new sources and consider including them in your literature review. Then, the process begins again by looking at the references cited in this second set of sources. Ethics demand that you actually procure a copy of each source, read it, and attribute it accurately. It is not acceptable to simply use another researcher's interpretation of or reference to another person's research. So take the time to hunt down each source and review it for inclusion in your literature review.

TABLE 3.1.1   Advantages and Disadvantages of Commonly Used Literature Review Sources

Sources	Advantages	Disadvantages
Books	Books provide good background information Even newly published books may contain on a topic for researchers who are unfamiliar information that is several years old. with a topic.	Even newly published books may contain information that is several years old.
Scholarly journals	Scholarly journals provide objective, reliable, and more current information than books.	Topic coverage is narrower and limited due to space constraints.
Newspapers and magazines	Newspapers and magazines provide timely and accessible information.	Information on methodology is often missing. Hence the information may not be objective or reliable.
Internet sources	Internet sources provide timely and accessible information.	Information may not be objective or accurate.
Experts	Experts provide practical and timely information.	Experts may be biased.

The literature review process can take weeks, even months, to complete. Indeed, locating, collecting, reading, and incorporating previously published research into your own literature review is tedious and time consuming. So how do you know when you are done? If a particular article or book is repeatedly cited by others, it is a good sign that it is critical to the literature and that it should be included in your literature review. For example, researchers interested in TASERs might find that Geoffrey Alpert and Howard Williams have written a lot on this topic (see, for example, Alpert et al., 2011 and Williams, 2008). In fact, both of these researchers are cited frequently by nearly all other researchers. Incorporating the research by these authors in your own literature review provides some assurance that you have located the most important studies in your literature review. Once you stop seeing new repeatedly cited works, you will know your literature review is relatively complete.

Note that sometimes the literature review process provides the necessary information to answer your research questions. For example, a police officer assigned to develop a new policy on high-speed vehicular pursuits may find enough guidance in the literature review to inform his or her department's policy on this issue. If so, then it makes little sense to conduct additional research. The existing research must meet the following criteria to be useful in this regard:

- it must be credible;
- it must be timely;
- it must have been conducted in a similar context; and
- it must use an acceptable research method.

If there is little to no credible research that already exists on your topic, you would be well served to go out and conduct research yourself. Research credibility is best determined by the objectivity of the researcher and the use of a peer review process. Research that is done by a person disinterested in its outcome is far more credible than research done by a researcher interested in advocating for a particular perspective. In addition, research that is submitted to a rigorous peer review process is usually considered credible. The peer review process has a way of either eliminating or improving poorly done and biased research.

Outdated research is another good reason to go out and conduct your own research. For example, over the past two decades we have seen dramatic changes in how police officers work. Hence, research on police procedures conducted 20 years ago is not timely. This is not to say that older research is completely irrelevant. James Q. Wilson's *Varieties of Police Behavior* was originally published in 1968, but it continues to influence policing today because of the way it describes how police officers approach their duties. But if most of the research is outdated, you have every reason to suspect that circumstances have changed enough to warrant a fresh look at the phenomenon.

Another good reason to move beyond the literature review stage and conduct your own research is if the existing research focuses on a context that is unique or substantially different from the one you are interested in studying. Research on a high-speed vehicular pursuit policy for a rural police department might not be relevant to an urban police department. If the research was limited to a particular locality, region, or country and you have reason to suspect that this location is fundamentally different from the location in which you are interested, further research is warranted.

Finally, before accepting research as valid and useful, it is important to evaluate the researcher's methodology. Was the sample collected randomly? Did the previous researcher define and measure the variables appropriately? Does the interpretation of the results make sense? Again, if there are methodological problems, your best bet might be to conduct your own study. But if the information is credible and gathered reliably, you can stop at the literature review. There is no real need for further investigation.

Getting to the Point 3.4—The literature review involves locating and understanding what previous researchers have learned about a topic. Researchers rely on several sources in this regard, including books, scholarly journals, newspapers and magazines, Internet sources, and experts. If the existing literature is credible, timely, context appropriate, and methodologically sound, there is no need to move past the literature review stage; the research question may be answered through the literature review alone.

Step 3: Refine the Research Question

As researchers conduct a literature review and learn what other researchers have discovered about a particular topic, they may refine their research question and begin to develop possible answers. For example, we may begin with the research question "*Does the availability of afterschool programs reduce juvenile delinquency?*" We find that many good studies on this exact same question have been conducted. But we also find that almost all the research has been conducted in urban areas. So we could refine the question and ask, "*Does the availability of afterschool programs reduce juvenile delinquency in suburban areas?*" or "*Is the relationship between afterschool programs and juvenile delinquency in suburban areas the same as the relationship found in urban areas?*" Our literature review helps us identify gaps and inconsistencies in the body of knowledge and this, in turn, helps us refine our research question.

Once we have settled on our research question, we need to develop some expectations about what the data might reveal regarding this question. In other words, we need to propose some possible answers to the question. Rather than merely guess what those answers might be, we look for theories that might give us possible answers. A theory is a statement, or set of statements, that attempts to explain the social world. Once we have our theory, we can develop a hypothesis, or a statement that predicts the answer to our research question. Consider the hypothetical example below.

MAKING RESEARCH REAL 3.1.2—BECOMING A COP

Subcultures exist in many professions. Physicians, lawyers, and professors, for example, tend to behave similarly and conform to the same standards of conduct within their professions. To the extent that police officers do the same thing, we can speak of a police subculture. Police officers, by and large, tend to act a certain way. And this may be due to the demands of the profession or to the personality types of individuals who are attracted to the policing profession. Either way, there is a process by which individuals new to the profession internalize the social norms of the policing profession. A researcher interested in this process may develop the following theory:

Understanding and adopting the norms of the policing subculture is related to long-term success in the policing profession.

To test this theory, the researcher may want to conduct interviews with newly hired police officers during the first years of their employment. The objective of this research would be to measure the extent to which these officers assimilate into the policing subculture. During the process of designing this research project, the researcher might develop the following hypothesis:

Individuals new to the policing profession who successfully adopt the norms of the policing subculture will be more likely to experience long-term professional success.

During the research process, the researcher will gather data to test the accuracy of this hypothesis. If the data supports this prediction, the theory will be confirmed.

Getting to the Point 3.5—The literature review process helps researchers refine their research question, identify a theory related to their research question, and propose a hypothesis that predicts the answer to their research question.

Step 4: Define the Concepts

So we have our research question and we have formulated our research hypothesis. Now we need to figure out a way to test this hypothesis. Consider the research hypothesis that impoverished neighborhoods will have higher crime rates. How can we actually test this? To begin, we need to define what we mean by 'impoverished neighborhood' and 'crime rate.' These definitions will eventually determine how we measure impoverishment and crime at the neighborhood level. The first stage of this process is called conceptualization. **Conceptualization** is a process by which researchers define the concepts in their hypotheses.

Conceptualization can be quite difficult in social science research. A physicist has the luxury of precise measurement. A pound of force is a pound of force. Social scientists are not so fortunate. Though it may be relatively easy to measure something like level of education, it is much more difficult to measure something like neighborhood satisfaction. Different social scientists will define these concepts in different ways. And that is acceptable. The key is to be as precise as possible and to communicate our definitions at the outset of our study. Here is a hypothetical example.

MAKING RESEARCH REAL 3.1.3—CONCEPTUALIZING JUVENILE CRIME

A researcher wants to study juvenile crime. At some point, early in the process, she must define the concept of 'juvenile crime.' In a sense, there are two concepts to define: 'juvenile' and 'crime.' Developing a conceptual definition for 'juvenile' is relatively easy. The researcher may define a juvenile as any person who is less than 18 years of age. Because most states do not charge children less than eight years of age with a crime, the researcher may want to be even more precise, defining a juvenile as any person who is between 8 and 17 years of age.

Defining 'crime' is more difficult. Does the researcher mean reported crime? What about crimes that were committed but undetected? Does the researcher include status offenses, which are behaviors that are only illegal when committed by a juvenile, such as a curfew violation? Should violations of school rules count as 'crimes'? The researcher must settle on some definition before moving forward with the research. In this case, she uses the following definition for 'juvenile crime':

> *Any behavior committed by an individual between the ages of 8 and 17 years old resulting in a conviction for a criminal offense punishable by a fine, a sentence to jail, or term of imprisonment in a juvenile detention facility.*

You may disagree with this researcher's conceptual definition. And, indeed, researchers often disagree with one another's conceptual definitions. But as long as researchers clearly define their concepts and do not overreach their conclusions, the conceptual definition is what the researcher says it is. The conceptualization stage is one of the few times when a researcher gets to be the decider.

Getting to the Point 3.6—Conceptualization is a process by which researchers define the concepts in their hypotheses. These definitions are important because they determine how researchers actually measure the concepts they use in their research.

Step 5: Create the Measures

Once the conceptual definitions have been developed, the researcher must decide on the best way to actually measure the concepts. We call this process **operationalization**. Here is an example of operationalization.

MAKING RESEARCH REAL 3.1.4—HOW RELIGIOUS ARE YOU?

A researcher wants to measure how religious people are. He refers to this variable as 'religiosity' and conceptually defines it as "the extent to which an individual's behavior is affected by the practices and precepts of his or her religious tradition." Many religions require regular attendance at worship services, so the frequency of attending worship services would measure one part of this concept. Some religions have dietary restrictions, so the extent to which a person desists from eating certain types of foods or eating any food at all during fasting periods would measure another dimension of this concept. Some religions require their members to dress a certain way, not work on certain days, avoid alcoholic beverages, and not cut their hair. The extent to which a person follows each of these practices would help us measure various dimensions of religiosity.

You can see how complicated measuring religiosity might become. It is likely that the researcher will have to ask several questions in order to fully measure this concept. Furthermore, in order to completely measure an individual's adherence to his or her religious traditions, the researcher must know a great deal about the precepts of various religions.

Getting to the Point 3.7—Operationalization is the process by which researchers decide on how they are going to measure their concepts as they have defined them. Often it is necessary to measure concepts along multiple dimensions.

Step 6: Design a Method

Remember that research is both a process and a product. As a process, research is about creating a method by which data can be collected and analyzed to respond to a question. Detailed information on the commonly used research methods in the social sciences [...]. Surveys, for example, are a common social research method. You have likely received a survey in your mail. Surveys can also be delivered over the telephone, on the Internet, and through person-to-person interviews. Experiments are another possible research method. They allow a researcher to control all factors that might influence an outcome and therefore isolate the effect of a single factor. In some types of research, researchers observe people and organizations in their natural environment. The list goes on and on.

There is no 'best way' to conduct research. The best method for one research project may fail miserably in another. Researchers generally pick a method that will answer their research question, work well in their research setting, and prove feasible and realistic given time and money constraints. Once the decision has been made as to which research method to use, it is the responsibility of the researcher to design it to meet his or her specific needs. The chapters [...] outline in detail the processes by which many of the commonly used social research methods are developed.

Things can go wrong in research and it is nearly impossible to predict the problems that might arise. Therefore, before an actual research method is used for collecting data, many researchers pre-test their methods. For example, a researcher who has decided to use a survey to collect data may find that some questions do not work well. Maybe it is the researcher's choice of words or maybe it is the instructions, but the questions may not produce the information that is needed. Pre-testing surveys on a small group of people will help researchers discover these problems before the actual survey is distributed. The following hypothetical vignette illustrates this point.

MAKING RESEARCH REAL 3.1.5—WHEN IT ALL FELL DOWN FOR PROFESSOR BROWN

Professor Brown is interested in the correlation between learning disabilities and delinquency among juveniles. He hypothesizes that juveniles who are diagnosed with attention deficit disorder, hyperactivity, dyslexia, and other learning disabilities are more likely to become delinquent. He observes that children with learning disabilities tend to have lower grades in reading and arithmetic. So he uses the students' grades on the latest state standardized test as a proxy for having a learning disability. In other words, instead of determining if a student has a learning disability, Professor Brown defines students with low standardized test scores as learning disabled. He then assesses whether students have committed a delinquent act in the past year and uses this as his measure of delinquency. He finds no correlation between learning disabilities and delinquency.

Where did Professor Brown go wrong? Well, for starters, his measure was not consistent with his conceptual definition. What Professor Brown did not know was that students diagnosed with learning disabilities are allowed numerous testing accommodations, such as extra time for standardized tests. So, a student with a learning disability could have performed well on the standardized test despite a disability. In the end, all the data that Professor Brown collected could not and did not answer his research question. Had he pre-tested his questionnaire on a small group of students, he might have identified these problems and fixed them before it was too late.

Getting to the Point 3.8—Researchers should pre-test their method to be sure that the research method(s) they use will produce the data necessary to actually answer their research question(s).

Step 7: Collect the Data

At this stage, you want to implement the research method you have selected and follow through on collecting your data. The type of data collection you do depends on the actual method you have selected. Some methods are relatively straightforward. For example, after a survey is developed and pre-tested, the researcher will spend time producing copies, addressing envelopes, affixing postage, and otherwise preparing to distribute the survey. Once the survey is sent out, the researcher will distribute follow-up letters to encourage responses or prepare for the data entry phase. Other methods are a bit more complicated. For example, field researchers may confront various challenges when observing behavior in a natural setting. What happens if it rains? What if a field worker gets sick? How should a dangerous situation be handled? These and many more questions should be asked and answered prior to the data collection phase.

Although it is important to follow the research process and schedule as originally developed, it may become necessary to make changes during this phase of the research process. Surveys with bad addresses get returned by the post office. Research subjects do not show up for scheduled interviews. Field researchers forget supplies or become fearful of their surroundings. Such mishaps are managed best by a **contingency plan**. A contingency plan is essentially a 'Plan B,' or an alternative plan of action for when problems arise. Here is an example from my own experience.

MAKING RESEARCH REAL 3.1.6—PROFESSOR COME GET ME!

In 2003, several of my graduate students approached me with a research proposal. They wanted to determine how much of a patrol officer's time is uncommitted to enforcement duties like answering calls for service, writing reports, conducting surveillances, making arrests, and conducting traffic stops. If a substantial amount of a patrol officer's time is 'free,' it is possible that they could be redirected to more proactive crime prevention duties. I agreed to supervise the research and submitted their proposal to the local police department for permission and to our university's Office of Research Administration for a human subjects review.

The only way to measure a patrol officer's use of time accurately is to ride along with officers and record the amount of time they spend doing various activities. We developed definitions for 'committed' and 'uncommitted' time, purchased stopwatches and clipboards for recording time, designed reporting forms, and selected a sample of officers to observe. Further, we pre-tested the process just to be sure it would work. We found a number of 'kinks' but those were easily resolved.

Being a former police officer, I knew that 'ride-alongs' could be dangerous. Indeed, all of the students had to sign a form releasing the local police department from any liability should the students be injured, or worse, during the ride-along. I also created a contingency plan. According to this plan, the police officers were to terminate the ride-along and to leave the student in a safe place, like a convenience store, when it appeared that they might be placed in a dangerous situation. For example, if the officer were to be dispatched to a robbery in progress or a domestic violence incident, he or she was to drop the student off at a safe place before responding to the call. I also gave each student an envelope containing $20 and a card with my cell number printed on it. I instructed them to call me or to use the cash for cab fare if they needed a ride home. The students performed dozens of field observations and called me on four occasions to ask for a ride home. All four calls were in the middle of the night. Although I lost a little sleep, I kept my students safe.

Getting to the Point 3.9—The process by which researchers collect data depends on their research methodology. Things can and do go wrong in the process of data collection. Researchers should develop contingency plans in case problems arise.

Step 8: Analyze the Data

A plan for data analysis should be developed early in the research process. If a researcher waits until the data are in before preparing for analysis, he or she risks not having the kind of data necessary to answer the research question. For example, a researcher wanting to measure the relationship between age and the frequency of criminal behavior would need to collect the ages and number of arrests for each of the research subjects. These two numbers would be used to produce a statistic called a correlation coefficient, which would indicate whether these two factors were related. If, on the other hand, the researcher asked the subjects to "Check the box beside the age range you fit in" and provided them four categories (15–25 years of age, 26–40 years of age, 41–55 years of age, and 56 years of age or older), he or she would not be able to calculate the correlation coefficient and answer the research question.

One of the most important decisions a researcher must make while preparing to analyze data is called an **a priori assumption**. A priori means before the fact. An a priori assumption is a statement, written in the form of a rule or guideline, about what the data must reveal for the researcher to confirm his or her hypothesis. If the research is quantitative in nature, the a priori assumption is basically a finding of statistical significance. If the research is qualitative in nature, the researcher must decide, a priori, how much evidence will be necessary to answer his or her research question. [...] For now, here are two hypothetical examples.

MAKING RESEARCH REAL 3.1.7—SCHOOL FIGHT EXPERIMENT

Two high school principals are concerned about the number of physical fights among students in their schools. Both schools have similar student populations in terms of size and demographic make up. One principal wants to hire security guards to deter potential fights. The other wants to hire a social worker to help students find more effective conflict resolution skills. The superintendent, unconvinced of either strategy, agrees to let them do what they want, but insists that they record the number of fights to determine which strategy is the most effective.

Prior to analyzing the results of the research at the end of the year, the researcher in charge of the project establishes a rule for deciding which of the two strategies is most effective. She decides that the school that has a statistically significantly lower number of fights compared to the other school and compared to the same school during the previous year will be the school whose strategy is most effective.

MAKING RESEARCH REAL 3.1.8—PERCEPTIONS OF SCHOOL SAFETY

A superintendent of an urban school district reads a story in the local paper in which a real estate agent is quoted as saying, "Fewer people want to live in the city because the schools there are so unsafe." This statement makes the superintendent downright angry. According to the most recent crime statistics, suburban schools have just as many fights as urban schools per capita. But whoever said that perceptions are always based on facts? The superintendent decides to conduct a study on how parents in the school district perceive the safety of their children's schools.

The superintendent plans a series of town meetings during which she intends to discuss school safety and ascertain parents' perceptions of school safety. These are essentially focus groups, a qualitative research method often used in product marketing. The superintendent thinks that these community meetings will reveal the most common factors that parents consider when developing perceptions of school safety. These factors might include graffiti and poorly maintained school properties. She intends to use the information from this study to develop a plan for improving the perception of school safety in her district. She knows that she cannot address every issue so she decides to focus on the most pressing issues. But how will she know which issues are most pressing? She decides a priori that an issue is pressing if more than one fourth of the parents at any one meeting identify it as a factor that influences their perceptions of school safety. Issues meeting this criterion will be the ones that the superintendent will focus her attention on improving.

So how do researchers actually go about analyzing data? Typically, when quantitative data arrive in the researcher's office, it is first entered into a computer program. To ensure that the individuals responsible for inputting the data are consistent, a set of **coding rules** should be established. For example, a survey may ask:

When you go out at night, how safe do you feel? (Check only one of the following boxes)

- *I am never afraid when I go out at night.$_1$*
- *I am occasionally afraid when I go out at night.$_2$*
- *I am frequently afraid when I go out at night.$_3$*
- *I am always afraid when I go out at night.$_4$*
- *I am so afraid that I never go out at night.$_5$*

Did you notice the subscript numerals at the end of each response? Entering a number is easier than entering the respondent's actual response. It also makes analysis easier. You may have noticed that the numbers (1–5) increase in value as the respondent's level of fear increases—the higher the value, the higher the level of fear. When researchers code data, they assign a number to different responses for the purpose of data entry. All individuals responsible for data entry must use these codes when entering individual responses for each question.

Once the data are coded and entered, researchers evaluate the completeness and accuracy of the data set. This is often called 'cleaning the data.' Incomplete and inaccurate records can be corrected or eliminated altogether. The actual data analysis is usually done with a statistical software program. Basically, the researcher will run statistical tests to determine if and how variables are related. Qualitative data analysis is a little more complex and usually involves organizing the results into various themes. The results of either form of data analysis are called 'findings.'

> **Getting to the Point 3.10**—A plan for data analysis is developed early in the research process. A priori assumptions establish what the data must reveal for a researcher to confirm his or her hypothesis. Researchers code, enter, and clean the data before running statistical tests or performing other types of data analysis.

Step 9: Interpret the Results

Completing a statistical analysis or organizing the results from a qualitative analysis is the easy part. Figuring out the meaning and practical significance of these findings is more art than science. Say we distribute a survey, collect and analyze the data, and find a relationship between neighborhood poverty and property-based crime. Why are these two variables related and what is the significance of this relationship for theory and policy? The interpretation of findings is often the most interesting part of research, but it is also the most difficult.

Findings are only meaningful in the context in which they arise and they are only as useful as the quality of the data. When findings are interpreted to mean more than they actually do, we say the researcher has 'overreached' his or her findings. For example, a researcher may find that 20 percent of the stops made by police officers involve African American drivers, while only 10 percent of the community's residents are African American. This researcher may conclude that the officers are guilty of racial profiling. This interpretation, however, would overreach the findings of this research. It could be that there is a higher percentage of African Americans in the driving population than in the residential population. It could also be that more African Americans reside in high-crime areas where more police officers are assigned to work and are therefore more likely to be observed and stopped. Finally, it could be that African American drivers commit more traffic violations and, hence, are stopped more often. All possible explanations or interpretations should be explored before reaching a conclusion.

> **Getting to the Point 3.11**—Research findings should be interpreted in the context in which they arise and are subject to the limitations of the available data. When findings are interpreted to mean more than they actually do, the researcher has overreached his or her findings.

TABLE 3.1.2   Common Sections in Scholarly Journal Articles

Section	Description
Abstract	A summary of the research, usually about 150 words or less, that describes what the researcher did and learned.
Introduction	An overview of the research that describes the purpose of the research, the research question and hypothesis, and how the article is organized.
Literature review	A review of what is known about a particular topic and a description of areas of agreement and disagreement among researchers on the topic.
Methodology	A description of the methods used by the researcher, including the sampling procedure, the measurement of variables, the data collection method, and the analytic techniques.
Findings	A summary of what the analysis revealed, including descriptive statistics.
Discussion	An interpretation of the research findings and a consideration of alternative explanations.
Conclusion	A summary of the research project, an evaluation of the strengths and weakness of the research, and/or a set of recommendations for policy changes or questions for future research.
References	A list, organized by author's last name, of the sources that were used by the researcher. This can also be referred to as a bibliography.

Step 10: Communicate the Findings

Once the analysis has been completed and the findings interpreted, the researcher turns his or her attention to writing the research report or otherwise communicating his or her findings. How a researcher goes about actually writing up a final research report depends on where it will be published, who is providing the funding, and how the research will be used. Most university professors submit their research to scholarly journals, which require a relatively standard format for reporting research results. Table 3.1.2 describes the sections that are commonly found in articles appearing in scholarly journals.

Research reports published by government agencies or research organizations often include the same sections as those of a scholarly journal article. The most prominent difference is in the abstract section. An abstract in a research report is sometimes called an Executive Summary. Both are very brief summaries of the research report. Research reports appearing in magazines and newspapers are not as formally presented. In fact, it can sometimes be difficult to find information on a researcher's methodology or analytical strategy in articles appearing in these types of publications. Scholarly articles and research reports are often written at a higher level of precision than articles written for publication in magazines or newspapers.

When academic researchers submit their findings for publication in scholarly journals, they must go through a double-blind peer review process supervised by a journal's editor. [...] Research reports written for criminal justice organizations, government agencies, or private clients often are submitted in draft format. This allows the agency or client to evaluate the report before it becomes public. The purpose of the review is still the same: to improve the quality of the research report. It is better to find and correct mistakes in the privacy of the peer review process than in the public arena.

Because the traditional publishing process can take a long time, researchers often present their findings at conferences or meetings of likeminded scholars and practitioners. These conferences are typically organized into different sessions wherein scholars and practitioners interested in similar topics share and discuss their latest research. Most criminal justice scholars attend the annual meetings of the Academy of Criminal Justice Sciences or the American Society of Criminology. Practitioners may attend any number of meetings such as meetings sponsored by the International Association of Chiefs of Police or the American Correctional Association. There are also numerous regional, state, and local organizations that hold regular meetings wherein research is shared.

Part of the process of presenting research findings is evaluating and communicating a research project's limitations. This is difficult for many researchers. Most researchers would prefer not to point out their mistakes or their project's limitations. It is important to remember, though, that all research has weaknesses and limitations. There is no such thing as a perfect research project. Identifying, even highlighting, a research project's weakness and limitations is an important part of the research process because it sets the stage for developing new research questions. It also helps other researchers assess the strength of a research project's findings. From a practical perspective, it is better to admit your own mistakes than to have somebody else point them out for you. Identifying the weaknesses and limitations of your research is the sign of a mature and competent researcher.

Remember that when communicating research findings, '*A picture is worth a thousand words.*' Most people are visual learners. This means that they learn best when they see things, as opposed to when they hear things. Pictures, including graphs and charts, are enormously helpful to anyone wanting to communicate ideas. Consider the comparison in Figure 3.1.2.

The following sentence appears in the written version of a research report. It uses words to describe what the researchers learned from their research.

> *Overall, it appears that education has a positive effect on income. The more education one has, the higher his or her income will likely be.*

Now, here is the same information presented visually.

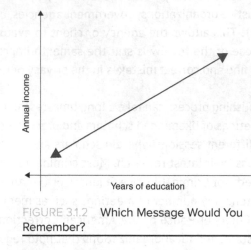

FIGURE 3.1.2   Which Message Would You Remember?

Both the words and the graph communicate the same information. Which of these are you likely to remember?

> **Getting to the Point 3.12**—The actual format of the research report depends on where it is published. Scholarly articles follow a standard organizational format that includes a literature review, information on methodology, a section on findings, and a discussion. Identifying the weaknesses and limitations of the research is critical when presenting research findings in publications or at conferences.

Final Thoughts

Researchers typically complete the ten steps of the research process in a particular order (see Figure 3.1.1). But it is also the case that researchers will revisit previous steps when they realize that something is not working or when they are not getting the data they need. The key to success in research is thinking through the entire research process before committing to a particular method. But it is also important to be flexible, to admit when something is not working, and to adjust your methods accordingly. This is what we mean by the research process being internally cyclical.

What about the 11th step, *Ask Another Question*? And you thought I forgot! The 11th step illustrates the externally cyclical nature of the research process. As mentioned previously, no research answers all our questions on a particular topic. In fact, good research raises more questions than it answers. And even good research has weaknesses and limitations. This produces gaps in the body of knowledge and the need for more research. At first this may seem frustrating, like the process never ends. But, it is also quite exhilarating to learn that there are endless opportunities to expand the body of knowledge. Above all else, stay curious, because curiosity is what expands our knowledge and makes us better at the things we do.

Getting to the Point/Chapter Summary

- The objectives of research are to answer research questions, to resolve disagreements among researchers, to fill gaps within the body of knowledge, and to produce more research questions.
- The research process is characteristically linear in that the steps must be completed in a certain order. However, the process is also internally cyclical, because researchers often have to revisit previous steps, and externally cyclical, because good research leads to additional research questions.
- Research questions should be actual questions that can be answered rather than statements that make some claim.
- The literature review involves locating and understanding what previous researchers have learned about a topic. Researchers rely on several sources in this regard, including books, scholarly journals, newspapers and magazines, Internet sources, and experts. If the existing literature is credible, timely, context appropriate, and methodologically sound, there is no need to move past the literature review stage; the research question may be answered through the literature review alone.
- The literature review process helps researchers refine their research question, identify a theory related to their research question, and propose a hypothesis that predicts the answer to their research question.
- Conceptualization is a process by which researchers define the concepts in their hypotheses. These definitions are important because they determine how researchers actually measure the concepts they use in their research.
- Operationalization is the process by which researchers decide on how they are going to measure their concepts as they have defined them. Often it is necessary to measure concepts along multiple dimensions.
- Researchers should pre-test their method to be sure that the research method(s) they use will produce the data necessary to actually answer their research question(s).
- The process by which researchers collect data depends on their research methodology. Things can and do go wrong in the process of data collection. Researchers should develop contingency plans in case problems arise.
- A plan for data analysis is developed early in the research process. A priori assumptions establish what the data must reveal for a researcher to confirm his or her hypothesis. Researchers code, enter, and clean the data before running statistical tests or performing other types of data analysis.

- Research findings should be interpreted in the context in which they arise and are subject to the limitations of the available data. When findings are interpreted to mean more than they actually do, the researcher has overreached his or her findings.
- The actual format of the research report depends on where it is published. Scholarly articles follow a standard organizational format that includes a literature review, information on methodology, a section on findings, and a discussion. Identifying the weaknesses and limitations of the research is critical when presenting research findings in publications or at conferences.

References

Alpert, G.P., Smith, M.R., Kaminski, R.J., Fridell, L.A. MacDonald, J. and Kubu, B. (2011). *Police use of force, Tasers and other less-lethal weapons*. Washington, DC: United States Department of Justice.

Bursik Jr., R.J. (1988). Social disorganization and theories of crime and delinquency: Problems and prospects. *Criminology, 26*(4), 519–539.

Crime Library (2012). Criminal profiling: Part I History and method by Katherine Ramsland. Retrieved from http://www.trutv.com/library/crime/criminal_mind/profiling/history_method/index.html (accessed February 2013).

San Francisco Chronicle (1998). Obituary of Pierce Brooks. Retrieved from http://www.sfgate.com.

Shaw, C.R. and McKay, H.D. (1942). *Juvenile delinquency and urban areas*. Chicago, IL: The University of Chicago Press.

Williams, H. (2008). *TASER electronic control devices and sudden in-custody death: Separating evidence from conjecture*. Springfield, IL: Charles C. Thomas, Ltd.

Wilson, J.Q. (1968). *Varieties of police behavior: The management of law and order in eight communities*. London: Oxford University Press.

The Vocabulary of Research

Mark L. Dantzker, Ronald D. Hunter, and Susan T. Quinn

What You Should Know!

The process of conducting and understanding research may seem to some like a foreign language. There are words, formulas, and so forth that may have more than one meaning or application. For example, the term *research* is often used in more than one context. It is quite common for students and teachers alike to use this term to describe a paper assignment that is actually a summary of existing literature. In contrast, the term *research* as used in this textbook refers to the process of conducting a scientific investigation of a specific phenomenon. Conducting research comes with a vocabulary that one must understand before one can proceed with the process of research. After completing this chapter, the reader should be able to:

1. Define theory and explain to the role that theory plays in research.
2. Describe the conceptualization process.
3. Describe what takes place during operationalization.
4. Define the terms variable, dependent variable, and independent variable.
5. Describe what a hypothesis is and how it differs from an assumption.
6. Present and discuss the types of hypotheses, including research, null, and rival.
7. Identify a population and discuss how it is related to a sample.
8. Define validity and reliability. Explain how these concepts are related.
9. Describe qualitative and quantitative research.
10. Discuss the steps in the research process, including theory, hypotheses, observations, and empirical generalizations.

The Language of Research

It is quite common for students and teachers alike to use the term *research* to describe a paper assignment that is actually a literature review. With respect to criminal justice and criminology, there is more to research than reviewing literature. The multiple uses of the term *research* is just one example of the need to understand the vocabulary associated with research methods. [...] the term *research* was defined. In this chapter, terms associated with research methods, such as *theory*, *hypothesis*, and *variable*, are defined and expanded.

The process of developing research can appear to be complicated with a lot of moving parts. However, the basics are simple and can be visualized in the form of a circle with four main parts: (1) theory, (2) hypotheses, (3) observations, and (4) empirical generalizations (Healy, 2013). Healy (2013) referred to this circle as the "Wheel of Science." Explanatory research typically begins with theory and then moves through the remaining four parts.

Theory

Theory is a statement or groups of statements that attempt to explain, predict, or understand a phenomena. An interesting debate could arise regarding the role of theory in research, reminiscent of the age-old argument: Which came first, the chicken or the egg? With respect to theory, one side of the debate argues that theories drive the research (theory-then-research), with a basis in deductive logic. Research that is based on deductive logic begins with a theory. From the theory, hypotheses are developed and observations are collected to test the hypotheses. Empirical generalizations are developed from the results of the hypothesis testing and either support or do not support the theoretical basis. Keep in mind that results that do not support the theory do not necessarily indicate that the theory is wrong. The value of a theory is often determined based on many tests of hypotheses based on the theory over years or even decades and not based on a single research study.

The other side of the debate argues that research creates the theory (research-then-theory), with a basis in inductive logic. Research that is based on inductive logic begins with observations from which empirical generalizations are developed that are used to create theory or theories to explain the observations (Adler & Clark, 2007; Bryman, 2008; Colton & Covert, 2007; Creswell, 2008; Healy, 2013). Deductive logic and inductive logic are both based on the Wheel of Science but with different starting points. Theory is the starting point for deductive logic, and observation is the starting point for inductive logic.

A theory is essentially a statement that attempts to make sense of reality. Reality consists of those phenomena that one can identify, recognize, and observe. For example, criminal behavior is observed. Therefore, people breaking the law are a reality. A question that arises from this reality is what causes people to break the law? It is here that theory becomes useful because it can explain an aspect of reality in general rather than just for individuals. Many criminological theories focus on causes of criminal behavior that include biological, psychological, and sociological factors. For examples of theories in criminology, see **Box 3.2.1**.

BOX 3.2.1 EXAMPLES OF THEORIES IN CRIMINOLOGY

Biological
   A person's physique is correlated to the type of crime one commits.
   Criminality is genetic.
   A chemical imbalance in one's brain can lead to criminal behavior.
Psychological
   Criminal behavior is the result of an inadequately developed ego.
   Inadequate moral development during childhood leads to criminal behavior.
   Criminals learn their behavior by modeling their behavior after other criminals.
Sociological
   Socializing with criminals produces criminal behavior.
   Society's labeling of an individual as deviant or criminal breeds criminality.
   Failure to reach societal goals through acceptable means leads to criminality.

Whether theories have any merit or are truly applicable is why research is necessary. Proving that a theory is valid is a common goal of criminological and criminal justice researchers. However, to research a theory, the first step is to narrow the focus onto a concept. A single research study will not be able to examine all aspects of all crimes; therefore, researchers must narrow their attention to study a focus that is manageable.

Conceptualization

A *concept* is best defined as an abstract label that represents an aspect of reality, such as an object, policy, issue, problem, or phenomena. Every discipline has its own concepts. In criminal justice and criminology, some concepts include crime, law, criminals, rehabilitation, and punishment. For example, criminals are individuals who have violated a law and may be punished within the criminal justice system. Punishments are the actions taken against someone who has violated a rule or law.

Concepts are viewed as the beginning point for all research endeavors and are often broad in nature. They provide the basis for theories and serve as a means to communicate, introduce, classify, and build thoughts and ideas. To conduct research, the concept must first be taken from its conceptual or theoretical level to an observational level. In other words, a concept must go from the abstract to the concrete before research can occur. This process is often referred to as *conceptualization*. In most research, it is seldom specified just how the concept is moved from the conceptual level to the observational level. This lack of clarity can cause readers to have problems in understanding what is being researched and why. Therefore, it is often helpful when the researcher can offer readers a clearer picture of the conceptualization process. Operationalization occurs after the conceptualization process.

Operationalization

Operationalizing involves the act of describing of how a concept is measured. This process is best described as the conversion of the abstract idea or notion into a measurable item. Operationalization is the taking of something that is conceptual and making it observable, or going from abstract to concrete. A single concept can be operationalized into multiple measurable items. For example, continuing with the criminal example from the conceptualization section, the concept of criminal could be operationalized into a measurable item that describes the type of crime committed by the offender (e.g., property, violent, other) or the number of crimes committed. The concept of punishment could be operationalized into a measureable item that describes the type of sentence (incarceration, community supervision, or other) or the length of the sentence (e.g., 6 months, 2 years, life without the possibility of parole).

Operationalization is one of the more important tasks before conducting any research. There is no one right way to approach this task. How this process is accomplished is up to the researcher. Yet, it is common for researchers to publish their results without ever explaining how their concepts were operationalized. This shortcoming has made it difficult for many students to comprehend fully the notions of conceptualizing and operationalizing variables. Therefore, when research is conducted that focuses on these two terms, it can be quite useful.

FROM THE REAL WORLD

Seldom do researchers report on their conceptualization process. However, when they do, it provides a better understanding of the research. From the following excerpt, can you determine the important concepts within the study?

Community empowerment is a concept used to describe individuals living in close proximity who as a group unite to combat a common problem. The focus of the group is the common problem. If a community is to be empowered, the residents must first be aware that a problem exists (community awareness) to such an extent that it is disturbing or troubling (community concern), resulting in organization of the community (community mobilization) to fight against it (community action). (Moriarty 1999, p. 17)

The following excerpt shows how a concept is operationalized. Community awareness was conceptualized as the level of knowledge about the use of alcohol and other drugs in the community. Four variables reflected community awareness: (1) drug usage in the neighborhood; (2) drug dealing in the neighborhood; (3) alcohol and drug prevention messages; and (4) availability of certain drugs (eight different drugs in all). The following are the actual questions used to establish each variable (Moriarty, 1999, p. 18):

- *Drug usage in the neighborhood: Respondents were asked, "How many people in this neighborhood use drugs?" Responses included "many, some, not many or no residents use drugs."*
- *Drug dealing in the neighborhood: Respondents were asked, "How often do you see drug dealing in this neighborhood?" The responses included "very often, sometimes, rarely, never."*
- *Alcohol/drug prevention message: Respondents were asked if they had heard or seen any drug or alcohol prevention messages in the past six months.*

- *Availability of certain drugs: Respondents were asked about the difficulty or ease of obtaining specific drugs in the county. The list of drugs included marijuana, crack cocaine, other forms of cocaine, heroin, other narcotics (methadone, opium, codeine, and paregoric), tranquilizers, barbiturates, amphetamines, and LSD. Each drug availability represents one variable.*

Variables

The primary focus of the operationalization process is the creation of measurable items known as *variables* and subsequently developing a measurement instrument to assess those variables. Variables are concepts that may be divided into two or more categories or groupings of "attributes" or characteristics. For example, *male* and *female* are attributes of the variable *gender*. The primary purposes of developing these variables are to measure a phenomenon and also to examine the relationship between two or more variables in explanatory research. When examining the relationship between variables, there are two types of variables involved: dependent and independent.

Dependent Variables

A dependent variable is a factor that requires other factors to cause or influence change in it. The dependent variable is the outcome factor or the factor that is being predicted. If a researcher is studying the impact or parental supervision on juvenile delinquency, then juvenile delinquency is the dependent variable. It is the dependent variable because changes in juvenile delinquency are being caused by changes in parental supervision.

Independent Variables

The independent variable is the influential or the predictor factor. In other words, these variables are predicted to cause the change or outcome of the dependent variable. Often used independent variables in the study of criminal behavior are demographic characteristics, such as age, gender, race, marital status, and education. When determining independent variables, it is important to keep in mind time order. Independent variables must come before dependent variables.

Identifying and recognizing the difference between the variables is important in research, but sometimes the details may get lost due to the amount of information within any one study. Therefore, when research specifically calls attention to the variables, it can be quite useful. Keep in mind that whether a variable is dependent or independent is defined by the researcher and not by the variable itself. Criminal behavior could be a dependent variable if the researcher is studying the impact of unemployment on theft behavior. On the other hand, criminal behavior could be an independent variable if the researcher is studying the impact of criminal behavior on the stability of marriage. The key to any research is to be able to operationalize the concepts into understandable and measurable variables. Failing to complete this task makes the creation and testing of the hypotheses more difficult.

Hypotheses

Once the concept has been operationalized into variables based on the theoretical basis, then most research focuses on testing the stated hypotheses. A *hypothesis* is a specific statement describing the expected relationship between the independent and dependent variables. There are three common types of hypotheses: (1) research, (2) null, and (3) rival.

Research Hypothesis

The foundation of a research project is the research hypothesis. This hypothesis is a statement of the expected relationship between the dependent and independent variables. The statement may be specified as either a positive or negative relationship. In a positive relationship, the dependent and independent variables are moving in the same directions. They are increasing, or they are both decreasing. In a negative relationship, the dependent and independent variables are moving in opposite directions. If the independent variable is increasing, then the dependent variable is decreasing. Or, if the independent variable is decreasing, then the dependent variable is increasing. The example of juvenile delinquency provides an example of a negative relationship, specifically an increase in parental supervision is predicted to decrease juvenile delinquency. This result may be expected because juveniles who are under increased supervision will have fewer opportunities to participate in delinquency.

Null Hypothesis

Some researchers argue that the results of the research should support the research hypothesis, including the existence of a relationship as well as the direction of the relationship between the dependent and independent variables. Others claim that the primary goal is to disprove the null hypothesis, which is a statement indicating that no relationship exists between the dependent and independent variables. Therefore, a null hypothesis may be that parental supervision does not impact juvenile delinquency. By rejecting the null hypotheses, the research goal has been fulfilled.

Rival Hypothesis

Before starting the research it is customary to establish the research hypothesis, which are generally the results the researcher expects to find based on the theoretical basis. However, sometimes the results may reject both the null hypothesis and the research hypothesis. This situation allows for the creation of what is called a *rival hypothesis*. The rival hypothesis is a statement offering an alternate prediction for the research findings. Continuing with the example of parental supervision and juvenile delinquency, the rival Hypothesis would be that as parental supervision increases, so does juvenile delinquency. This unexpected result may occur because juveniles who are under increased supervision may rebel and act out due to the stress of being constantly under supervision.

It is usually the goal of the research to be able to reject the null hypothesis. Testing the research hypothesis becomes central to the research, making identifying the hypothesis an important aspect of the research. Yet, although hypotheses often take center stage in research, there is another type of statement that can find its way into the research: assumptions. However, these types of statements should be avoided whenever possible.

Assumptions

Hypotheses are educated guesses about the relationship between variables and must be proven by the research results. In contrast, an assumption is a statement accepted as true with little supporting evidence. From a research perspective, assumptions are problematic. It is expected that with statements of inquiry or fact that there be substantiating research. It seems generally inconsistent in scientific research to have assumptions (Banyard & Grayson, 2009; Creswell, 2008).

FROM THE REAL WORLD

In examining the effect of participatory management on internal stress, overall job satisfaction, and turnover intention among federal probation officers, Lee, Joo, and Johnson (2009) offered three hypotheses: (1) organizational variables are more important than individual variables in predicting an officer's turnover intention; (2) among organizational variables, participatory climate, internal stress, and overall job satisfaction, respectively, have a significant direct effect on an officer's turnover intention; and (3) participatory climate and internal stress also have a significant indirect effect on an officer's turnover intention.

Assumptions can be defined as statements one accepts as being true with little or no supporting evidence, a stance inappropriate to scientific research (Gillham, 2009). However, it is difficult to conceptualize a piece of research without having some assumptions about the topic of the study. Some assumptions may be needed in the development of a working hypothesis or hypotheses, to help guide thought about the topic of interest, and to help shape the design of the study. It is good research practice to identify and acknowledge any a priori assumptions of which the researcher is aware while the research study is in the planning stages.

However, assumptions can often lead to research. For example, because of the believed natural caring instincts of women, an assumption might be made that women would make better police officers than men. Because there is little evidence to validate this assumption, and it is not a readily accepted statement, at least among men, there is a need to research this assumption. In this situation, the researcher could move beyond the untestable assumption that women would be better officers because they are more caring by converting the assumption into hypotheses that can be tested. Variables could be created to measure what is meant by caring and what is meant by officer performance.

Theory, concept, operationalize, variable, hypothesis, and assumption are all key words in the language of research. Still, they are just the building blocks for other words with which one should be familiar.

Other Necessary Terms

There are many other terms a student should be familiar with before undertaking a research effort. Because these remaining terms are covered in greater detail in later chapters, only a brief definition is offered here.

Unit of Analysis

A unit of analysis is the level at which the researcher will focus his or her attention. It could be individuals, groups, or social artifacts depending on the nature of the research. If the proposed study is examining the influences of individual criminal behavior, then the level of analysis is the individual. However, if the proposed study is crime rates, then the unit of analysis would be the social artifacts, specifically crime reports at the state, county, or local levels.

Population

A population is the complete group or class from which information is to be gathered. For example, if a researcher was studying policing in Atlanta, Georgia, then all Atlanta police officers would be the population. Although it would be great if every member of a population could provide the information sought, it is usually logistically impractical in that it is both inefficient and wasteful of the researcher's time and resources. Therefore, most researchers choose to obtain a sample from the targeted population.

Sample

A sample is a smaller subset chosen from within a target population to provide the information sought. Choosing this group is referred to as *sampling* and may take one of several forms, including probability and nonprobability sampling. Sampling is important enough to warrant an entire chapter of its own later in the text. Some examples of sampling are:

> Random: A random sample is one in which all members of a given population had the same chances of being selected. Furthermore, the selection of each member must be independent from the selection of any other members.
>
> Stratified Random: This sample is one that has been chosen from a population that has been divided into subgroups called *strata*. The sample is comprised of members representing each stratum.
>
> Cluster: Cluster refers to a multistage sample in which groups are randomly selected and then individuals within the groups are randomly selected.
>
> Snowball: This sample begins with a person or persons who provide names of other persons for the sample who in turn provide the names of additional persons.
>
> Purposive: Individuals are chosen based on the researcher's belief that they will provide the necessary information.

Once the sample has been identified, the information is collected. The various collection techniques are covered in detail in a later chapter. In collecting this information two concerns for the researcher are the validity and the reliability of the data collection device.

Validity

Validity is a term describing whether the measure used accurately represents the concept it is meant to measure. There are four types of validity: (1) face, 2 content, (3) construct, and (4) criterion.

Face validity is the simplest form of validity and refers to whether the measuring device appears, on its face, to measure what the researcher wants to measure. Using a ruler to measure time would appear odd and not useful; however, using a ruler to measure distance appears to be valid. Face validity is primarily a judgmental decision. It is the most used form of validity, perhaps due to its simplicity. In content validity, a measuring device is examined to determine how well it covers the concept in question; specifically each element is examined within the measuring device. Only using income to measure socioeconomic status is missing important elements, such as education and occupation measures; thus it is incomplete and lacks content validity. Construct validity refers to the fit between theoretical and operational definitions of the concept as well as the level of expected agreement between the measure and other variables. For example, a positive relationship might be expected between fear of crime and the likelihood of protective behaviors, such as not walking alone at night. Criterion validity represents the degree to which the measure relates to an external criterion. It can either be concurrent (comparing self-reports of property crime victimization to property crime reports) or predictive (the ability to accurately foretell future events or conditions, such as use of the Scholastic Aptitude Test (SAT) to predict performance in college).

Reliability

Reliability refers to how consistent the measuring device would be over time. If the study is replicated, will the measuring device provide consistent results? The two key components of reliability are stability and consistency. *Stability* means the ability to retain accuracy and resist change. *Consistency* is the ability to yield similar results when replicated. Keep in mind that a measure can be reliable but not valid. Each year as daylight savings time begins, many people will forget to reset their clocks. If for the next week, an individual does not reset his clock, it will sound consistently when it reads 7:00 a.m.; however, it will in actuality be 8:00 a.m. (you may be able to use this as an excuse for being for work once, but beyond that would be pushing your luck).

Data

Having established the validity and reliability of the measuring device, the sample can now be approached for information. The information gathered is known as *data*. Data are simply pieces of information gathered from the sample that describe events, beliefs, characteristics, people, or other phenomena. These data may be qualitative or quantitative.

Qualitative Versus Quantitative Research

The debate over qualitative versus quantitative research simply comes down to a question of concepts as ideas or terms versus numerical values. Broadening this distinction in easy terms offers quantitative research that refers to counting and measuring items associated with the phenomena in question, whereas qualitative research focuses on concepts and verbal descriptions (Given, 2008).

In recent years there has been a trend among scholarly journals to demand more quantitative than qualitative research. This preference is because qualitative research is often criticized as not being "scientific" (Bergman, 2009; Creswell, 2008; Given 2008). Both methods are appropriate and necessary to criminal justice and criminological research. However, either qualitative or quantitative research may be preferred depending on the goal or purpose of the research.

Qualitative Research Defined

Qualitative research is defined as a nonnumerical explanation of one's examination and interpretation of observations with the goal of identify meanings and patterns of relationships (Creswell, 2008; Hagan, 2006; Maxfield & Babbie, 2009). This type of research encompasses interpreting action or meanings through a researcher's own words (Adler & Clark, 2007) rather than through numerical assignments. For example, saying someone is aggressive and confrontational is a qualitative observation, but saying that someone has been arrested five times for disorderly conduct is a quantitative observation. Such analysis enables researchers to verbalize insights that quantifying of data does not permit. Continuing with this example, the qualitative observation could be expanded to include specific details related to the aggressive and confrontational behavior, such as alcohol or drug consumption prior to the incidents. It also allows one to avoid the trap of false precision, which frequently occurs when subjective numerical assignments are made. If the disorderly conduct offender were assessed by a counselor using an assessment device that included the item "How aggressive is the arrestee on a scale of one to five with one being the least aggressive and five being the most aggressive," this example would be quantitative but is subjective based on the judgment of an individual. These quantifications are misleading in that they convey the impression of precision that does not really exist.

Merits and Limitations of Qualitative Research

The insights gained from qualitative research and their usefulness in designing specific questions and analyses for individuals and groups make this form of research invaluable in the study of criminal justice and criminology. However, the costs and time involved in such studies may not be logistically feasible (Bergman, 2009; Drake & Jonson-Reid, 2008). One of the major complaints about qualitative research is that it takes too long to complete. Other complaints about qualitative research include that it requires clearer goals and cannot be statistically analyzed (Creswell, 2008; Given, 2008; Maxfield & Babbie, 2009). There may also be problems with reliability in that replication may prove quite difficult. Lastly, validity issues may arise from the inability to quantify the data.

Quantitative Research

Unlike qualitative research, the definition of which has been controversial and often inconsistent, definitions of quantitative research are quite consistent: It provides a means of describing and explaining a phenomenon through a numerical system (Berg, 2008; Fowler, 2009; Maxfield & Babbie, 2009). In other words, quantitative research is not based on a possibly subjective interpretation of the observations but is a more objective analysis based on the numerical findings produced from observations. One could look at data often collected by correctional agencies as an example of quantitative research, such as the length of prison sentences (often measured in months or years), the number of prior convictions, or the number of days offenders stay out of trouble upon release. Keep in mind that subjectiveness can be interjected into quantitative analysis, as in the previous example of the counselor using his or her judgment with an assessment device.

Because of the potential for bias and the criticisms of qualitative research as being unscientific, most criminal justice and criminological research tends to be quantitative in nature. A quick review of the leading journals that publish criminal justice and criminology research supports this assertion. There are many issues that are not suitable for numerical assignments; to apply quantitative measurements would be inaccurate and misleading. Some of the more intense theoretical debates, such as the merits of the death penalty, are based on personal beliefs about human nature that are shaped by deep-seated religious, political, and moral convictions. As a result, perceptions of these tend frequently to be more influenced by emotion and ideology than by scientific study. This reasoning does not mean that quantitative research cannot be conducted, only that it is difficult to do so.

The Research Process

Having been introduced to research and its language, you can now see how the described process fits into the Wheel of Science model. This process begins with a theory, usually identifying some concept. The concept is then conceptualized and operationalized creating variables, including dependent and independent variables. Completing the identification of both the independent and dependent variables leads to developing the hypothesis. Finally, a sample is chosen, information (data) is gathered from the sample, the information is converted into the proper data for analysis, and the results are reported. This process becomes functionally clearer as the text progresses.

What You Have Not Done Before

Developing researchers may believe that they have done qualitative research through the literature reviews and comparative and historical research done for previous courses. If done in a systematic and logical manner consistent with the scientific method, perhaps this is true. But have numerical values been assigned, data collected using that assignment, and the results analyzed? It is doubtful, unless one has a strong background in math and science or has been fortunate enough to have been involved in an empirical research project (for those who are still struggling with methods phobia, fortunate is defined here as having benefited from the knowledge and insights of the experience rather than from the pleasure of the experience). This deficiency is one that the authors hope to aid in correcting. A college graduate who values and is capable of critical thinking and independent learning needs to be able to conduct quantitative research. It will prove valuable not only in an academic career but in future work tasks or civic duties. It is surprising to find how many things there are in life that warrant "looking into." In addition, quantitative research is actually easier than qualitative research.

Summary

Becoming proficient in research requires knowing the language. Several terms have been introduced that are important to mastering research as a language. The main terms include theory, concept, conceptualization, operationalization, variables, hypothesis, and sample. There are two types of variables: independent and dependent. A sample is a subset of the selected population. Other terms are validity (face, content, construct, and criterion), reliability, and data. With knowledge of these terms, the research process can be taken to another level.

References

Adler, E. S., & Clark, R. (2007). *How it's done: An invitation to social research* (3rd ed.). Belmont. CA: Wadsworth.

Banyard, P., & Grayson., A. (2009). *Introducing psychological research* (3rd ed.). New York, NY: Palgrave Macmillan.

Berg, B. (2008). *Qualitative research methods for the social sciences* (7th ed.). Columbus, OH: Allyn & Bacon.

Bergman, M. M. (2009). *Mixed methods research*. Thousand Oaks, CA: Sage.

Bryman, A. (2008). *Social research methods*. New York, NY: Oxford University Press.

Colton, D., & Covert, R. W. (2007). *Designing and constructing instruments for social research and evaluation*. San Francisco, CA: Wiley.

Creswell, J. W. (2008). *Research design: Qualitative, quantitative, and mixed methods approaches* (3rd ed.). Thousand Oaks, CA: Sage.

Drake, B., & Jonson-Reid, M. (2008). *Social work research methods: From conceptualization to dissemination*. Columbus, OH: Allyn & Bacon.

Fowler, F. J. (Ed.). (2009). *Survey research methods* (*applied social research methods*). Thousand Oaks, CA: Sage.

Gillham, B. (2009). *Developing a questionnaire* (2nd ed.). New York, NY: Continuum International.

Given, L. M. (2008). *The SAGE encyclopedia of qualitative research methods*. Thousand Oaks, CÀ: Sage.

Hagan, F. E. (2006). *Essentials of research methods in criminal justice and criminology* (2nd ed.). Columbus, OH: Allyn & Bacon.

Healy, J. F. (2013). *The essentials of statistics: A tool for social research*. Belmont, CA: Wadsworth.

Lee, W.-J., Joo, H.-J., & Johnson, W. W. (2009). The effect of participatory management on internal stress, overall job satisfaction, and turnover intention among federal probation officers. *Federal Probation, 73*(1), 33–41.

Maxfield, M. G., & Babbie, E. R. (2009). *Basics of research methods for criminal justice and criminology* (2nd ed.). Belmont, CA: Wadsworth.

Moriarty, L. J. (1999). The conceptualization and operationalization of the intervening dimensions of social disorganization. In M. L. Dantzker (Ed.), *Readings for research methods in criminology and criminal justice* (pp. 15–26). Woburn, MA: Butterworth-Heinemann.

Conclusion

The research process includes 11 distinct, yet interconnected steps. Getting started with this process may take some practice, time, and energy. In this chapter's Building Your Research Proposal section, a helpful technique for developing a research question is introduced. Although it may seem early, chapter 9 (the final chapter of this text) discusses the need to start writing your research paper/proposal early on. It is never too early to develop an outline that includes each of the required research proposal/paper subheadings and how you plan to address each area. The thoughtful organization of this information will come in very handy as you write your research proposal/report (see chapter 9).

Chapter 3 Reflection Questions

1. List and define the 11 steps involved in the research process.
2. Identify and summarize a theory of crime or victimization. Locate a scholarly journal article that "tests" that theory. Summarize the article. How did the researchers test that specific theory? Did the researchers find support for that theory?

Building Your Research Proposal

Chapter 3: Ask a Research Question, and Consider Theoretical Connections

Step 1: Recall the general area(s) of interest you identified in the Building Your Research Proposal exercise at the end of chapter 1.

☐ Law enforcement/policing ☐ Courts/law ☐ Corrections/reentry ☐ Victimology/victim services ☐ Criminological theory/nature, extent, causes, control of crime ☐ Other _____ (List)

Step 2: Copy the area you identified into the box provided.

Step 3: Identify three potential ideas for a research study/project that relate to your general area of research interest. (Please use additional space if necessary.) This can be based on your existing interests or any other sources you would like to explore (internet search, news, library search engines, etc.). If you are unsure or need inspiration, type the area you identified in step 1 into the search engine to explore published studies that relate to your general area of interest.

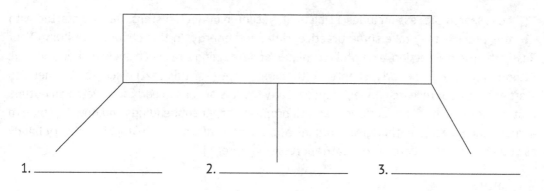

1. _____   2. _____   3. _____

Step 4: Of the three identified, choose the specific research area of the greatest interest to you. Construct a research question or hypothesis related to this topic.

Step 5: Identify and define a theory that relates to your area of research interest. Discuss how this theory relates and how it can inform your research proposal/study.

Research Partnerships with Criminal Justice and Community Organizations

Introduction

Partnerships between researchers and criminal justice and/or other organizations are essential for producing findings or evidence that can be used to inform organization/agency efforts and decision-making. In this chapter, the authors discuss the importance of building police–researcher partnerships, strategies for facilitating and making these partnerships mutually beneficial, and barriers that hamper the development of these partnerships. Although the content in this chapter presents information specific to promoting effective police–researcher partnerships, many of the issues discussed apply to practitioner/agency partnerships between researchers and a myriad of community and institutional organizations, including legal, institutional, and community corrections; agencies that serve crime victims; and other social service agencies. Whether you aspire to be a practitioner or a researcher, this chapter is for you.

How to Make Police–Researcher Partnerships Mutually Effective

Lisa Tompson, Jyoti Belur, Julia Morris and Rachel Tuffin

Evidence-based policing is grounded in the notion that practitioners use the best available evidence to inform their decision-making; the implicit assumption being that practitioners are open to new ideas stemming from research evidence. Such receptivity in operational policing circles has, however, been documented as being stubbornly low (Kennedy, 2010; Weisburd and Neyroud, 2011). This is not unique to policing and has been observed across other professions that are generally assumed to be research driven (see Guillaume, Sidebottom and Tilley, 2012 for examples).

Police resistance to research evidence, when it exists, has been attributed to a myriad of factors, not least the legacy of the critical police research era, during which the police were 'the subject of research and the unwitting recipient of researcher's attentions' (Rojek, Martin and Alpert, 2015). That is, research in the mid-twentieth century was typically 'on' the police, rather than 'with' or 'for' the police (Cockbain and Knutsson, 2015). The result was a body of research largely (but somewhat justly) critical of the police, often without adequate appreciation of the practical challenges faced by the service. In the decades that followed, many scholars have documented disconnect between what academics study and what matters to different tiers of police practitioners (e.g., see Willis and Mastrofski, 2016). In light of this, the police's disinclination to embrace research findings is hardly surprising.

Police receptivity to research is influenced by many factors (Telep, 2016). Thus a multipronged approach is required to engender an attitudinal change in the police at an organisational level so that they are open to research findings. The challenge for proponents of evidence-based policing is to make research evidence less 'academic'—that is, esoteric and marginal—but more 'practical' and of operational relevance.

Echoing others (e.g., see Lum et al., 2012), in this chapter we argue that police involvement in research partnerships, from defining the problem through to the implementation of an intervention, can increase the practical relevance of the findings. Moreover, police 'ownership' of research has the potential to secure support for the findings to be accepted and integrated into practice (Weisburd and Neyroud, 2011). As an after-effect, the 'co-production' of research (see Crawford, this volume) may bring the philosophy of the scientific process into sharp focus for police practitioners and, through this experiential learning, elevate their receptivity to research evidence.

Being open to evidence is, of course, the first step. Credible evidence should lead to an adaption of police practice, which in turn ought to result in better performance. However, translating research findings to implementable changes in police practice is much more challenging and complex than many academics appreciate (Engel and Whalen, 2010; Rojek et al., 2015). The traditional model of the police as 'research customers' and the academics as 'research providers' is thus outdated and unproductive in influencing practice. A 'coalition for a common purpose' might be more fruitful (Strang, 2012), although this is not neccesarily an organic process. Hence, both police practitioners and researchers need to change how they do their business—which could be conceived of as organisational change—if they want to collaborate in partnerships.

With austerity budgets forcing police agencies to rethink the efficiency and effectiveness of their responses (Huey and Mitchell, 2016), and the prevailing political climate favouring evidence-based policing, effective police–researcher partnerships have never been so sorely needed. The aim of this chapter is to present a logic model of an idealised effective police–researcher partnership. In other words, we propose a plausible and sensible model of how an initiative (police–researcher partnerships) will work under certain conditions. In doing so, the intention is to provide a road map for those embarking on a partnership endeavour. In particular, this narrative is for researchers who wish to engage with practitioner communities, to encourage them to think about their demeanour and the interpersonal skills they deploy when building relationships. Receptivity to craft-based1 police practice by researchers is of equal importance to receptivity to research by police practitioners. We hope the model will stimulate thinking and provide a means of evaluating existing partnerships by offering a way of structuring (perhaps tactic) knowledge on how partnerships work.

The chapter begins by considering the links between receptivity to research and the professionalisation agenda before summarising the UK College of Policing's activities to promote a cultural shift towards an evidence-based policing profession. Next, we review the documented barriers to police–researcher partnerships. We then describe our approach to conceptualising police–researcher partnerships, before presenting a logic model that traces the process of setting up police–researcher partnerships, focusing on four essential stages that support effective partnerships.

Moving towards Being an Evidence-Based Police Profession

Police receptivity to research findings is largely confined to individual officers in individual police forces. The penetration of evidence-based policing in a police operating model is thus variable across countries, across forces within a country, across ranks within an organisation, and is not particularly joined up amongst early adopter officers (Telep, 2016). One of the main reasons for police lack of receptivity to research findings more generally (Weisburd and Neyroud, 2011) and amongst specific forces and ranks in particular (Cordner and Biebel, 2005) can be attributed to the strength and omnipresence of a police subculture that revers skills and experience. Three notable features of this subculture need highlighting. First, it is not monolithic, but consists of several subcultures specific to different levels and ranks within the service (Reuss Ianni and Ianni, 1983; Manning, 1993; Chan, 1996). Second, individual police officers are not passive receptors of the occupational subculture, but actively interpret and absorb or resist it (Fielding, 1988; Reiner, 1992; Chan, 1996). Finally, occupational subculture does not exist in a vacuum but is influenced by the external social, political, legal, and organisational context (Chan, 1996).

Thus, measures to increase police receptivity to becoming more evidence based (implicitly increasing receptivity to research) need to be addressed at the individual, operational, and organisational levels, accompanied by changes in the wider sociopolitical context to provide the impetus for such change. Chan (1996) uses Bourdieu's relational theory concepts of 'field' and 'habitus' (Bourdieu and Wacquant, 1992) to explain the process of engendering change as a dynamic interaction, whereby police actors use 'their habitus (cultural knowledge) to interpret and react to their structural conditions (field) to produce and to modify practice' (O'Neill, 2016: 477). Thus, there is a strong argument made for refashioning the role of police through a change in social expectations; in other words, a change in the structural conditions in which they operate and in the expectations from the police, in order to bring about desired receptivity to change within the occupational subculture (Loftus, 2010).

Arguably, transforming policing from a craft into a profession would be the necessary precursor to police officers welcoming research evidence into their decision-making (Kennedy, 2015). Efforts to induce this transition are currently underway at the UK College of Policing, with a number of incentives being offered to practitioners and researchers to support such a sea change. These might usefully be conceptualised as the external influences of the field modifying the policing habitus.

The UK's College of Policing

The College of Policing (CoP) was established in 2013 as the professional body for the police in England and Wales. At the heart of the college's activity is a strong drive to ensure that policing becomes an evidence-based profession, supported by standards, guidance, and training that are built upon evidence. The end goal is to foster a profession that produces reflective and enquiring practitioners, who make decisions by integrating evidence into their professional experience, and who are active participants in developing the profession. Research receptivity is an intermediary stage in this journey.

To embed this scale of change in any complex system is not straightforward or undemanding. The college uses a number of different (explicit and implicit) levers to encourage a shift in professional practice. Explicit and implicit levers include the selection and assessment of officers and staff (e.g., for promotion); the design and delivery of evidence-based policing modules throughout the national policing curriculum; the delivery of national policing guidance, standards, and associated training curricula; the development of an evidence-based career pathway; and capacity-building exercises such as the Evidence Base Camp courses which are designed to teach research methods with real-world examples. Importantly, the college also oversees the provision of grants for police–researcher partnerships through schemes such as the 2015 £10m Police Knowledge Fund. This emphasises building practitioner research capability over the longer term and the genuine co-production of knowledge.

The active involvement of police in conducting research is thought to be vital in building an evidence-based profession for two reasons. The first is a logistical issue—the dearth of good quality studies in policing means that academics working alone simply cannot supply the volume of studies demanded to fill the current evidence gaps. The second reason is more fundamental. Palmer's (2011) research documented that police officers tended to rely on and prefer professional experience over research evidence. Yet the more those officers knew about research, the less they believed the police had sufficient knowledge within their organisation to respond to crime. Palmer (2011) further revealed that the more police officers are exposed to research, the more willing they are to do research; and finally, when research is part of their professional experience, the more likely they are to use it. Actively involving practitioners in research is thus not only important to increase the output of quality studies in policing and plug key knowledge gaps, but also as a lever for getting evidence into practice.

Practitioners with a positive experience of a research partnership are subsequently ideally placed within their organisations to become 'opinion leaders' on evidence-based policing principles. Given the powerful nature of peer influence in a 'closed' culture like policing (Reiner, 1992) and that practitioners privilege information from institutional sources (Palmer, 2011; Lum et al., 2012), we suggest that this is an effective mechanism through which to galvanise a cultural change towards receptivity of research. Our assumption is that a cultural revolution might best begin internally, with these key individuals promulgating an appetite for evidence to be ingrained into practice. The first step to realising these aims, however, is the positive experience of a research partnership, which is by no means guaranteed, for reasons that we now unpack.

Organisational Culture as a Barrier to Partnership Harmony

Police officers and academics lead vastly different working lives. Each hails from a distinct organisational culture with divergent values, different reward systems, and conflicting languages (Rojek et al., 2015). Historically the exchanges between the police and researchers have been wryly dubbed 'the dialogue of the deaf' (MacDonald, 1986: 1), which captures the lack of communication and lingering mutual mistrust from the critical police research era (Engel and

Whalen, 2010; Wilkinson, 2010). The differences in the two working cultures are frequently cited as the main barriers to collaborative working (e.g., see Bradley and Nixon, 2009).

The police are said to be action oriented and decisive (Foster, 2003). They operate in an ever-changing political and organisational environment and are regularly exposed to the very worst of human nature. 'Street smarts' are often a presumed requisite for the countless situations a police officer might face, to the denigration of intellectual or 'book smarts' (Kennedy, 2015). In stark contrast, researchers are trained to be critical and reflective thinkers. In terms of research interests, the police seek clear and unambiguous findings that translate into operational changes to local problems (Lum et al., 2012; Rojek et al., 2015). Academics have traditionally been more concerned with testing and developing criminological theories (Madensen and Sousa, 2015) and are comfortable with uncertainty (Strang, 2012). As a consequence, both parties hold a different world view on what type of knowledge is valuable and worth investing time and resources in (Buerger, 2010). Hence, the lack of a natural overlap between each partner's objectives makes the practical relevance of much research questionable for the police (Rojek et al., 2015).

These dissimilar philosophical positions are compounded by the timescales and the reward systems in which both parties tend to work (Lum et al., 2012). Policing is characterised by dynamic operational circumstances, requiring real-time solutions to be administered as situations and problems unfold. Practitioners are consequently rewarded for producing concrete results that satisfy their various stakeholders (e.g., the media, the public, and politicians) (Rojek et al., 2015). Researchers, on the other hand, are rewarded for scholarly productivity. Prestigious publications that advance academic careers require high-quality methods that take considerable time to execute and require reflective and slow deliberation throughout the research process. This timing mismatch can consequently compromise the relevance of the research to practitioners (Weisburd and Neyroud, 2011).

Two dominant themes are recurrent in the literature on the barriers to effective partnership working: *trust* and *communication*. These are somewhat interdependent and can either reinforce or undermine each other. As in all human relationships, trust is paramount. The police culture is one that is necessarily secretive (Kennedy, 2015) and, at the same time, is closely scrutinised by the media, the public, and politicians. Whereas scientific communication is a public affair, the police prefer to deflect critical media attention (Fleming, 2010). Police sensitivity to negative press coverage is formative in the development of trust between partners.

The researcher's motives for engaging in a partnership are also central to trust. The police are all too aware that the research community needs them more than they need the researchers to do their work (Engel and Whalen, 2010). Any sense of the partnership being one-sided or exploited by the researcher will not gain traction; 'data robbers' will not be tolerated.

A recurrent criticism from the police is that researchers do not appreciate the 'daily rigours' of police work and, consequently, can neglect to work to the police's objectives (Fleming, 2011: 141). In reality few researchers have practical experience of policing and are likely unaware of the idiosyncratic operational and political constraints under which the police often work. A lack of operational exposure for the researcher can result in research findings that are not sensitive to implementation practicalities, which will fail to be seen as credible by the police (Engel and Whalen, 2010).

Police and academic cultures are then manifestly different or, as Laycock (2014: 397) remarks, 'the cultural equivalents of oil and water spring to mind'. An effective partnership, defined here as mutually beneficial and producing reciprocated knowledge, requires partners to transcend these differences in pursuit of a common objective. As we expand on later, this can be achieved by all partners valuing each other's strengths and acknowledging the weaknesses so that there is mutual respect for the breadth of knowledge and skills across the spectrum of the partnership which can be put to the best use (Fleming, 2011).

Conceptualising Police–Researcher Partnerships

The literature on encouraging police–researcher partnerships has identified a number of factors that facilitate or hinder a partnership working (e.g., see Fleming, 2011, 2012; Rojek et al., 2015). However, this knowledge remains prescriptive rather than processual. Here we attempt to synthesise this information into a logic model that traces the process of how effective partnerships should operate.

The model presented here is the result of a thought experiment, but one that is underpinned by a synthesis of the literature on partnership working and extensive individual, and collective, experience of working with, and as, police researchers. We additionally gathered survey data from practitioners and academics with experience of partnership work to test some of our suppositions generated from the literature and our practical experience. This survey was administered and promoted in various practitioner-oriented events.[2,3] Because we sought participants with experience of partnership working in the previous five years, the response rate was low,[4] with 44 responses overall, and 22 respondents with previous partnership experience (see results in Appendix 4.1.1). The survey data are hence used to support our contentions, but fall short of acting in the capacity of 'evidence'. In addition a working version of our partnership model was presented to a group of practitioners at an evidence-based policing event in the UK, with the objective of testing and validating our nascent model. This exercise generated valuable feedback that helped refine the model.

Effective Partnership Working

Partnerships can take many forms and degrees of formality. Central to all are some basic requirements that contribute towards a partnership being effective, namely 1) mutual areas of interest, 2) trust, 3) communication, and 4) feedback to and from police practitioners. Although prerequisites for all police–researcher partnerships, the intensity and depth of these individual 'ingredients' differs depending on the maturity of any particular partnership and the scale of the research objectives.

To elaborate, Rojek and colleagues (2015: 31), borrowing from the International Association of Chiefs of Police, outline three categories of partnerships, which differ in their level
of commitment:

1. *Cooperation*—short-term and informal partnerships that may involve such efforts as
    the agency seeking advice from a researcher or simply providing the research partner
    data for analysis.
2. *Coordination*—more formal partnerships that centre on a specific project or goal, such
    as contracting a researcher to conduct a specific analysis or jointly securing grant
    funding with a researcher to evaluate a specific initiative. The partnership ends with
    the conclusion of the project.
3. *Collaboration*—formalized long-term partnerships where police agencies and research-
    ers work together on multiple projects over time. An example of such a partnership
    could involve a 'memorandum of understanding' or contract between an agency and
    university or researcher for engaging in ongoing and multiple research efforts.

Cooperation partnerships represent a fledgling, but not established, relationship between the
partners. It is likely that these partnerships involve ad hoc unfunded projects that commonly
occur between individuals, rather than institutions. Many variations of these partnerships
exist. Sometimes, in a more traditional setup, the terms will be agreed to at the outset and
the researcher will be provided data to analyse off-site. Other times this partnership will pivot
around the researcher providing technical support or advice to the practitioner. Problem-oriented
policing partnerships and researchers embedded in police agencies (e.g., see Braga and Davis,
2014) take yet other forms.

A deepening of the four components outlined earlier will move a cooperation partnership into
a coordination, or even collaboration, partnership. (We should stress at this point that although
these partnership styles are presented in a somewhat sequential fashion, collaboration partnerships are the only style that require pre-existing partner relationships.) Real life is often messy,
and partnerships may fall within the margins of different models rather than neatly into any
one category. What may begin as a professional acquaintance in a cooperation partnership can
evolve into a personal relationship through the cementing of trust and mutual understanding
of each partner's professional worlds.

We assert that regular partner interaction is the mechanism through which trust and communication are established and relationships between partners develop. The frequency and
intensity of interaction also directly influence the nature of knowledge dissemination between
the practitioner and researcher, because each interactive occasion provides an opportunity for
learning more about the other partner's organisational culture and constraints. Collaboration
partnerships involve extensive interaction, strong levels of trust, and personal relationships
and result in the authentic two-way exchange of knowledge (Rojek et al., 2015). Cooperation
partnerships, in contrast, usually result in one-way knowledge transfer from the researcher to
the police practitioner. Coordination partnerships fall somewhere in between the other two
partnership styles on the continuum of knowledge flow direction (Rojek et al., 2015).

If our assumptions about how partnerships might elevate receptivity to research have merit, then positive experiences of partnership working are vital to promulgating the principles and influence of evidence-based policing. In our opinion, collaboration partnerships represent the pinnacle of co-produced research and embody crystallised trust and sustainable research agendas. Arguably, one of the chief precursors to collaboration partnerships are coordination partnerships, and it is on these latter partnerships which we specifically focus in this chapter.

Our model portrays an idealised version of the essential ingredients needed to make effective partnerships work. This draws from our collective experience of the relationship dynamics required in applied police research and is supplemented by feedback garnered from practitioners. In essence the model seeks to invert the barriers identified in the literature, because 'barriers and facilitators to partnerships are not separate issues, but two sides of the same coin' (Rojek et al., 2015: 41). We do though fully acknowledge that our model is a crude representation of how things work on the ground. (To accurately model the complexity and diversity of partnership processes would result in an incomprehensible schematic with an excess of divergent paths and feedback loops.) For example, we are assuming here that pre-existing relationships are not necessary in a partnership and there is a blank slate for building interpersonal relations. In practice, researchers embarking on these kinds of endeavours have either established networks of police contacts or are connected with police practitioners through a third party. Reputations and first impressions may, therefore, influence both partners' initial opinions of the other.

Coordination-Style Partnerships

Coordination partnerships are purposeful; they involve explicit objectives and people working together in pursuit of a shared agenda. They may be new in terms of the relationships between partners, and the stimulus for these partnerships may be conditions for funding which stipulate co-production of research. This model presented in Figure 4.1.1 comprises four stages: 1) initiation, 2) planning, 3) building trust, and 4) applying knowledge. In this we pay particular attention to the practical aspects of initiating and maintaining such partnerships, which are sorely neglected in the academic literature (Cockbain, 2015).

Stage 1: initiation

Identifying the beginning step of a partnership is harder than it sounds. The first (working) version of the model proposed that coordination partnerships could be initiated by either of the partners and that a mutual area of interest would precede the pursuit of grant funding. The practitioners in our validation exercise, however, challenged this assumed sequence. Several participants stated that the identification of a funding source was the impetus to liaise with researchers over mutual areas of interest. Another participant was confident that a funding source could always be found for a well-formulated research proposal. The model was thus refined to reflect these two scenarios. Other entry points are equally possible. The responsibility for securing funding is more likely to fall to the research partner because, generally speaking, researchers are familiar with the procedures for writing grant proposals and identifying funding bodies sympathetic to a research topic (see questions 1 and 2 in Appendix 4.1.1).

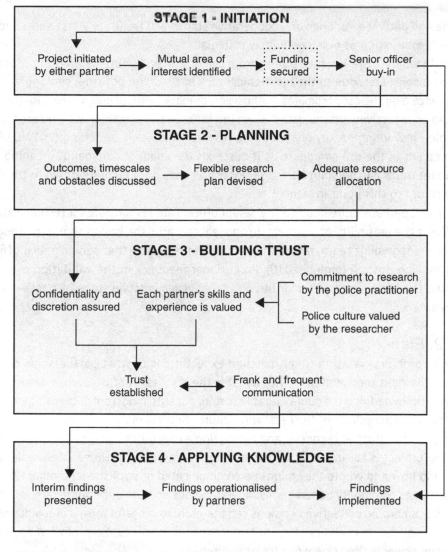

FIGURE 4.1.1   Logic Model of an Effective Coordination Partnership

Identifying reciprocally beneficial research goals requires dialogue to explore each partner's rationale and negotiation to find compatible objectives (Madensen and Sousa, 2015). It also helps if each partner knows what knowledge gaps they wish to fill. Police research priorities may be susceptible to stakeholder influence (e.g., the government or public opinion) and may differ across the rank structure of the agency. The police may also find articulating their knowledge gaps, in terms of research requirements, difficult (Goode and Lumsden, 2016). The challenge for the researcher is to work with the practitioner to identify what the research objective is, its context and influences, and, crucially, the desired outcome. This may require tactful negotiation and some degree of adjustments by both partners to arrive at a joint acceptable research aim. Hence researchers need to learn how to share the process of research with practitioners, which takes time and patience. An open and cooperative stance will facilitate a first impression of the researcher's motivation as being genuinely collegial.

The final step of stage 1 is that 'buy-in' from senior officers is obtained. This is important for two main reasons: first, due to the hierarchical rank structure in policing, senior officers wield great influence over their subordinates. Enthusiasm, or indeed simple pragmatism, for the research project can be effectively promulgated down the ranks to the practitioners who are likely to be responsible for working on key phases in the research. Although, as Strang (2012: 216) points out, 'agreement at the top can dilute as it descends the chain of command', meaning that the endorsement (for a partnership) from a senior officer may not percolate down to the frontline staff. We return to this point in stage 3.

Second, and perhaps more importantly, senior officers are responsible for resource allocation, which affects the feasibility of a project. In an ideal scenario, the buy-in should be sought from the senior management team, rather than an individual, given that senior police officers are prone to moving posts (Fleming, 2010). Practitioner feedback in the validation exercise also emphasised the importance of senior buy-in at the *implementation* stage of a research project (see more later).

Stage 2: Planning

To alleviate problems relating to mismatched expectations of what partnerships can deliver, and when, the next logical step in the model is the discussion of outcomes, timescales, and obstacles. Acknowledging that unfavourable results are still important sources of evidence can help to temper perceptions of 'success' and 'failure'. Setting out clear terms of reference and a project plan can further reconcile any conflicting expectations across partners of how the partnership project is to run, what outcomes might be produced, whose intellectual property they are, and how and where they might be communicated or published. Fleming (2011) notes that these issues commonly generate misunderstandings and can undermine relations between partners. Documenting collective decisions can therefore be a useful means of maintaining commitment from all partners and can help to protect against misconceptions of what each partner's role is in the project. The survey results from question eight in Appendix 4.1.1 lend weight to this recommendation: 'clear communication and negotiation at the outset of the projects' and 'better management of police expectations' were purported to be good solutions to the issue of timeliness by participants in open-ended questions (not shown).

Policing is founded on shifting political and operational sands. Partnership research thus requires the adoption of a plan which includes flexibility regarding the allocation of resources (Rojek et al., 2015). Resourcing demands for, say, a critical incident or public outcry can naturally take precedence over partnership working (Foster and Bailey, 2010; Stephens, 2010). Relatedly, research often encounters unforeseen delays. Research that wishes to retain 'currency' (Wilkinson, 2010) needs to adapt to changing circumstances and recognise that police practitioners face internal pressures (Fleming, 2012). Sometimes this may require revising the research plan entirely; other times it may necessitate a recalibration of resources and timescales.

Having practitioner input at the planning stage is thus crucial, as practitioners are more familiar with the types of abstractions and hurdles likely to be encountered during the research. The 'co-production' (see Crawford, this volume) of the research plan is hence very important (see question 6 in Appendix 4.1.1). However, Wilkinson (2010) observes that researchers are not always comfortable with 'interference' in their professional habits. The same might be said of the police—the participants in the validation exercise said that although the police like to ask questions, they do not like to be questioned by others.

It would seem that both partners might benefit from suspending their usual customs and being accommodating to the shared goal. In this vein, Madensen and Sousa (2015: 76) recommend that 'researchers should not cling to form at the expense of substance'. By this they mean that research methods should be appropriately tailored to the presenting situation, and the researcher, or 'pracademic' (see Huey and Mitchell, 2016), should take care to translate relevant theoretical concepts into insights that can feed into practice. Understanding how the research findings will be used is essential for the researcher when explaining the research design and the robustness of the findings to the practitioner. At times, less rigorous methods (from an academic perspective) are arguably a better fit for many policing circumstances and can yield useful insights for the police, but might then have to be cautiously used by practitioners to make causal inferences or definitive arguments.

Stage 3: Building Trust

Building trust is embedded into the whole partnership lifecycle, but intensifies as the research is executed. Two fundamental requirements: 'confidentiality and discretion assured' and 'each partner's skills and experience is valued', are precursors to the establishment of trust in stage 3. The first can be achieved through careful and transparent agreements for the provision of data sharing and intellectual property rights, but may also be augmented by a researcher's reputation. The second is more challenging. In part it is dependent on the 'right' people being involved in the partnership (Goode and Lumsden, 2016), who possess personality traits—such as open-mindedness and good communication skills—to engender reciprocated understanding and respect (Fleming, 2012).

Two key mechanisms enable this mutual respect: a 'commitment to the research by the police practitioner' and 'police culture valued by the researcher' (Rojek et al., 2015). The former requires buy-in from the partnership team, which is different than buy-in from senior officers. Although senior officers may hold sway over subordinates, it is critical that the police practitioners in charge of executing the research understand the rationale behind the project and what constitutes fidelity to the research plan (Strang, 2012). Being able to communicate the real-world application of the research findings to the police is a distinct advantage at this stage of the process (Fleming, 2010).

The literature suggests that researchers ought to value police culture (Rojek et al., 2015). Sometimes the researcher will be 'embedded' within the police department in which the project is being done (Braga and Davis, 2014) in order to immerse them in the culture. If this is not feasible, a researcher must convey a readiness to understand, and be respectful of, police heritage, processes, and operational constraints (Stanko, 2007). To gain legitimacy in the eyes of the police, researchers must be prepared to be repeatedly tested (Engel and Whalen, 2010), to prove they are motivated and that their behaviour is trustworthy. Visibility, approachability, availability, and willingness to work on tasks outside the scope of the project all contribute to achieve this goal (Rojek et al., 2015).

Many police practitioners might determine that personality dynamics are fundamental to this stage of the process; however, in reality researchers can hone their emotional intelligence to gain social acceptance within the police organisation. This includes cultivating softer skills such as carefully listening and observing, showing interest in the views of others, asking pertinent neutral questions, using straightforward language, and being courteous and respectful of police traditions and processes (Brown, 2015). Such intelligence can be developed through 'self-awareness and self-reflection' (Cockbain, 2015: 31). It is hence helpful for the researcher 'to be carefully attuned to organisational politics and to be able to navigate them smoothly' (Holgersson, 2015: 111). It is worth noting, however, that police culture is not homogenous or 'unitary' (Reiner, 1992; Kennedy, 2015), but differs subtly both within and between police agencies, and researchers need to be aware of these differences.

It is also critical for the researcher to acknowledge the craft- or practice-based knowledge held by the police. Failure to do so can impede the development of trust, limit access to research subjects, and undermine the willingness of the police practitioner to cooperate (Engel and Whalen, 2010; Lum et al., 2012). The police's practical wisdom can contribute insights to the project and refine the research plan, and thus should be an integral component to the co-produced research.

That each partner's skills and experience are valued rests on a mutual appreciation that neither partner holds the monopoly of knowledge, or experience, on the research topic. It requires an acknowledgement that each partner brings complementary strengths and contributions to the partnership (Fleming, 2011; Willis, 2016). If these factors are in place then a reciprocal relationship based on trust can flourish, but in recognition that it is fragile and may need constant renegotiation.

Continual communication between partners both influences and strengthens trust; hence these are interdependent in Figure 4.1.1. This ameliorates police concerns about feeling detached from developments in the research (Fleming, 2011) and, in particular, nasty surprises. Frequent and frank communication also speaks to the police practitioner's need for timely results (Rojek et al., 2015) and keeps the researcher abreast of organisational changes that might (negatively or positively) affect the research (Fleming, 2011). Communication is especially vital in the face of controversial findings being broadcasted by the media (which may happen towards the end of a project). When this happens, senior police managers need to be fully informed about the nature of the research and the factors that might have influenced the findings—or compromised the effectiveness of an initiative. In doing so, they are poised to handle questions from the media in a constructive manner.

Conflict is somewhat inevitable in partnerships due to the different priorities and personalities involved. A partnership with a custom of effective communication will be well placed to recognise and acknowledge conflict when it arises and to agree a position that satisfies the partnership's objectives. Face-to-face interaction is generally assumed to be preferred by practitioners (Cockbain, 2015). This facilitates sensitive interpretation of the research process and findings and encourages clarification questions (Huberman, 1994). However, written updates, in the form of emails and interim reports, can augment these meetings (see question 10 in Appendix 4.1.1).

Stage 4: Applying Knowledge

Interim findings feature strongly in the cycle of continuous communication in Figure 4.1.1. Police practitioners can feel uneasy if they are not kept informed of how the research is developing, particularly if there is a perception that the researcher is working independently of the policing agency (Fleming, 2011). Provisional interim findings also stimulate debate on whether refinements to the methods or data collection are required and forewarn partnership members if the findings are looking unfavourable. They are particularly useful vehicles for softening the impact of challenging findings (Laycock, 2015). Such reports can also be used to anticipate potential implementation problems.

Interim findings need not follow a traditional report structure, but may be more influential when delivered as practitioner-friendly briefings, practical 'toolkits', executive summaries, and/ or technical applications (Telep, 2016; Holgersson, 2015). Engel and Whalen (2010: 108) advise researchers to write clearly and take care not to use language that 'implies intellectual superiority'. Relatedly, different strata of the police (e.g., frontline officers and managerial officers) will have different knowledge needs and therefore multiple written communication styles may be required (Stephens, 2010).

The penultimate step in the model of coordination partnerships is the operationalisation of the findings by all partners. This counters the historic tendency for research findings to be divorced from the operational context in which they are forged (Engel and Whalen, 2010). Involving all partners in the translation of the research findings draws on the collective strengths across the partnership; researchers can advise on the strength and reliability of the findings, and police practitioners can advise on the practical reality of the implementation plan. Doing so has the potential to result in a greater acceptance of the final outcomes of the research project and increase the likelihood of inducing organisational change (Guillaume et al., 2012).

Arguably the final stage in a coordination partnership is the implementation of the research findings—the change in practice. This is no easy task. Delivering organisational change is challenging, and especially so if it comes off the back of research that identifies a deficiency in police practice (Rojek et al., 2015). The political and organisational environment may not support such change (e.g., see Mastrofski, 2002), and change agents may feel apprehensive of delivering innovations, particularly if there is a strong culture of blame in their particular police agency. Maintaining communication and good interpersonal relations between the partners is crucial here, as is support from senior officers. Participants in the validation exercise raised the issue that practitioners who had helped generate the research findings often have to go up the chain of command for approval for resources to implement those findings. Having a senior officer who is convinced of the merits of the research, and who values the findings, is more likely to grant approval rather than someone removed from the partnership.

Although we present the model as somewhat linear, in reality it is likely that there are count-less feedback loops; the building of trust pervades the entire process but has a particular role in building relationships (Madensen and Sousa, 2015). However, it is also possible that all of these steps are somewhat interdependent. Each of the stages in the model is reliant on human factors, and the people involved have to be of a certain disposition to patiently deal with the myriad of interpersonal exchanges that might be needed to overcome barriers to the partnership. Partnerships are undoubtedly an ongoing process rather than a series of one-off events, and hence key participants need to be committed to a journey, as well as a destination.

Discussion and Conclusion

If the aspirations of evidence-based policing (EBP) are to be realised, research needs to become an integral part of the dialogue in police decision-making. To make this happen, police practitioners need to understand, and value, the nature of research evidence and engage critically with the findings so that they might translate them into their operational contexts. Equally, researchers need to respect and value the craft-based practice that has been built over the history of policing.

In this chapter we have argued that police–researcher partnerships are the linchpin to a cultural shift towards evidence-based policing. When effective, partnerships have the poten-tial to elevate receptivity to research evidence. We suggest that partnerships do this via three mechanisms: 1) by giving the police (joint) ownership of police research, which is hypothesised to secure investment into the evidence-generation process and the findings (Weisburd and Ney-roud, 2011); 2) by increasing the relevance of police research, through influencing the research questions studied and by injecting practical wisdom into the implementation of the findings (Rojek et al., 2015); and 3) through the inherent experiential learning within the partnership process that demystifies and humanises the scientific process (Palmer, 2011).

Partnership harmony is not a given, however, and requires organisational change from both research and police partners. In Figure 4.1.2 we use force field analysis to summarise the fundamental obstacles that might crop up in a partnership working process and how these might be neutralised. These are represented as 'forces against' partnerships on the right and 'forces in support' on the left. The strongest barrier—absence of trust—is positioned at the top right, because this underpins the entire partnership process. As discussed previously, communication is closely intertwined with trust, but is deserving of its own category. The police chain of command (i.e., management style) and organisational stability (i.e., the ten-dency of human and other resources to be in flux) comes next in the list of forces against, with the barrier of obscure operational relevance of operational findings being in the bottom right. The left-hand side of Figure 4.1.2 reflects the strategies we have proposed that might counterbalance these forces against.

Figure 4.1.2 might serve as a risk assessment tool for someone embarking on a new part-nership. It prompts thinking about the setup of a partnership in terms of relationship building,

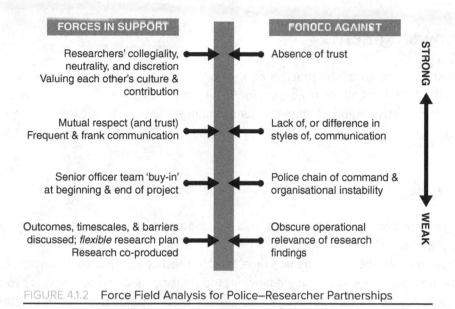

FIGURE 4.1.2   Force Field Analysis for Police–Researcher Partnerships

communication, and governance. It forces the researcher to consider how to make the research (or other output) operationally relevant and how to maintain buy-in from senior officers.

To anyone who has worked in partnerships, the model we present in this chapter will seem rather obvious. It is, however, the first attempt (of which we are aware) to bring together all of the crucial partnership ingredients and loosely order them in sequence. We have proposed four stages in a typified cooperation partnership process: 1) initiation, 2) planning, 3) building trust, and 4) applying knowledge. Throughout each phase there needs to be trust, communication, a conjoining of motives to undertake research, and feedback to police partners. With most (if not all) of the essential ingredients in place, it is possible that a mutually beneficial partnership that produces reciprocated knowledge might flourish. We hope this model stimulates thinking on how to test whether the processes we have outlined are operating as suggested, perhaps through the participatory action research favoured by applied researchers (Wood, Fleming and Marks, 2008; Bradley and Nixon, 2009).

In conclusion, there is mounting impetus—from external and internal sources—for policing to move towards being an evidence-based profession. In contribution to this goal, in this chapter we contend that police–researcher partnerships are an important mechanism through which police receptivity to research, and researcher receptivity to craft-based practice, might be elevated. Truly effective partnerships are those that surpass organisational agendas and evolve into symbiotic and personal alliances. These have the potential to cement the value of research into police consciousness and put evidence at the heart of decision-making.

Acknowledgments

We are grateful to all of the practitioners who took part in our validation exercise and to Nicky Miller from the College of Policing for facilitating the session. The chapter was strengthened by constructive feedback from the Kongsvinger workshop participants and, in particular, Betsy Stanko.

Notes

1   Police *craft* refers to the knowledge, skill, and judgment officers acquire through their daily experiences.
2   These included the International Crime and Intelligence Analysis conference, a College of Policing–sponsored event on evidence-based policing, and the survey was promoted on POLKA (Police Online Knowledge Area), which is accessible to all police practitioners in the UK.
3   Interested parties may contact the corresponding author for a copy of this survey.
4   Several participants at the events attended said that they didn't have this experience and therefore did not fill in the survey.

References

Bourdieu, P. and Wacquant, L. J. D. (1992). *An Invitation to Reflexive Sociology*, Cambridge: Polity Press.

Bradley, D. and Nixon, C. (2009). 'Ending the "dialogue of the deaf": Evidence and policing policies and practices. An Australian case study', *Police Practice and Research*, 10(5): 423–35.

Brown, R. (2015). 'Tip-Toeing through the Credibility Mine Field: Gaining Social Acceptance in Policing Research', in E. Cockbain and J. Knutsson (eds) *Applied Police Research*, pp. 34–44, Abingdon, Oxon: Routledge.

Buerger, M.E. (2010). 'Police and research: Two cultures separated by an almost-common language', *Police Practice and Research: An International Journal*, 11(2): 135–43.

Chan, J. (1996). 'Changing police culture', *British Journal of Criminology*, 36(1): 109–34.

Cockbain, E. (2015). 'Getting a Foot in the Closed Door: Practical Advice for Starting Out in Research into Crime and Policing Issues', in E. Cockbain and J. Knutsson (eds) *Applied Police Research*, pp. 21–33, Abingdon, Oxon: Routledge.

Cockbain, E. and Knutsson, J. (2015). 'Introduction', in E. Cockbain and J. Knutsson (eds) *Applied Police Research*, Abingdon, Oxon: Routledge.

Cordner, G. and Biebel, E.P. (2005). 'Problem-oriented policing in practice', *Criminology and Public Policy*, 4: 155–80.

Engel, R. and Whalen, J. (2010). 'Police-academic partnerships: Ending the dialogue of the deaf, the Cincinnati experience', *Police Practice and Research*, 11(2): 105–16.

Fielding, N. (1988). *Joining Forces: Police Training, Socialization, and Occupational Competence*, London and New York: Routledge.

Fleming, J. (2010). 'Learning to work together: Police and academics', *Policing: A Journal of Policy and Practice*, 4(2): 139–45.

Fleming, J. (2011). 'Learning to work together: Police and academics', *Australasian Policing*, 3(2): 139–45.

Fleming, J. (2012). 'Changing the way we do business: Reflecting on collaborative practice', *Police Practice and Research*, 13(4): 375–88.

Foster, J. (2003). 'Police Cultures', in T. Newburn (ed) *Handbook of Policing*, pp. 196–227, Devon, UK: Willan.

Foster, J. and Bailey, S. (2010). 'Joining forces: Maximizing ways of making a difference in policing', *Policing: A Journal of Policy and Practice*, 4(2): 95–103.

Goode, J. and Lumsden, K. (2016). 'The McDonaldisation of police–academic partnerships: Organisational and cultural barriers encountered in moving from research on police to research with police', *Policing and Society*, 9463(February): 1–15.

Guillaume, P., Sidebottom, A. and Tilley, N. (2012). 'On police and university collaborations: A problem-oriented policing case study', *Police Practice and Research*, 13(4): 389–401.

Holgersson, S. (2015). 'An Inside Job: Managing Mismatched Expectations and Unwanted Findings When Conducting Police Research as a Police Officer', in E. Cockbain and J. Knutsson (eds) *Applied Police Research*, pp. 106–16, Abingdon, Oxon: Routledge.

Huberman, M. (1994). 'Research utilization: The state of the art', *Knowledge and Policy*, 7(4): 13–33.

Huey, L. and Mitchell, R.J. (2016). 'Unearthing hidden keys: Why pracademics are an invaluable (if underutilized) resource in policing research', *Policing*, doi: 10.1093/police/paw029

Kennedy, D. (2010). 'Hope and despair', *Police Practice and Research*, 11(2): 166–70.

Kennedy, D. (2015). 'Working in the Field: Police Research in Theory and in Practice', in E. Cockbain and J. Knutsson (eds) *Applied Police Research*, pp. 9–20, Abingdon, Oxon: Routledge.

Laycock, G. (2014). 'Crime science and policing: Lessons of translation', *Policing*, 8(4): 393–401.

Laycock, G. (2015). 'Trust me, I'm a researcher', in E. Cockbain and J. Knutsson (eds) *Applied Police Research*, pp. 45–66, Abingdon, Oxon: Routledge.

Loftus, B. (2010). 'Police occupational culture: Classic themes, altered times', *Policing and Society*, 20(1): 1–20.

Lum, C., Telep, C.W., Koper, C.S. and Grieco, J. (2012). 'Receptivity to research in policing', *Justice Research and Policy*, 14(1): 61–96.

MacDonald, B. (1986). 'Research and Action in the Context of Policing: An Analysis of the Problem and a Programme Proposal', unpublished document of the Police Foundation of England and Wales.

Madensen, T.D. and Sousa, W.H. (2015). 'Practical Academics: Positive Outcomes of Police-Researcher Collaborations', in E. Cockbain and J. Knutsson (eds) *Applied Police Research*, pp. 68–81, Abingdon, Oxon: Routledge.

Manning, P. (1993). 'Toward a Theory of Police Organization: Polarities and Change', paper given to the International Conference on Social Change in Policing, Taipei, 3–5 August 1993.

Mastrofski, S.D. (2002). 'The Romance of Police Leadership', in E. Waring and D. Weisburd (eds) *Advances in Criminological Theory: Crime and Social Organization*, pp. 153–95, vol. 10, New Brunswick, NJ: Transaction Publishers.

O'Neill, M. (2016). 'Revisiting the classics: Janet Chan and the legacy of 'changing police culture', *Policing and Society*. Retrieved from http://dx.doi.org/10.1080/10439463.2016.1165997.

Palmer, I. (2011). *Is the United Kingdom Police Service Receptive to Evidence–based Policing? Testing Attitudes towards Experimentation*, MSt. Thesis, Cambridge University, UK.

Reiner, R. (1992). *The Politics of the Police*, 2nd edition, Hemel Hempstead: Harvester Wheatsheaf.

Reuss Ianni, E. and Ianni, F. (1983). 'Street Cops and Management Cops: The Two Cultures of Policing', in M. Punch (ed.) *Control in the Police Organization*, pp. 251–74, Cambridge, MA: MIT Press.

Rojek, J., Martin, P. and Alpert, G.P. (2015). *Developing and Maintaining Police-Researcher Partnerships to Facilitate Research Use: A Comparative Analysis*, New York: Springer-Verlag.

Stanko, B. (2007). 'From academia to policy making: Changing police responses to violence against women', *Theoretical Criminology*, 11(2): 209–20.

Stephens, D.W. (2010). 'Enhancing the impact of research on police practice', *Police Practice and Research*, 11(2): 150–4.

Strang, H. (2012). 'Coalitions for a common purpose: Managing relationships in experiments', *Journal of Experimental Criminology*, 8(3): 211–25.

Telep, C. (2016). 'Police Officer Receptivity to Research and Evidence-Based Policing: Examining Variability Within and Across Agencies', *Crime and Delinquency*, doi: 10.1177/0011128716642253

Weisburd, D. and Neyroud, P. (2011). *New Perspectives in Policing: Police Science—Toward a New Paradigm*, Harvard Executive Session on Policing and Public Safety, Washington, DC: National Institute of Justice.

Wilkinson, S. (2010). 'Research and policing—looking to the future', *Policing*, 4(2): 146–8.

Willis, J.J. (2016). 'The romance of police pracademics', *Policing*, 10(3): 315–321, doi: 10.1093/police/paw030

Willis, J.J. and Mastrofski, S.D. (2016). 'Improving policing by integrating craft and science: What can patrol officers teach us about good police work?', *Policing and Society*, doi: 10.1080/10439463.2015.1135921

Wood, J., Fleming, J. and Marks, M. (2008). 'Building the capacity of police change agents: The nexus policing project', *Policing and Society*, 18(1): 72–87.

APPENDIX 4.1.1   Partnership working survey answers

	Police	Researcher
Who initiated your most recent partnership?		
Co-initiated by police practitioner and researcher	2	1
The police practitioner	3	1
The researcher	0	3
Other (please specify)	1	0
TOTAL	6	5
Who was responsible for obtaining the funding for your most recent partnership?		
All partners	1	0
No funding/work done 'in kind'	0	1
The police practitioner	3	0
The researcher	2	4
TOTAL	6	5
How was the partnership funded? Please choose all options that apply.		
Research council/EU commission	2	1
Charity/third-sector organisation	1	0
Government (e.g., home office, local authority)	2	3
University	1	0
Police agency	1	2
No funding	0	1
TOTAL	7	7
In your opinion was this police–researcher partnership:		
More beneficial to the police practitioner than the researcher	2	1
More beneficial to the researcher than the police practitioner	1	0
Mutually beneficial	3	4
TOTAL	6	5
Based on your most recent experience, would you consider continuing another project with the same partner?		
No	1	0
Unsure	0	1
Yes	5	4
TOTAL	6	5
How important is practitioner experience in shaping the research plan?		
Very important	6	3
Somewhat important	0	2
Not very important	0	0
TOTAL	6	5

APPENDIX 4.1.1 *(Continued)*

Does the time required to conduct research inhibit its relevance to operational decision-making?		
No	4	1
Somewhat	2	2
Yes	0	2
TOTAL	6	5

How do you think this [timeliness] issue could be overcome? Please select up to three options.		
Clear communication and negotiation at the outset of the project	3	1
Better management of police expectations	2	3
Interim findings reported regularly	1	2
Flexible research plan to suit police requirements	1	0
Other (please specify)	4	3
TOTAL	11	9

In your experience, is there effective communication between police and research partners?		
No	1	0
Somewhat	2	2
Yes	3	3
TOTAL	6	5

How can communication between partners be strengthened? (Please select up to two options)		
Co-location of partners	1	1
Regular face-to-face interaction	5	3
Regular email correspondence	2	2
Regular telephone calls	0	1
Regular interim progress reports	2	2
TOTAL	10	9

How important is trust between the police and the researcher to the success of the partnership?		
Somewhat important	0	1
Very important	6	4
TOTAL	6	5

What factors can strengthen trust between practitioners and researchers? (Please select up to three options)		
Previous experience of successful partnerships with other partners	2	2
Previous experience of successful partnerships with the same partner	1	3
Exposure to research	3	3
Exposure to police culture	4	1
Good interpersonal relationships	5	3

Reputation of partners	0	1
Minimal change in personnel during the partnership	3	2
TOTAL	18	15
Based on your overall experience of research partnerships, what is the most useful outcome that you value?		
A solution to a problem/actionable information	1	2
Access to new information or resources	1	0
Knowledge exchange	0	0
Learning new perspectives	1	1
Strong interpersonal relationships	1	1
Understanding the other partner's working culture	0	1
Other (please specify)	2	0
TOTAL	6	5

Conclusion

This chapter provided strategies for facilitating mutually effective partnerships between the police and researchers, highlighting a four-stage sequence that includes (1) initiation, (2) planning, (3) building trust, and (4) applying knowledge. Practitioners/professionals should be involved and provide input at all stages of the research process as "ownership of research has the potential to secure support for the findings to be accepted and integrated into practice." Whether you aspire to be a practitioner/professional within the criminal justice or social services field or a researcher, never hesitate to reach out and explore the possibility of forming mutually effective partnerships to design and execute research whose outcomes are vital to informing effective policies and practices that "put evidence at the heart of decision-making."

Chapter 4 Reflection Questions

1. What is evidence-based policing?
2. What are some barriers that prevent the formation of effective partnerships between police and researchers?
3. List and briefly discuss the four basic requirements that contribute to effective partnerships between researchers and practitioners.
4. List and briefly describe the three categories of partnerships.
5. Explore the National Institute of Corrections evidence-based practices web page (https://nicic.gov/evidence-based-practices-ebp). Identify one study of interest. Read and summarize the study. Based on the outcomes of this research, what evidence-based practices are recommended?

Building Your Research Proposal

Chapter 4: Consider and Explore Researcher-Agency Partnerships

Reflect on the research question/hypothesis developed in the previous chapter. Identify a local agency with whom you could form a partnership to execute this research. How would you approach this agency? What should you consider? What steps can you take to build trust and ensure that this relationship will be mutually beneficial?

Reviewing the Literature

Introduction

The first article in this chapter, "The Literature Review Process," presents and discusses various types of literature reviews, selecting and narrowing research topics/questions, and locating and selecting sources of information for inclusion. Dawidowicz defines a literature review as "an examination of scholarly information and research-based information on a specific topic." A literature review is a vital component of a scholarly research paper as the process allows the researcher to (1) determine whether any research has been conducted on a similar topic/in a similar area; (2) assess the methods (such as secondary data, surveys, interviews) researchers have used to examine a similar topic; (3) evaluate what this research has found; and (4) uncover areas for which additional research is needed to address gaps in the literature.

The second selection, "Structuring the Literature Review," presents examples/excerpts of reviews of scholarly research from published research papers. The Building Your Research Proposal assignment for this chapter requires the reader to locate and write summaries for three scholarly journal articles that align with the research question developed within earlier assignments. Readers are also asked to consider ways to revise original research questions or hypotheses after reading, summarizing, and reviewing those articles.

The Literature Review Process

Paula Dawidowicz

A literature review is an examination of scholarly information and research-based information on a specific topic. In other words, it's a review of what's *known*, not suspected or assumed, about a specific subject. Its goal is to create a complete, accurate representation of the knowledge and research-based theory available on a topic.

An integral part of a research process, then, is gaining an understanding of what is and isn't known about the reality of a situation, event, or circumstance. One simple explanation for the need to work toward that understanding is this: If people don't know reality, then how can they develop a research study or a plan to address a problem or concern with any effectiveness? An understanding of reality is essential to avoid creating a plan that addresses fiction rather than reality. So, researchers, regardless of academic level or professional position, use appropriate quality literature to accomplish their goals. Although this aspect of a literature review will be discussed in greater depth later in this book, its importance to the integrity of a literature review is so great that it becomes part of the basic definition.

Before proceeding much farther, though, it's useful to reconsider the nature and purpose of a literature review for a moment. By using the current body of knowledge to develop a literature review, a researcher can extend the information making up that body of knowledge and, in turn, extend the understanding of the topic being researched. In other words, when a literature review is followed by original research like that done in a dissertation, doctoral study, or thesis, the body of knowledge (or amount of knowledge) on that topic can actually be increased. That increase in knowledge allows people to both plan more appropriately as they design programs and also design further research that, in turn, adds even more to the body of knowledge on the topic they're examining.

In other words, knowledge of current research and literature versus knowledge of potentially biased or inaccurate information in the popular press can allow practitioners to develop programs and research that can create change. By the same token, theories and actions developed based on information acquired through popular press sources may, if accurate at all, tell researchers only one thing—what the people who wrote that material were thinking about the topic. Bias and objectivity will also be considered later.

Types of Literature Reviews

Literature reviews can be done at all levels of education. They're also often used in business, government, and nonprofit environments as part of individuals' and organizations' planning processes. Needless to say, each of these literature reviews can be distinctly different. These different types of literature reviews can be broken into three basic categories: simple, applied, and academic.

Essentially, a simple literature review is done to gain a brief overview of a topic. The quality of sources is important, but it is not essential that the sources be purely academic. Often such simple reviews are a short compilation of ideas, so popular sources can prove appropriate and useful. However, even in a simple review, popular sources versus academic sources are identified as such so that their value can be judged accordingly.

Applied literature reviews are used in business, in government, and in other professional environments where fact finding is important to a decision making or planning process. Often such reviews involve practical considerations like marketability and profitability figures. Such reviews still have much in common with the literature reviews being discussed here. They almost always include a section on the nature of the change being considered. They require objectivity, and they require accuracy. They will examine the relative value and relevance of different information sources, as well as the latest insights surrounding the results of similar programs or actions. In fact, the most successful proposals have substantive reviews of literature and relevant material on their topic and, as a result, follow the same principles provided in this book.

Academic literature reviews are the review type discussed most often in this book although, as stated here, all three types of reviews benefit from the principles and methods presented in the chapters that follow this one. Academic reviews are designed as either stand-alone products for classes or as precursors to conducting some type of study or project based on current research-based best practices. They require a number of qualities to be of value: accuracy, quality resources, objectivity, thoroughness, and strong analysis. They also require attention to detail, good organization, and a depth of knowledge other reviews may not.

The differences between each of these categories will be described in the following discussions on selecting and narrowing a topic, selecting literature sources, and identifying goals. However, as you read the remainder of this book, remember that, whether a literature review is for an office project, a high school class, or a dissertation, the same principles will apply to each in order to maximize success.

Selecting a Topic

The process of developing a literature review begins with selecting the right topic. Regardless of the level of education for which the review is being written or the professional environment in which it will be used, the topic should be one that will sustain interest for the length of time it will take to complete the extensive research required to finish the project. In the case of a simple review, that time period might only be a few weeks. In the case of a dissertation, the time frame could be much longer—sometimes up to two years.

In all cases, developing a literature review will involve developing a question or questions. What is it that needs to be answered? What is the curiosity or the purpose? These answers will help frame the question or questions and will help determine the content of a successful literature review, so they're very important.

If it's an academic review, the research question should be designed to fill a gap in information available in literature about a topic. In other words, it should provide people with information peer-reviewed research hasn't already provided. It should address a research need. The literature review's goal, then, will be to determine what is known, what is still needed, and how a specific study being considered can help fill that need.

If it's an applied review, it will to survey known information about a topic and help identify information that is not yet known so that best decisions for action or for further examination of a situation can be made. In other words, filling a gap in the literature isn't the main goal. The main goal is an understanding of existing and missing knowledge. The question or questions used should guide that kind of applied knowledge acquisition.

If it's a simple review, the question will normally be more general, as will the survey of the literature conducted. The question will be one that dictates an overview of the information provided in numerous sources on the topic being considered. It will also be one that lays the groundwork for future research of greater depth. In other words, it will provide insight into areas that will each be reviewable in greater depth in future research.

Consider Your Time Period

How long can a literature review take to develop? If it's a literature review for a secondary school or undergraduate class (a simple review), it might take from a month to three months. If it's a literature review to support a grant proposal, a project development plan, or a case study of a program (for an applied review), a literature review development process might take no more than a month or might take as much as a year. The time constraints will be determined by the depth of research required and the broadness of the topic at hand. For example, literature reviews required to support some government grant proposals can be as much as 200 pages, which will take a considerably longer time than the 20-page reviews required for other projects. Senior projects, Master's theses, or doctoral dissertations can take up to a year.

Consider How to Narrow the Topic

Narrow the topic until the question or hypothesis is specific enough for a comprehensive literature review to be completed. Managing to narrow a topic is often one of the biggest problems researchers face, regardless of educational level or professional environment. As humans, people often want to address the big problem—how to cure low income student failure, how to increase productivity in a company with several productivity-related issues to consider, or similar complex questions—which is simply too large to be answered in a reasonable period of time and in a reasonably sized document. There are simply too many pieces of knowledge that must be known and, among them, too many pieces of knowledge that are missing for the information to be acquired and written about thoroughly and effectively enough. If that were not the case, all children would be doing well in school and all companies would be succeeding,

Narrowing Your Topic

First, people benefit from drafting several questions to get a feel for how different questions can address different aspects of the topic being considered. Then, people can examine those questions to see whether they need answers to subquestions that are part of answering the larger question. If there are important subquestions, either plan on including those questions in your research or narrow your topic to explore only one of those subquestions.

Keep in mind that if your question has subquestions you may not be able to answer the large question until you've conducted a study on the smaller question. Why? Your subquestion may have its own subquestions. Let me give you an example.

You're interested in studying why female adolescents in urban areas don't major in mathematics and science in college as often as males. Your question is:

> What factors make female adolescents in urban areas less likely to enter mathematics and science higher education programs?

Your subquestions could be:

- What cultural factors, if any, make female adolescents in urban areas less likely to enter mathematics and science higher education programs?
- What educational factors, if any, make female adolescents in urban areas less likely to enter mathematics and science higher education programs?

If we make a small change to your major question, you'll find some sub-questions need to be answered before the major question can be addressed effectively. Here's an example: What factors make females less likely to enter mathematics and science higher education programs?

One subquestion might be:

- What cultural factors, if any, make female adolescents less likely to enter mathematics and science higher education programs?

However, with that subquestion, you need to break your literature review questions into smaller subquestions, like:

- What familial factors, if any. ...
- What community-related factors, if any ...
- What cultural factors, if any ...

Identifying Subquestions

If you're not limiting your research to a specific location or even a certain research population in a specific location, your topic may be too big for you to meet the requirements to research it thoroughly enough to create a solid literature review or solid study. The fact is questions that are too large—that involve too many factors, too large a population, or too large a geographic area—require you to have so much background knowledge of your topic to draw valid, supportable research-based conclusions that you may never be able to finish your literature review, your research study, or your business proposal. Limiting questions, populations, environments, or topics can be essential for your success.

If you're doing a literature review for a case study or an applied project, or if you're doing a simple literature review, you won't need to be as detailed in your analysis. In the first case, you've already greatly limited your populations' potential variable characteristics. In the second place, you're not expected to draw the type of detailed conclusions as are necessary for an academic literature review.

Small Research Questions and Larger Research Questions Have a Distinct Relationship

Normally, the small questions are answered by research studies over a period of time, all of which incorporate a literature review to help people gain an understanding of the realities of their topic. In the social sciences, the large questions normally can't be answered before those years of sub-question research occur. Once those smaller studies occur, the new information generated is combined to create a new, higher level of understanding.

If you want additional help with the question planning process, examine the brainstorming and organization sections of this book. Using those methods can help you identify topics and factors to consider as potential question and subquestion areas.

Further Narrowing Your Topic

Having discussed questions and subquestions, and how they define your literature review, it may seem ironic to now add the idea of narrowing your topic. However, one characteristic of a literature review that the consideration of questions and subquestions illustrates is that it's not just a matter of identifying all of the factors and characteristics of your sample population that you need to consider as you create a review. You need to create realistic limits to the topic you study. Otherwise, you'll never be able to do a thorough enough literature review to gain a solid understanding of your topic and its variables.

Regardless of the type of literature review you prepare, you will not have to read every article on your subject. For both applied and academic reviews, though, you will have to read enough to get a thorough picture of the body of research and the spectrum of perspectives that are available. To accomplish this without making your literature review your life's purpose (or the equivalent in time required to complete it effectively), you may have to narrow your topic.

Narrowing your topic becomes even more imperative in part because, with too broad a topic, your efforts in research collection can encompass so many topics and so much information that you can lose focus. As a result, a literature review that is already unwieldy can quickly become totally overwhelming. As you narrow your topic, consider the following:

1. Who will be interested in your question? Why is it important to them?
2. What period of time do you need to consider in your review? For some discussions, a history of the work on the topic is important. For others, only recent knowledge and activities are important.
3. What type of literature does your review topic require? This question is the focus of the next section.

Remember, as you consider how to narrow your topic, that a literature review is different from a research report. Often research reports focus on literature that supports your perspective. However, a review of the literature should cover work that supports not just your initial perspective, but also enough other perspectives to create an unbiased understanding of your topic. Again, for assistance with narrowing your topic, you can review the brainstorming and organization sections of this book.

So, as you consider who will be interested in your question, why it's important, how much time it will take to consider it, and what types of literature you will use, remember you're not considering just one perspective. You're considering multiple perspectives to draw objective conclusions.

Selecting Literature Sources

What types of literature are useful in a literature review? In any review of literature, you'll use research-based articles. You'll also read locally written articles relevant to your topic and situation or event. As mentioned earlier, you do not have to read every article available on your topic to complete a comprehensive review. In addition, depending on the project involved, it can be preferable if you're doing a simple literature review or an applied literature review to do a more focused review of literature so that your information doesn't become unwieldy.

Local Sources Versus Research-Based Sources

That said, the process of identifying your literature review sources can be a long one. Depending on your topic and the type of review you're doing, you'll want to use some quality research-based sources and you'll want to include some sources that are local to the situation or event you're examining. For most applied literature reviews and for all academic literature reviews, research-based sources will be peer-reviewed journals.

What ratio of these two types of sources—local and peer-reviewed—will you want to use? That depends on your literature review and purpose. For simple literature reviews, an equal mix of local and research-based sources is normally appropriate. For an applied literature review that is part of an on-site case study, you will normally need more local sources than research-based sources. However, your ratio will be dictated by your topic and goals. If the literature review is part of a grant application or similar product, the significant bulk of sources used will be research-based sources. Finally, for an academic literature review, local sources will be used only as part of your evaluation process, which is discussed later in this book.

How many sources do you need for your literature review? There is no numerical answer for that question. The answer is that you need enough sources to let you gain a solid, unbiased picture of your topic. You'll want to have several sources that draw the same conclusions about a topic, but after that you'll want to begin search for other perspectives and conclusions about your topic. Remember, the goal is to create an unbiased discussion of aspects of your topic. More details on how to do that are covered in the section on brainstorming in this book.

Research-Based Sources

In academic literature reviews, the majority of articles will be drawn from peer-reviewed and refereed journals. Such articles are printed in journals because the journals' reviewers have determined that the information shared in them is valuable and meets rigorous research and analysis standards. The reviews of the articles are done by reviewers who do not know who wrote the papers, so the decision to publish a given article is based on the work done rather than the name of the author. This helps guarantee that the information presented in such journals is strong and has integrity.

Books versus Peer-Reviewed Articles

As you search for research-based sources, you may come across numerous books you feel are appropriate for your literature review. They're written by a professor at Harvard or Yale, or perhaps by a world-renowned expert on your topic. They contain enlightening information.

Should you use those sources? There is no simple answer, since those sources may have value. The authors will have documentable background in your topic. However, there are a couple of other considerations. First, everyone has some type of bias, regardless of how much people work to control it. Even experts in a field may not see a situation as clearly as they might. Second, there is no blind peer review of the information shared in books.

A blind review of an article is a review of that article by several (normally three) researchers in the field who are not given the author's name. Instead, the article and the study it describes are judged on their own merit. The reviewers separately examine the basic framework (basic perspective or philosophy) of the article developed as a result of the literature review (similar to yours) that the author conducted and partially presented in the article itself. Was that framework developed as a result of an unbiased examination of previous research?

Reviewers also consider whether the research procedures and analysis met academic standards—large enough participant samples, appropriate samples, appropriate data sources or participant questions, and appropriate meticulous analysis. They also consider whether the conclusions drawn appear appropriate based on the data acquired. Were the conclusions logical? Were they appropriately limited or generalized to the group examined?

Only if an article meets required academic standards is it published, which is very different from the publication of a book. You can see the rigor to which peer-reviewed articles are subjected. You can understand, also, why books are not considered as valuable, when developing a literature review, as peer-reviewed articles.

Selecting Research-Based Sources

So, how do you find the research-based sources you use? Often, when you conduct a search of peer-reviewed articles, you'll find you either have a large volume of articles from which to choose or you have almost none. Since there are few topics that are totally unresearched, if you find you have few sources, you might want to consider trying new search terms. If you find you have too many sources, you might want to consider adding some additional search parameters that will limit your large number of articles a little more.

Once you have a group of peer-reviewed articles from which to choose, you'll need to narrow the number. A good first step is to review the articles' abstracts to discover the type of research done, perspectives used and, potentially, the results of the research. Since your goal is to read material on as many different perspectives, and presenting as much new information as possible that's relevant to your topic, abstracts give you an opportunity to flesh out a planned reading list. Remember, you will have already narrowed your topic so you can successfully develop your literature review. Be careful not to veer from that narrowed topic.

Selecting Local Sources

Since local sources can be biased and, potentially, manipulative, they have a limited value in most literature reviews. However, they can help people understand the human dynamic—how people feel about a topic or situation, how people feel about other people, or how people react to a certain event. These sources can also provide details of events that may not be available otherwise.

Here are some examples of situation-specific or event-specific sources:

1. newspaper articles that give details, statistics, and other facts related to your topic and your particular situation or event.
2. newspaper articles that share people's opinions about your topic or about the event or situation you're examining.
3. journals of individuals who experience the situation or event you're examining.

4. Historical accounts of the topic, situation, or event you're examining,
5. video recordings or broadcasts on a topic, situation, or event.

Although some of these sources have a specific use—providing statistics, numbers, participants, and more—about your situation, they're not always appropriate to use. At times, those facts can be trusted, and at times they can't. You as the researcher must be a discerning user. Whenever possible, check your facts with several sources.

Local sources that describe people's feelings or that quote people do not provide objective information. However, by providing people's opinions and emotions, they tell you how people are responding to a situation. This knowledge is important in *academic literature reviews*, but is particularly important in *applied* and *simple literature reviews*. It is something that must be considered when evaluating an environment for which you are either developing or evaluating a plan of action, or developing a research study. So, these articles have value as long as they are not confused with objective research.

When developing an *academic literature review* or, in most cases, a project to address a need, though, you will find yourself relying more on academic research sources. These sources will most often be peer-reviewed articles that provide a detailed review of the topic you're examining. You'll use articles in various peer-reviewed journals and other materials that you can apply to your specific environment or situation. More information about peer-reviewed sources is provided in a following chapter on the nature and quality of sources available for your use.

In addition, a discussion of tailoring a literature review to the specifics of the situation you are considering occurs later in the book. Here, I will focus on peer-reviewed sources to foster your ability to both conduct and present high quality analytical literature reviews and will only touch minimally on the use of other sources.

Peer-Reviewed Articles

Peer-reviewed articles fall into several categories. They include reviews of relevant literature created by others, literature summaries (reports on articles, not analyses), study reports, policy discussions, and examinations of quantitative and qualitative methodologies. Each type of study has a specific purpose and value to dissertations, depending on the topic.

However, just because a piece of literature is a study report does not mean it's a study report appropriate for a literature review. It needs to be the report of a study published in a peer-reviewed journal. Each of these types of literature is reviewed in some detail here and in greater detail later.

A literature summary does just what its title says it will do. It summarizes a number of articles on a topic. The summary is not of the articles as a whole. It includes a summary of only those portions that are related to the topic being studied. As part of this summary, the articles and information are examined for relative value and validity.

A study report is similar, although it focuses on a study that has been conducted. It covers every step from framework through conclusions, presenting the information in a comprehensive manner. The presentation includes a discussion of the various perspectives considered in the process of developing the framework upon which the study was based.

A policy discussion analyzes rationale for a policy or the effects of a policy. The analysis is done using peer-reviewed journals. Such policy discussions are valid because of their attempts at objectivity. If at any point the material presented is not as objective as possible, the author can lose credibility.

Identifying Goals

To summarize, the goal of a literature review is to gather the most current information from the body of knowledge on a given topic you are researching. Some of that information will be contradictory and will present different perspectives. In your literature review, you will present the information, consider its value, and draw conclusions based on that presentation and consideration.

Structuring the Literature Review

Mildred L. Patten and Michelle Newhart

A literature review's main purpose is to summarize the existing scholarship. It is a standard part of a research report whose role is to introduce themes and topics in previously published articles and books that orient the reader to the conversation about the topic. Often, it presents persuasive information to help make a case about the importance of the topic and research.

Literature reviews start most writing that reports original research, including journal articles, theses, dissertations, and sometimes student papers. When the literature review is a part of a larger work, it comprises about 20% of that piece of work. It may be only a few paragraphs in a shorter length article or consist of a chapter in most dissertations. [L]iterature reviews can be published as standalone articles, but the most common type of literature review is the one found at the outset of an empirical article. We will focus on this example in this topic.

In empirical articles, the literature review often appears at the beginning, and may flow directly from the introductory paragraph or follow directly after an introduction. It may or may not be labeled with a heading, depending on journal style and length of article. It provides context for the presentation of original research, followed by sections about the study's hypotheses, methods, and findings, and a concluding section that discusses the broader implications of the findings, as well as their limitations.

A straightforward recipe for starting a literature review is to define key terms and establish the importance of the research topic. There are a few tried and true ways to establish a topic's importance. One is to provide a compelling key statistic. Example 1 is the first paragraph of an original research article on fear of cancer recurrence among breast cancer survivors, taken from the journal *Health Psychology*.

Example 1

> Breast cancer affects 1 in 8 women in North America (American Cancer Society, 2011; Canadian Cancer Society, 2011). The majority of breast cancer patients successfully complete treatment and become survivors. Studies show that survivors have unmet needs (i.e., supportive care needs that, according to the survivor, have not yet been appropriately addressed; Harrison, Young, Price, Butow & Solomon, 2009), the most frequently cited one being fear of cancer recurrence (FCR; Baker, Denniston, Smith, & West, 2005; Herschbach et al., 2004; Lebel, Rosberger, Edgar, & Devins, 2007). FCR has been described as the sword of Damocles that hangs over patients for the rest of their lives (Baker et al., 2005). FCR is defined as "the fear or worry that the cancer will return or progress in the same organ or in another part of the body" (Simard & Savard, 2009; Vickberg, 2003). The current literature suggests that moderate to high levels of FCR affect 33% to 56% of cancer patients (Llewellyn, Weinman, McGurk, & Humphris, 2008; Vickberg, 2003). FCR is associated with impairment in functioning, psychological distress, stress-response symptoms, and lower quality of life (Dow, Ferrell, Leigh, Ly, & Gulasekaram, 96; Mellon, Northouse, & Weiss, 2006; Vickberg, 2003).[1]

The authors begin with a compelling statistic. Note that each claim made in this paragraph is supported by citations. The language is careful. This is an important aspect of the literature review portion of academic work [...]. It is critical that the premises on which the article is based are not simply the author's opinion but reflect the findings of existing research, and that claims do not overstate the conclusions in the original source[s]. For instance, when the authors state, "Studies show" that survivors have unmet needs, the citation includes more than one study. Overstating the findings of prior research or sloppiness in describing them will undermine the credibility of not just the literature review but the report as a whole.

Statistics are not the only evidence that is connected to sources; the author is careful to define the major terms related to the study that will follow. Key terms should be clearly defined. Definitions may also include concrete information on what is included within a term, or how it is measured. For instance, the main term, fear of cancer recurrence, or FCR, is both defined and linked to important outcomes. When the authors discuss "unmet needs," they begin to clarify what needs are included (supportive care needs).

Literature reviews often start with a combination of definitions and statements of supporting evidence (with statistics, if any) indicating the importance of the problem area.[2] Note that definitions are not invented by the authors. It is acceptable to quote a published conceptual definition, as long as the source is properly cited. Definitions and statistics are central elements to establish a topic that will be presented in the research. Other strategies for making a persuasive argument include establishing that a trend is increasing or decreasing, arguing for the importance of the trend, making a case that a particular topic has not been adequately covered in other studies, or providing facts that may surprise the reader about something familiar to them. All three strategies help to make a case for the importance of the contribution the new research can make.

Example 2 comes from the literature review in a peer-reviewed article on cyberbullying. This article had a separate introduction and literature review. The introduction included definitions of bullying and cyberbullying in making the claim (with citations) that bullying is not new, but cyberbullying is on the rise. This excerpt shows the first sentences from the Literature Review section:

Example 2

Prior to 2002, no research existed on the topic of cyber-bullying (Hinduja & Patchin, 2012). However, researchers have found that two-thirds of students reported that cyber-bullying is just as serious as traditional bullying, if not worse, as people often feel shielded from the ramifications of their actions and, therefore, may state things they would not ordinarily say in person (Strom et al., 2012). Further research conducted on 124 middle school students found that 32% of its participants felt that cyber-bullying was a problem in their school (Accordino & Accordino, 2011). Interestingly, research suggests that the highest frequency of cyber-bullying is found in public schools, followed by all-girl private schools, with the least cyber-bullying incidents occurring at private charter schools (Mark & Ratliffe, 2011).[3]

In this example, you can see some commonly used elements of the literature review in action. The report claims that there was little research prior to 2002. Statistics claim that many students are affected, and establish that the issue is important to students. There is also a fact of interest (where bullying most frequently occurs) that might surprise or contradict what someone expects about the trend in cyberbullying. All claims presented are tied to sources, and all relate directly to the specific areas that the research in the report will cover.

Notes

1 Lebel, S., Beattie, S., Arès, I., & Bielajew, C. (2013). Young and worried: Age and fear of recurrence in breast cancer survivors. *Health Psychology, 32*, 695–705. doi:10.1037/a0030186
2 See Appendix C for examples of beginnings of reviews.
3 Herrera, J., Kupczynski, L., & Mundy, M. (2015). The impact of training on faculty and student perceptions of cyberbullying in an urban south central Texas middle school. *Research in Higher Education Journal, 27*, 29 pages.

Conclusion

Reviewing the literature is a vital, integral part of the research process. The literature review represents a substantial portion of a research proposal or paper, with a purpose of summarizing published studies that closely relate to the topic being researched. The bullet points included within the Building Your Research Proposal section below (question 3) provide valuable information and guidance for reading and summarizing scholarly journal articles.

Chapter 5 Reflection Questions

1. What is a literature review?
2. Why is the literature review "an integral part of the research process"?
3. What are the types of literature reviews?
4. What are the various sources of information that may be included in a literature review?

An additional source of information that provides helpful hints to assist you with learning to read a scholarly journal article may be found at https://libguides.usc.edu/evaluate/scholarlyarticles.

Building Your Research Proposal

Chapter 5. Conduct a Literature Review and Revise/Refine Your Research Question

1. Restate the research question or hypothesis you developed in the Building Your Research Proposal section in earlier chapters. If you are still not certain about what you would like to focus on, you can restate your general category of research interest.

2. Conduct a search of peer-reviewed journal articles via your institution's library or other online scholarly journal article search engine (such as Google Scholar) using key words from your question or hypothesis. If you are still not certain about your area of focus, you can use general terms, such as "law enforcement" or "corrections" so that you can be inspired by what other researchers have examined. Select three articles that relate to your specific research idea.

3. Read and answer the following questions for each article. Once you have completed that work, summarize each of the five points in a paragraph that includes an in-text citation (Author(s) year).

   • What did the researcher(s) examine?
   • What population/sample was utilized?
   • What methods were used?
   • What were the findings/results of this study?
   • What were the study limitations and authors' suggestions for future research?

4. Develop a References page. Cite **each** article reviewed in APA style. See Purdue University's Online Writing Lab for excellent resources specific to citing references in APA style (the most widely accepted formatting guide in the criminal justice; https://owl.purdue.edu/owl/research_and_citation/apa_style/apa_style_introduction.html).

APA Reference Formatting
Author, A.A. (year of publication). Title of article. *Title of Journal, volume*(issue), page–page.

5. Based on your review of the articles summarized, identify ways you may modify or refine your original research question.

Research Design and Measurement

Introduction

After a researcher has selected a topic, developed a research question/hypothesis, reviewed the literature, and refined the research question/hypothesis, they must select a blueprint or plan for gathering information to address the question/hypothesis guiding the study. The first article in this chapter, "Introduction to Research Design," reveals that "a research design is essentially a plan that maps the course of action for a research project" and is "driven by the research question." The authors continue by differentiating between experimental designs (rarely used within criminal justice research) and quasi-experimental designs and present levels of measurement for variables employed within these types of research (nominal, ordinal, interval, and ratio). The next article, "Research Designs," by the same authors, discusses designs that are more commonly used within criminal justice–related research, including descriptive, historical, cross-sectional, longitudinal (trend, cohort, and panel), and case study, and present specific types of research, including correlational, causal-comparative, and evaluation research. As you read this chapter, think about which approach may be the most beneficial to addressing the research question or hypothesis you posed in earlier chapters/assignments.

Harwood's two selections provide practical applications for measuring single and multiple variables. In the "Measuring a Single Variable" selection, measurement considerations for hypotheses/research questions that contain one variable are discussed, and several possibilities for information (data) that can be used to answer a research question are presented (surveys, observation using data that have already been collected for a different purpose). In

Harwood's second selection, "Measuring Multiple Variables," examples for formulating research questions or hypotheses that include more than one variable are presented. Although non-criminal justice–related examples are utilized in these two chapters, you are urged to apply the research question/hypothesis you have developed to complete these exercises.

Introduction to Research Design

Mark L. Dantzker, Ronald D. Hunter, and Susan T. Quinn

What You Should Know!

A research design is essentially a plan that maps out the course of action for a research project. Before choosing a research design, it is important to recognize the goals of the study. For example, is the study attempting to determine the causes of homicide? All of the choices regarding research design are driven by the research question—specifically, what is the researcher trying to find or determine? After completing this chapter, the reader should be able to:

1. Define empiricism and discuss how it relates to criminal justice research.
2. Identify and discuss the three criteria for causality.
3. Contrast idiographic and nomothetic causal explanations.
4. Contrast necessary and sufficient cause.
5. Compare experimental and quasiexperimental research designs.
6. Discuss the three elements of experimental research design.
7. Describe the classical experiment research design.
8. Compare the classical experiment research design to the pretest-posttest, protest only, and factorial research designs.
9. Describe the four levels of measurement: nominal, ordinal, interval, and ratio.
10. Identify the questions that can be used to help correctly identify a variable's level of measurement.

Empirical Observation

Thinking back to an introductory course in criminology and criminal justice or a course in criminological theory, students may realize they have already received an introduction to empiricism. Cesare Tombroso, the founder of the Positive School of Criminology, used empiricism in his study of criminals. Lombroso's study of criminals focused on observing and measuring physical characteristics, such as facial features. Earlier scholars also used empirical techniques. For example, Quetelet and Guerry compared the crime rates of geographic areas in France.

Empiricism is defined as seeking answers to questions through direct observation, specifically sensations and experiences, to arrive at conclusions about the world in which we live (Jeffery, 1990). The use of the scientific method, with its focus on structured inquiry rather than casual observation, is what makes empiricism important. This emphasis on trying to see things as they are rather than idealistically is the basis on which positive criminology is founded. Rather than just quoting an "eye for an eye," empirical techniques can be used to gather and evaluate data as to the effectiveness of correctional programs, to decide which patrol strategy is more cost effective, or to determine whether extralegal factors influence conviction rates.

Causality

In applying empirical observation to criminal justice research, the focus is on causal relationships. Simply stated, what behaviors or events lead to other behaviors or events? When trying to answer that question, one seeks to determine causality. One of the main questions in criminal justice and criminological research is what "causes" people to commit crime? By determining the causes of criminal behavior, the criminal justice system could develop interventions to decrease or prevent crime.

Idiographic and Nomothetic Causal Explanations

The examination of numerous explanations to describe why a single event occurred is known as *idiographic explanation*. Historians tend to use this method to explain the occurrence of events, such as explaining why the terrorist attacks on September 11, 2001 occurred. Police officers investigating a homicide are searching for an idiographic explanation. They are trying to determine why a single homicide occurred and not trying to determine why all homicides occur. When researchers in criminal justice and criminology aim to determine why behaviors (such as homicide) or events occur in general, rather than to explain a single event, they are using *nomothetic explanations* (Berg, 2008; Bergman, 2009; Gavin, 2008).

Rather than trying to provide a total picture of every influence in a causal relationship, nomothetic explanation focuses on one or a few factors that could provide a general understanding of the phenomena being studied. Nomothetic explanations of causality are based on probabilities. In other words, what factors may increase or decrease the likelihood of behaviors or events? For example, city officials who want to determine how to reduce vandalism in areas of tourism determine that increasing surveillance, such as increasing the presence of police, decreases occurrences of new vandalism.

The Criteria for Causality

In investigating to determine if there is a causal relationship between the events or issues that being studied, three criteria must be observed (Adler & Clark, 2007; Dunn, 2009): (1) time order—the independent variable (the variable that is providing the influence) must occur before the dependent variable (the variable that is being acted on); (2) association—a relationship between the independent and dependent variable must be observed; and (3) elimination—the apparent relationship is not explained by a third or external variable.

For example, one sees individual A struck by person B. Person A then falls down. Using the criteria for causality, one would conclude that the striking (independent variable) led to the falling (dependent variable). It occurred before the falling and was clearly related to that which was witnessed. If no other event (a third variable, such as a second blow struck by person C) occurred, then it is reasonable to assume that the criteria for causality have been met.

Necessary and Sufficient Cause

In investigating causality, one must meet the previously mentioned criteria (time order, association, and elimination of the impact of an external variable), but there is no requirement to demonstrate a perfect association. In other words, every time changes occur in the independent variable, changes may not occur in the dependent variable because the relationship is based on probabilities or likelihoods. In probabilistic models, such as those used in most inferential research, one often finds exceptions to the rule. *Necessary cause* refers to a condition or event that must occur for another event to take place. For example, to collect a paycheck, one must be employed. The cause must be present for the effect to occur.

When the presence of a condition ordinarily causes the effect to occur, this is known as a *sufficient cause*. The cause usually, but not always, creates the effect. Playing golf in a thunderstorm may not result in being struck by lightning every time (the authors still do not recommend it), but the conditions are sufficient for the lightning strike to occur. In social science research, it is preferred co identify a necessary cause for an event but to do so is often impossible. Instead, one is more likely to identify causes that are sufficient.

Experimental Research Designs

Although it is most often used in the natural sciences, research requiring a true experimental design occasionally may he attempted by social scientists. Though it is more likely for criminal justice and criminological researchers to use quasi-experimental research designs, it is important to understand experimental research designs. Typically, experimental research designs are used in assessing cause-and-effect relationships in which a specific group experiences something and this group is compared to another group that did not experience the something. The classical experiment is considered the gold standard of experimental research designs and includes all three major components of experiments: (1) random assignment, (2) experimental and control groups, and (3) pretesting and posttesting (Campbell & Stanley, 1963; Maxfield & Babbie, 2009). Experimental research designs that are modifications of the classical experiment include the pretest-posttest, posttest-only, and factorial experiment research designs.

In classical experiment research designs, the first step is to determine which subjects will be assigned to the experimental or control groups using random assignment. Random assignment is essentially flipping a coin to determine to which group each subject will he placed. This process should result in experimental and control groups that are roughly equivalent. Subjects in the experimental group are exposed to the experimental stimulus, which is based on the hypothesis's independent variable (Campbell & Stanley, 1963; Maxfield & Babbie 2009). For example, if the purpose of a study is to investigate the impact of an intervention designed to increase the empathy of violent offenders toward crime victims, then the hypothesis would be that exposure to the intervention would increase empathy of violent offenders toward crime victims. After violent offenders who were serving time in prison were selected to participate in the study, they would be randomly assigned to the experimental or control groups.

The subjects in the experimental group participate in the empathy intervention, but he subjects in the control group do not. The inclusion of the control group allows for the elimination of the impact of external variables, which is one of the criteria for determining causality. The structure of the classical experiment research design also addresses the time order element of the causal criteria. The experimental research designs can be used to address the issue of time order because one has the ability to control when the experimental group is exposed to the experimental stimulus. Additionally, one can control how much exposure occurs by determining how often the duration occurs and how long the subject is exposed to the experimental stimulus. Borrowing a term from medicine, this is known as "determining the dosage."

Both the experimental group and the control group complete pretesting and posttesting. The pretest and posttest are typically the same measure designed to assess changes in the dependent variable. Continuing with the example of the empathy intervention, the subjects (violent offenders) in the experimental group would complete the same survey designed to assess the level of empathetic attitudes before (pretest) and after (posttest) the intervention. The control group would also undergo pretesting and posttesting even though these subjects were not exposed to the experimental stimulus (empathy intervention). The inclusion of pretesting and posttesting in the experimental research design allows for assessment of the changes in the level of empathy before and after the intervention within the experimental group and control group as well as comparing the impact of the intervention between the experimental and control groups.

O X O
O   O
t_1 t_2 t_3

FIGURE 6.1.1   Classical Experiment Research Design

In the classical experiment research design, one can see that all elements of the experimental research designs are present, including random assignment, control and experimental groups, and pretesting and posttesting. In **Figure 6.1.1,** O represents observations, and X represents the experimental stimulus. The experimental group is displayed on the first line with O X O, indicating an observation (pretest), experimental stimulus, and then the second observation (posttest). The control group is displayed on the second line with O O, indicating an observation (pretest) and then a second (posttest) but no experimental stimulus.

The third line shows the time order, with t_1 representing the first time period, t_2 representing the second, and t_3 representing the third.

The other experimental research designs—pretest-posttest, posttest-only, and factorial experimental research designs—are variations of the classical experiment with elements either subtracted or added. The pretest-posttest experimental research design **(Figure 6.1.2)** differs from the classical experiment research design in that it does not contain a control group, which also negates the need for random assignment.

FIGURE 6.1.2 Pretest-Posttest Research Design

This experimental design allows for the comparison between pretest (before exposure to the experimental stimulus) and posttest (after exposure) (Campbell & Stanley, 1963). Using the empathy intervention example, the pretest-posttest design would allow for comparisons between before and after the intervention. Therefore, one could not determine if the same changes would have occurred without the intervention since the results of a control group's pretest and posttest are not available to compare to the results of the experimental group. Furthermore, the exclusion of the control group from the pretest-posttest research design means that the presence of external variables cannot be eliminated in the analysis. For example, a victim of a violent crime may have been a guest speaker at the prison between the pretest and posttest, which could impact the results since the effect of this event may have had an impact on empathy in place of or in addition to intervention itself.

The posttest-only experiment research design **(Figure 6.1.3)** differs from the classical experiment research design in that there is no pretest. Subjects are still randomly assigned to the experimental and control groups but only receive the posttest. In the posttest-only research design, comparisons can be made between the experimental and control groups, which allows for the elimination of the impact of external variables. However, the exclusion of the pretest does not allow assessment of the impact of the experimental stimulus, since a baseline observation is not available (Campbell & Stanley, 1963; Maxfield & Babbie, 2009). Researchers may argue for the use of the posttest-only research design if they perceive the pretest as having an impact on the behavior of the subjects and convoluting the results. For example, subjects in the experimental and control group may consciously or subconsciously change their reported Behavior on the posttest due to perceiving the desired results of the study from taking the pretest. However, the value of the pretest in being able to compare the results to the experimental and control group posttest results typically outweighs the concern of the unintended impacts of the pretest.

FIGURE 6.1.3 Posttest-Only Research Design

FIGURE 6.1.4 Factorial Experiment Research Design

Unlike the pretest-posttest and posttest-only experiment research designs, the factorial experiment research design **(Figure 6.1.4)** adds to the classical experiment research design. Rather than having one experimental stimulus, the factorial design has two or more experimental stimuli. The experimental stimuli may differ based on dosage (Campbell & Stanley, 1963; Maxfield & Babbie, 2009). For example, the subjects in the first experimental group (X_1) for the empathy study may receive a single, hourlong exposure to the experimental stimulus (the intervention), and the subjects in the second experimental group (X_2) may receive one two-hour session per week for 11 weeks. The type of experimental stimuli can also differ, such as one being a therapy session and another as simple as watching a video. Even though the factorial experiment research design can contain an unlimited number of experimental stimuli, one should keep in mind what the primary goal of the research is and focus the experimental stimuli on the primary goal.

The primary advantage of the experimental design is its ability to isolate the experimental variation and assess its impact over time. Individual experiments can be limited in scope and require little time, money, and number of subjects. In addition, it is often possible to replicate the results: Because an experiment is a controlled environment, the procedures can be replicated and the results compared. The major disadvantage is artificiality. Processes that occur in a controlled setting may not actually occur in the natural setting. Violent offenders randomly assigned to participate in the empathy intervention may not decide to participate on their own so the usefulness of the results are called into question.

With respect to criminal justice and criminology, this type of research is often expensive and logistically difficult to perform. One of the most difficult issues is obtaining consent when the research involves human test subjects. However, sometimes consent is easier to obtain if the experiment could prove useful to the subjects. For example, assume a new drug has been created that could suppress sexual desires. A group of convicted pedophiles are asked if they will participate in a study in which part of the group will receive the new drug, whereas the other half are given a placebo. After a certain number of weeks, both groups are tested for sexual response to certain stimuli, and the results are compared.

Another major problem in conducting true experimental research is the difficulty in being able to maintain and control the environment in which the experiment is conducted. The environment in which criminal justice and criminology research is conducted is often far from stable and is filled with possible interfering variables. As a result of the control and consent issues, along with costs and other logistical problems, it is rare to see a criminologist conduct true experimental research. These difficulties have not stopped some efforts to conduct this form of research. Some examples found in criminal justice include the Kansas City Preventive Patrol Experiment, the Minneapolis Domestic Violence study, and San Diego's one- versus two-person patrol units.

FROM THE REAL WORLD

For one year starting in 1972, the Kansas City Police Department implemented the Kansas City Preventive Patrol Experiment to determine the impact of police patrols on the occurrence of crime. In the study, three areas were selected, and different levels of routine patrols were implemented. In one area there were no routine patrols, and officers only answered service calls. In a second area, the levels of routine patrols were not changed, and this area acted as the control group.

In a third area, the levels of routine patrols were more than doubled or even tripled. It was hypothesized that the higher levels of routine patrols would decrease the occurrence of crime. However, the results indicated little impact of the routine patrols on the occurrence of crime (Kelling, Pate, Dieckman, & Brown, 1974).

Reality dictates that few experimental research projects are possible in criminal justice and criminology. The limitations, however, can be addressed to some degree with a quasi-experimental design, which retains some, but not all, elements of the experimental research design.

Quasi-Experimental Research Design

Unlike the true experimental design in which the researcher has almost complete control over relevant factors, the quasi-experimental design offers only some control. The quasi-experimental research design allows for the approximation of conditions similar to an experiment. However, this research design does not allow for the random assignment of subjects to experimental and control groups, nor does it include the ability to control or manipulate the experimental stimulus. Random assignment in particular is difficult to implement in criminal justice or criminological research due to ethical and legal concerns.

Although easier to implement than the true experimental design, the quasi-experimental design has its difficulties, making it less appealing to most social scientists. The main difficulty lies in the interpretation of the results, specifically being able to separate the effects of a treatment from the effects caused by the initial inability to make comparisons between the average units in each group. Since random assignment is not performed within quasi-experiments, the groups are not truly equivalent. Quasi-experimental research design is most commonly used in evaluation research to assess new approaches in the criminal justice system and to solve problems with direct applications to the criminal justice system. The empathy intervention was used as an example of an experimental research design. However, the assessment of the empathy intervention would be more likely to be completed using a quasi-experimental research design. Subjects choose whether to participate and then changes in the level of empathy before and after the empathy intervention are compared between subjects who participate and subjects who do not participate. One issue with this example is that the subjects who choose to participate may be different from those who do not participate. Specifically, they may be more likely to display empathy in the first place.

Overall, there are a number of research designs from which to choose. The design chosen depends largely on what the researcher is seeking to discover, explain, or describe. Other considerations when choosing a research design include economics, logistics, and time. Ultimately, the researcher must decide which design allows for the best results.

Quantitative Levels of Measurement

Experimental and quasi-experimental research is typically quantitative. Quantitative data have variables with various levels of measurement, including nominal, ordinal, interval, and ratio.

Based on the previously mentioned definition of quantitative research, *measurement* is viewed as the assignment of numerical values or categorical labels to a phenomenon for the purpose of analysis. Determining what level of measurement to use can often be a confusing part of conducting quantitative research. The four levels of measurement range from low (nominal is the simplest variable) to high (ratio is the most complex variable).

Nominal Level Variables

The simplest level of measurement is the nominal level. At this level, measurement is categorical with no specified order within the categories of the variable. An example of a nominal level variable is month of birthday, with the categories of January through December. The categories are mutually exclusive. In other words, the categories do not overlap. A single item cannot fit into more than one of the variable categories. For example, a variable describing vehicles with the categories two-door, four-door, truck, sedan, minivan, and SUV would have overlap between the categories, such as a two-door truck. Since there is overlap between the categories, they are not mutually exclusive. The way to fix this problem would be to specify separate categories; for example, the single vehicle variable would become two variables, the first being the number of doors and the second being the vehicle type.

Ordinal Level Variables

The next level of measurement is the ordinal level. This level moves beyond being merely categorical by assigning a rank or a placement of order to the categories of a variable. As in the nominal level variables, the categories ordinal level variable are mutually exclusive. Although in using this level of measurement, numbers may be assigned for ranking purposes (e.g., on a scale of 1–10), these numbers are not scores, but are simply viewed as a demonstration of where the respondent believes the item to fall. For example, in looking at the difference between the seriousness of criminal offenses in which murder is labeled as a 9, robbery a 5, and theft a 1, there is a four-unit difference between each type, but one cannot explain what that difference truly represents. Another example is that the types of prisons may be broken down into the categories of minimum, medium, and maximum.

Most often ordinal measures are found in attitudinal surveys, perceptual surveys, quality of life studies, or service studies. For example, individuals could be given a list of occupations that respondents could be asked to rank in order of how stressful they perceive each to be, from most stressful (10) to east stressful (1). Although they would write any number between 1 and 10, the listed order would only tell what the individuals perceive. There is no way to determine how much difference there is in the perceived stressfulness between each occupation. A common type of ordinal level variable is a Likert scale, which consist of five categories. For example, students may be asked to respond to the statement "Research methods will play a vital role in my career in the field of criminal justice" by choosing one of five provided responses, including "strongly disagree," "disagree," "neutral," "agree," and "strongly agree."

Interval Level Variables

The third highest level of measure is interval, which has scores instead of categories. With scores, there is an expected equality in the distance between choices on the continuum. The use of scores rather than categories allows the use of more sophisticated techniques during data analysis. There is no absolute zero or starting point for interval data. Because numbers assigned have an arbitrary beginning, the usefulness of the information may be limited. For example, the difference between an IQ of 135 and 150 is the same 15-unit difference as between 150 and 165. However, there is no distinction as to what the difference means. One can comment on the differences but cannot explain what that difference means. To be able to do so requires ratio level data. For practical purposes, interval level variables typically are treated as ratio level variables for the purpose of analysis.

Ratio Level Variables

The highest level of measurement is ratio. This level is primarily characterized by an absolute beginning point of zero, and the differences between scores are equal and can be explained. Two of the more common ratio level variables are age and income. For an age variable, the respondent would provide their exact age, typically in years. For an income variable, the respondent would provide their exact income, usually for a single year. An example of the absolute zero relevance for the ratio-level variable would be a subject that provides a 0 as a response to an income question because they were unemployed during the time period. With respect to research, ratio measures can be collapsed into ordinal measures, such as the individual scores of a ratio level income variable being collapsed into an ordinal level variable with the following categories: under $10,000, $10,000–$24,999, $25,000–$49,999, over $50,000.

Many people, including students, find it frustrating to accurately determine a variable's level of measurement. Sometimes, this situation is due to confusion on the part of the individual, but at other times the variable information is poorly worded. Asking the following question can help determine a variable's level of measurement. First, are the variable's possible outcome scores (numeric) or categories (named units or ranges of values)? If the variable's possible outcomes are scores, then the variable is ratio. If the variable's possible outcomes are categories, then the next question is: do the categories have an order? One way to check for order is to move a middle category to the top or bottom. If the categories look out of order or off, then the categories do have an order. If the categories have an order, then the variable is ordinal. If the categories do not have an order, then the variable is nominal. These questions should help guide the determination of a variable's level of measurement.

The level that is chosen has an important impact on how the data are collected and analyzed. Researchers can move down from a higher level of data to a lower level during data analysis, but they cannot move up to a higher level from a lower level.

Summary

This chapter provides an introduction to research design. Research design is based on empiricism with the goal of establishing causality (or more likely, association). The basis for research design is experimental research, including classical, pretest-posttest, posttest-only, and factorial experiment research designs. Even though experiments are difficult to implement in criminal justice and criminological research, understanding the basics are important since it provides the basis of quasi-experiments as well as the cross-sectional and longitudinal research designs (discussed in the next chapter). Experimental research is largely quantitative; thus, identifying the variable level of measurement, including nominal, ordinal, interval, and ratio, is important.

References

Adler. E. S., & Clark, R. (2007). *How it's done: An invitation to social research* (3rd ed.). Belmont, CA: Wadsworth.

Berg. B. (2008). *Qualitative research methods for the social sciences* (7th ed.). Columbus, OH: Allyn & Bacon.

Bergman, M. M. (2009). *Mixed methods research*. Thousand Oaks, CA: Sage.

Campbell, D. T., & Stanley, J. C. (1963). *Experimental and quasi-experimental designs for research*. Boston, MA: Houghton Mifflin.

Dunn, D. S. (2009). *Research methods for social psychology*. Sussex, England: Wiley.

Gavin, H. (2008). *Understanding research methods and statistics in psychology*. Thousand Oaks, CA: Sage.

Jeffery, C. R. (1990). *Criminology: An inter disciplinary approach*. Englewood Cliffs, MA: Prentice Hall.

Kelling, G. L., Pate, T., Dieckman, D., & Brown, C. E. (1974). *The Kansas City preventive patrol experiment: A technical report*. Washington, DC: Police Foundation.

Maxfield, M. G., & Babbie, E. R. (2009). *Basics of research methods for criminal justice and criminology* (2nd ed.). Belmont, CA: Wadsworth.

Research Designs

Mark L. Dantzker, Ronald D. Hunter, and Susan T. Quinn

What You Should Know!

A conscious effort is required to conduct research and to use the most appropriate design. A multitude of methods are available to conduct research, and the method chosen by any researcher may be reflective of a style he or she is most comfortable with, believes will provide the best results, or selects based on the research question. This chapter examines the various designs from which researchers can choose. After completing this chapter, the reader should be able to:

1. Discuss the issues to consider in selecting a research design.
2. Describe how a historical research design is conducted.
3. Explain how a descriptive research design is conducted.
4. Compare and contrast cross-sectional and longitudinal research designs.
5. Discuss the various types of longitudinal research design, including trend, cohort, and panel.
6. Describe how a case study research design is conducted.
7. Describe correlational and causal–comparative studies.
8. Discuss evaluation research.

Research Designs

To complete any type of research successfully, it is important to establish a feasible plan or blueprint, known as a *research design*. This plan primarily responds to the common five Ws (who, what, where, when, and why) and H (how) of investigation. Because criminal justice and criminological researchers have a choice of research designs, it is important to be able to match the design properly to the desired outcomes. In selecting a research design, a number of issues should be considered. Creating an outline is recommended to ensure that all relevant issues have been considered. **Box 6.2.1** is an example of such an outline.

BOX 6.2.1 ISSUES TO CONSIDER IN SELECTING A RESEARCH DESIGN

Purpose of research
    Identify the purpose of the research project, which should be clearly indicative of what will be studied.
Prior research
    Review similar or relevant research. This review promotes knowledge of the literature.
Theoretical orientation
    Describe the theoretical framework on which the research is based.
Concept definition
    List the various concepts that have been developed and clarify their meanings.
Research hypotheses
    Develop the various hypotheses that will be evaluated in the research.
Unit of analysis
    Describe the particular objects, individuals, or entities that are being studied as elements of the population.
Data collection techniques
    Determine how the data are to be collected, who will collect it, who will be studied, and how will it be done?
Sampling procedures
    Specify sample type, sample size, and procedures to be used.
Instruments used
    Describe the nature of the measurement instrument or data collection device to be used.
Analytic techniques
    Determine how the data will be processed and examined. What specific statistical procedures will be used?
Time frame
    Pinpoint the period of time covered by the study. This will include the time period examined by research questions and the amount of time spent in preparation, data collection, data analysis, and presentation.
Ethical issues
    Address any concerns as to the potential harm that might occur to participants. Also deal with any potential biases or conflicts of interest that could affect the study.

FROM THE REAL WORLD

The Bureau of Justice Statistics produced the report *Homicide Trends in the United States, 1980–2008*. This report describes homicide patterns and trends based on the Federal Bureau of Investigation's Supplementary Homicide Report. Information is provided on victim and offender demographic characteristics (age, race, gender), victim/offender relationships (intimate, family, infants, elders), circumstances (felony, sex related, drug related, gang related, argument, workplace), weapon involvement (gun, arson, poison), and homicides with multiple victims and/or offenders.

Descriptive Research Design

A descriptive research design focuses on the description of facts and characteristics of a given population, issue, policy, or any given area of interest in a systematic and accurate manner. The descriptive research design focuses on answering the "what" question in research design, but it cannot provide an answer to the question of "why" a phenomenon is occurring. The information obtained in descriptive studies can provide insights not recognized in prior research and provide the basis for additional studies focused on explanation. For example, studies reporting police patrol trends and crime rates may provide the basis for a study to examine the impact of police patrol patterns on crime rates.

Historical Research Design

The historical design is the study of actions, events, and phenomena that have already occurred (Berg, 2008; Creswell, 2008; Givens, 2008). This design allows the researcher to systematically and objectively reconstruct the past through the collection, evaluation, verification, and synthesis of existing documenting information to test a hypothesis. It can assist in determining why or how an event occurred and whether such an event could happen again. A historical research design is also a means by which researchers may compare and contrast events or phenomenon that have occurred.

There are many sources of existing information, including text-based information, visual and auditory information, and secondary data. Text-based existing information may include news reports, public records, or even private diaries. Often one thinks of text-based information as the basis of historical research designs; however, pictures or maps as well as audio and visual recordings can provide useful information. A researcher may use crime rate maps to examine the impact of the opening or closing of businesses on crime over time. Or, photographs and audiovisual clips could be used to examine the impact of propaganda on the treatment of disadvantaged groups during times of conflict.

Another source of existing information is secondary data, which is the data that has already been collected for another purpose. Secondary data is used extensively in criminal justice and criminological research. Researchers may collect data for their own studies and then make that data available through repositories, such as the Inter-university Consortium for Political and Social Research (ICPSR). Government agencies also collect a considerable amount of information for management and evaluation purposes. Recidivism, the recurrence of criminal behavior, is an important issue in criminal justice research and can be measured using records from correctional and court agencies.

One of the most debated topics in criminal justice and criminology is the deterrent effect of capital punishment. A common hypothesis for capital punishment supporters is that the death penalty serves as a better deterrent against committing homicides than life imprisonment. To study this hypothesis a historical research design is appropriate and, for example, could include a study of homicide rates in the United States between 1950 and 1997. Although just studying the numbers might provide an interesting conclusion, the true historical research design study requires inclusion of possible influencing factors, such as U.S. Supreme Court decisions, sentencing patterns, social episodes (e.g., a war), and population growth. A successful historical study considers all relevant information to provide proper conclusions.

The historical design is an economically efficient means for conducting research. Considering the vast array of records available related to criminal justice, there is no shortage of possible research topics. A shortcoming of this design is the difficulty of expanding beyond what is documented, therefore limiting the scope of the research. Researchers are limited to the information in the files and seldom have means to follow up or get clarification of the available information. In addition, there is the old computer maxim of "garbage in garbage out." The research is only as good as the data that is contained in the records. If there is inaccurate information or missing data in the original source material, the research suffers.

FROM THE REAL WORLD

To determine the impact on recidivism of matching youth with services consistent with the clinical recommendations that they had received, Vieira, Skilling, and Peterson-Badali (2009) conducted a study in which data were collected and compiled from a variety of secondary data sources. These sources included clinical charts; participants' court reports; each youth's scores on a risk and need measure (Youth Level of Service/Case Management Inventory); probation notes; parent and mental health service reports; and school records, probation files, and court records. The researchers found that having only a few of the recommended services was associated with an increase in the number of new convictions and a decrease in the amount of time until recidivating.

Both descriptive and historical research designs can be cost-effective and logistically easier to conduct than other designs. However, they present researchers with limitations as to what variables can be examined and the extent of the information available. They may also be more 'time sensitive', which means that data may only be available for a certain time frame and the information obtained may be limited in its usefulness.

Cross-Sectional Research Design

The primary concept of the cross-sectional research design is that it allows for the study of a phenomenon at one point in time. These studies are best suited for exploratory or descriptive research but can be used in explanatory research by attempting to study the association between variables. Cross-sectional studies provide a snapshot of the phenomenon and do so by examining the relationship between variables at one point in time. For example, Violanti et al. (2009) examined whether suicide ideation, planning suicide, and suicide attempts were more likely to occur among police officers because of their exposure to suicides. For their study they did a cross-sectional study involving 115 randomly selected police officers from a mid-sized urban police department of 930 officers. One drawback to the cross-sectional study design is that it is difficult (or even impossible) to determine time order of the independent and dependent variables, which is an issue addressed in longitudinal research design.

Longitudinal (or Time Series) Research Design

Perhaps a police agency is interested in following the activities of members from a rookie police class from graduation through their first 5 years of service. They may be primarily interested in the turnover rate, promotions, occurrence of injuries, accommodations and complaints, and levels of job satisfaction. The best research design for this type of study is longitudinal, or time series. This type of research design allows for the investigation of specifically identified patterns and events, growth, or change by collecting data at two or more distinctive time periods. It also allows for determining the time order of the independent and dependent variable, which the cross-sectional research design struggles to accomplish, and is therefore particularly suited for explanatory research as well as exploratory and descriptive research. This type of research can be costly and time-consuming; thus cross-sectional research design is used more often. Examples of longitudinal research designs include trend studies, cohort studies, and panel studies.

FROM THE REAL WORLD

In a study of binge drinking among college students, Wechsler et al. (1994) surveyed a total of 17,592 students at 140 colleges in the United States regarding binge drinking and the consequences of the reported drinking behavior at one point in time, such as being hungover, doing something that you regretted, missing classes, forgetting what happened, getting behind in school work, arguing with friends, engaging in unplanned sexual activity, not using protection during sex, getting injured, damaging property, getting into legal trouble, and needing medical treatment for an alcohol overdose. Binge drinking was defined as having four or more drinks in a row for women and five or more drinks in a row for men. According to the study, almost half of the students (44 percent) reported at least one instance of binge drinking within the last two weeks.

Trend Research Design

Trend research design examines changes in a general population over time. For example, data is collected for the census every 10 years from all individuals residing in the United States. One might compare results from several census studies to determine what demographic changes have occurred in that population, such as employment or income changes. Another example is the General Social Survey, which annually surveys a sample representative of the adult population in the United States. Surveys might indicate that opinions on the death penalty fluctuate over time depending on social conditions not related to crime or changes in the incidences of murder or the occasional occurrences of sensational murders.

Cohort Research Design

Cohort research design involves studies that focus on the changes occurring in specific sub-populations over time, such as age groupings. This research design is highly flexible and could be used to examine social, political, or economic changes or have a more specific focus. For example, a cohort research design may be used to examine the one-year recidivism rates of inmates released from a state facility during 2010.

In a famous criminological study, Wolfgang, Figlio, and Sellin (1972) examined delinquency among a cohort of juveniles, specifically males born in 1945, who were living in Philadelphia, Pennsylvania, on their 10th birthday. The researchers were particularly interested in the age that delinquent behavior began as well as when delinquent behavior stopped for this cohort. The findings from this study significantly impacted future research and practice in juvenile justice. In addition to primary data, many cohort studies use secondary data, making it cost effective.

Panel Research Design

Panel research design studies the same set of people at two or more distinct points in time. Unlike the cohort studies, these subjects may not have a single unifying characteristic, such as an age cohort. By using the same individuals, couples, groups, and so forth, researchers are able to more precisely examine the extent of changes and the events that influenced them. However, due to attrition because of the effects of deaths, movements from the area, refusal to continue as subjects, and other factors that cause the sample to lose members, these studies are logistically difficult to continue over an extended period of time. For example, the National Crime Victimization Survey interviews a member of a selected household every six months.

FROM THE REAL WORLD

Hunter and Wood (1994) were interested in the relationship between severity of sanction and unarmed assaults on police officers. They obtained assault data on officers for all 50 states. They compared these data with the sanctions applied for unarmed assaults on police officers within each respective state during 1991. They then compared the rates in states that had felony sanctions for weaponless assault on police officers to their neighboring states from 1977 through 1991. This strategy resulted in the longitudinal analysis of four groups of states. Analysis of results in these groupings did not reveal support for the hypothesis that more sanctions would decrease the incidence of weaponless assaults on police officers.

Case Study Research Design

The case study research design allows for the intensive study of a given issue, policy, or community in its social context at one point in time even though that period may span months or even years (Adler & Clark, 2007). It also may be used to study specific individuals or groups. The case study research design includes close scrutiny of the background, current status, and relationships or interactions of the topic under study. Case study research design often focuses on a specific phenomenon, such as community policing.

FROM THE REAL WORLD

The National Longitudinal Survey of Youth 1997 (NLSY97) is a panel study of a nationally representative sample of youth who were 12 to 16 years old as of December 31, 1996. The first NLSY97 survey of the youth and the youth's parent took place in 1997, and the panel members continue to be surveyed on an annual basis, with the most recent survey occurring in 2013. The study is focused on entry into the workplace but contains a considerable number of criminal justice variables.

Case studies may be longitudinal in that they sometimes observe a case or cases over a certain length of time. These observations are closely linked with the observing of potential independent variables that may be associated with changes in the dependent variables. There are three basic features to this design (Dunn, 2009; Hagan, 2006; Maxfield & Babbie, 2009): (1) qualitative or quantitative descriptions of a variable over the extended period of time, (2) a context wherein the researcher can observe changes in the variables, and (3) the potential for developing measurement instruments and the testing of their reliability over time.

Case study research designs are not limited as to what can be studied and are particularly useful in exploratory research. However, they can be costly and time prohibitive and may not provide an explanation for the results. If one wants to know why something is or has occurred and possible correlating factors, then a correlational design may be more appropriate.

Determining Correlations and Causations

Research often has the goal of determining that there is a causal relationship between two variables (causal-comparative research) or at the very least an association (correlational research). The selected research design will determine the ability to determine causation or correlation. Most studies are trying to determine correlation between two variables.

FROM THE REAL WORLD

Chappell's (2009) abstract states the following:

Community policing is the operating philosophy of the majority of American police departments in the new millennium. Though most departments claim to engage in community policing, research has shown that implementation of the strategy is uneven. One way to investigate the implementation of community policing is to study patrol officer attitudes toward community policing because prior research has shown that attitudes are related to behavior. The present study used qualitative data in a case study research design to explore the extent to which patrol officers have endorsed and implemented community policing in one medium-sized agency in Florida. Furthermore, the research sought to gain insight into the organizational barriers that prevented officers from adopting community policing in their daily work. Results indicated that although most officers agreed with the philosophy of community policing, significant barriers, such as lack of resources, prevented its full implementation in this agency. Implications of the findings and directions for future research are discussed. (p. 5)

Correlational Research

A popular research design is one that allows researchers to investigate how one factor may affect or influence another factor, or how the one factor correlates with another—the correlational design. In particular, this type of design focuses on how variations of one variable correspond with variations of other variables. An example is a study of the level of education of police officers and promotion rates, arrest rates, or job satisfaction. The goal of this research design is to obtain correlational coefficients that are statistically significant (discussed in a later chapter). For example, a cross-sectional study examining the association between drug use and academic performance is a correlational research design, but its design does not allow for the determination of a causal relationship.

Causal—Comparative Research

Why do men rape? Why do teenagers turn to gangs? Why do individuals become serial killers? To answer these types of questions, a causal-comparative (or ex post facto) design is useful. This design allows the researcher to examine relationships from a cause-and-effect perspective, which is done through the observation of an existing outcome or consequence and searching back through the data for plausible causal factors. The criteria to determine causality is often not met outside of the experimental research designs. Of the previously discussed causal criteria, being able to account for the impact of an external variable is particularly problematic. Thus, causal—comparative research is less common than correlational research.

FROM THE REAL WORLD

Adding to the literature on whether gang membership is uniquely related to victimization experiences for females compared to males, Gover, Jennings, and Tewksbury (2009) produced a correlational study in which they examined the relationship between gender, gang membership, and three types of victimization. They used data from the 1999 South Carolina Youth Risk Behavior Survey, an ongoing state and national survey conducted by state contracts for the Centers for Disease Control and Prevention, Division on Adolescent and School Health. Their results indicate gang membership is significantly related to the risk of victimization regardless of gender.

FROM THE REAL WORLD

Stevens's (1999) study of the relationship between drug addiction and criminal activity among incarcerated women who were in a prison drug rehabilitation program could be viewed as a causal-comparative design. This study addressed the belief that drug addiction gave rise to criminality among females. Yet the results of the data did not support this belief. One implication of this finding was that drug addiction in itself is not necessarily a causal factor for producing crimes of violence, especially among females.

Evaluation Research

To this point, almost all the research designs discussed are used after an event, situation, or other unexplained phenomenon occurs and one wants to understand it better. These designs are quite useful to academic researchers as well as practitioners. A practitioner may want to know how something will work or what might occur when something not previously done is attempted. Evaluation research is particularly important if managers or administrators want to make sweeping policy implications. To gain support for these types of changes, the managers or administrators would have to demonstrate that the changes would have the desired impact.

Evaluation research can assist in the development of new skills or approaches. It also aids in the solving of problems with direct implications for the "real world." This type of research typically has a quasi-experimental research design. For example, a police agency is debating whether to add a nonlethal weapon, a stun gun, to what is available to its officers. To see how stun guns might be used and what outcomes might result from their use, an evaluation research design would use a select group of officers who are issued stun guns for a set period of time. Each time the weapon is used, a report explaining the reason and results must be filed. At the end of the data collection period, the reports are analyzed; depending on the results, stun guns would be issued to all officers or certain officers, or the recommendation might be not to issue these weapons at all.

Evaluation research is important for the criminal justice practitioner—researcher because it assesses the merits of programs or policies being used (or under consideration for use) in the field. Whereas more basic research seeks to develop theoretical insights and much applied research seeks to determine if a theory can actually be applied in the field, evaluation research allows practitioners to determine the costs and effectiveness of the program or project that is being or has been implemented. For this reason, evaluation research that studies existing programs is frequently referred to as *program evaluation*.

FROM THE REAL WORLD

To investigate the effectiveness of Thinking for a Change, a widely used cognitive behavioral curriculum for offenders, Lowenkamp, Hubbard, Makarios, and Latessa. (2009) evaluated the impact of the program using a group of felony offenders placed on probation. The experimental group consisted of probationers who were referred directly to the program from court, and the comparison group included probationers who were not referred to the program. The results of the study found that the offenders who participated in the program had a significantly lower recidivism rate than similar offenders who had not been in the program.

Summary

Selecting a topic and creating the research question are just the beginning of conducting research. One of the most important steps is choosing an appropriate research design. Although one of the most popular designs is survey research, which is also a means of collecting data in the other designs, other possible methods include:

Descriptive—describing the facts and characteristics of a given population, issue, policy, or any given area of interest in a systematic and accurate manner.

Historical—studying actions, events, and phenomena that have already occurred to systematically and objectively reconstruct the past to test a hypothesis.

Cross-sectional—studying the issue of phenomenon at one point in time.

Longitudinal—investigating patterns and sequences of growth or change as a function of time, including trend, cohort, and panel studies.

Case study—studying intensively the background, current status, and environmental interactions of a given social unit, such as individual, group, institution, or community.

The researcher must clearly understand what compromises exist in the internal and external validity of his or her design and proceed within these limitations. The chosen design should best meet the needs of the research goals.

References

Adler. E. S., & Clark, R. (2007). *How it's done: An invitation to social research* (3rd ed.). Belmont, CA: Wadsworth.

Berg, B. (2008). *Qualitative research methods for the social sciences* (7th ed.). Columbus, OH: Allyn & Bacon.

Chappell, A. T. (2009). The philosophical versus actual adoption of community policing: A case study. *Criminal Justice Review, 34*(1), 5–28.

Creswell, J. W. (2008). *Research design: Qualitative, quantitative, and mixed methods approaches* (3rd ed.). Thousand Oaks, CA: Sage.

Dunn, D. S. (2009). *Research methods for social psychology.* Sussex, England: Wiley.

Given, L. M. (2008). *The SAGE encyclopedia of qualitative research methods.* Thousand Oaks, CA: Sage.

Gover, A. R., Jennings, W. G., & Tewksbury, R. (2009). Adolescent male and female gang members' experiences with violent victimization, dating violence, and sexual assault. *American Journal of Criminal Justice, 34*(1/2), 103–118.

Hagan, F. E. (2006). *Essentials of research methods in criminal justice and criminology* (2nd ed.). Columbus, OH: Allyn & Bacon.

Hunter, R. D., & Wood, R. L. (1994). Impact of felony sanctions: An analysis of weaponless assaults upon American police. *American Journal of Police, 12*(1), 65–89.

Lowenkamp, C.T., Hubbard, D., Makarios, M. D., & Latessa, E. J. (2009). A quasi-experimental evaluation of thinking for a change: A "real-world" application. *Criminal Justice and Behavior, 36*(2), 137–149.

Maxfield, M. G., & Babbie, E. R. (2009). *Basics of research methods for criminal justice and criminology* (2nd ed.). Belmont, CA: Wadsworth.

Stevens, D. J. (1999). Women offenders, drug addiction, and crime. In M. L. Dantzker (Ed.), *Readings for research methods in criminology and criminal justice* (pp. 61–74). Woburn, MA: Butterworth-Heinemann.

Vicira, T. A., Skilling. T A., & Peterson-Badali, M. (2009). Matching court-ordered services with treatment needs: Predicting treatment success with young offenders. *Criminal Justice and Behavior, 36*(4), 385–401.

Violanti, J. M., Fekedulegn, D., Charles, L. E., Andrew, M. E., Hartley, T. A., Mnatsakanova, A., & Burchfiel, C. M. (2009). Suicide in police work: Exploring potential contributing influences. *American Journal of Criminal Justice, 34*(1/2), 41–46.

Wechsler, H., Davenport, A., Dowdall, G., Moeykens, B., & Castillo, S. (1994). Health and behavioral consequences of binge drinking in college: A national survey of students at 140 campuses. *Journal of the American Medical Association, 272*(21): 1672–1677.

Wolfgang, M. E., Figlio, R. M., & Sellin, T. (1972). *Delinquency in a birth cohort.* Chicago, IL: University of Chicago Press.

Doing the Research

Measuring a Single Variable

Jake Harwood

Cassandra works for the *Daily Centurion*, the campus newspaper at Middle State University. Her editor has asked her to "find out how much students are reading the student newspaper." The editor is asking for *information* and wants an answer (as opposed to a guess or an opinion). In this case, the answer will involve numbers—an answer in hours per week or something similar would help Cassandra answer the question. Where will she start?

Measurement: Turning Social Behavior Into Numbers

Cassandra needs to **measure** something. Let's call it *Centurion* reading. And she is assuming that *Centurion* reading *varies*—some students read the paper a lot and some don't ever read it. It would be weird if everyone on campus read the newspaper exactly the same amount, right? Anything that varies is called a **variable.** How should Cassandra measure the variable *Centurion* reading? Before proceeding, think about how *you* would go about measuring this variable. In the space below, write a brief description of how you would measure it.

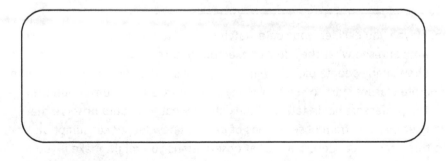

USING READER RESPONSE BOXES

There are reader response boxes throughout this book. Taking a couple of minutes to respond in these areas will be valuable for helping you engage with the content and in subsequent review for exams. Go ahead—scribble away!

There are a few different approaches to this sort of measurement problem. In your earlier response, you probably described something like one of the following:

a) **Self-report:** Maybe you decided that you could ask people how much they read the newspaper. Whether or not you went this route, think now in a little more detail about how you might do that. And yes—just asking people "How much do you read the newspaper?" is an option here, but think about the vague responses you might get if you just asked that. ("A lot!" "I dunno." "Once a week or so." "Whenever I get around to it.") Think about how to ask the question in a way that you'll get answers that are meaningful.

Write a question or questions here and think about the answer options people might have. Are people allowed to respond in any way they want, or will you give them a limited set of options?

b) **Observation:** Maybe you decided you could watch people in a location where newspapers are available and see what they do. For example, you could observe a newspaper stand and see how many people pick the paper up (versus don't), or you could observe classrooms before classes start to see how many students are flipping through the paper before the professors begin talking. Think about what *you* could observe that would let you get *numbers* from observations of people's newspaper consumption. Write two to three sentences describing what observations you might make if you were trying to measure newspaper reading by observation.

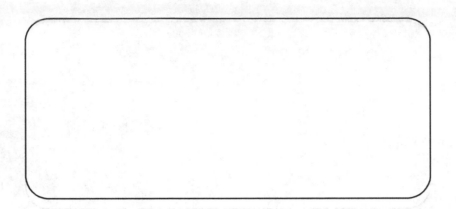

c) **Existing data ("archives")**: Sometimes you get lucky and data already exist that measure what you are interested in. In the newspaper-reading example, for instance, perhaps at the end of each day, a university truck drives around campus picking up all the unread papers from the distribution stands and sends them to a recycling agency. If the university or the recycler keeps track of the volume of papers, then you could get a decent idea of how many people are taking a paper with a simple subtraction calculation:

[total number of papers printed] − [total sent to recyclers] = total "read"

How might *you* measure readership using information that already exists? [Hint: Think about new technology here—readership includes online reading, so are there data that exist there That might help you?]

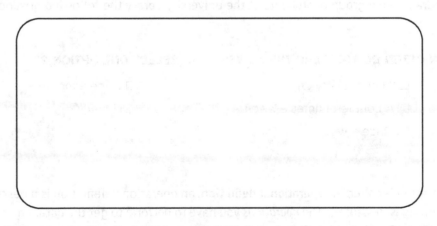

Before continuing, look back at your initial strategy for measuring *Centurion* reading. Did it use self-report, observation, or existing data? After having thought about those three types of data collection, which one would you go with now?

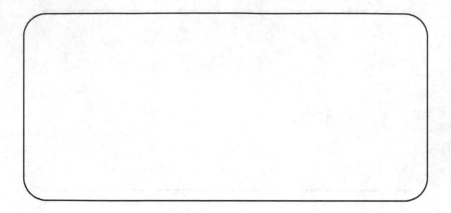

Cassandra's First Measurement Plan

Cassandra went through the same process you did in terms of brainstorming some different ways to answer this question. She realized that to do good observations would take a lot of time—she didn't have enough time in her schedule, and her research project (like many such projects!) has a very limited budget. Similarly, it was a nice idea to look at how many papers get recycled, but it turns out that on her campus, nobody keeps track of that, so she couldn't use such information. She also thought about using website views (that was my earlier hint about technology), but her information technology department couldn't help her get that information. Sigh. So, Cassandra decided to go with self-report measurement.

Cassandra asked a group of students at the university library the following question:

HOW OFTEN DO YOU READ THE NEWSPAPER (SELECT ONE OPTION)?

☐ Almost every day   ☐ Once a month

☐ A couple of times a week   ☐ Never

☐ Once a week

This question is called an **operational definition**: an operational definition is a description of *how* something is measured—the *operations* you have to perform to get the data. An operational definition for taking someone's temperature might be something like "Take a thermometer, stick it in the person's ear, read off the number."

In the boxes that follow, describe three pros and three cons of Cassandra's operational definition and her broader research strategy. Think carefully about the way her question is worded, the response options she provides, and the people whom she is asking the question.

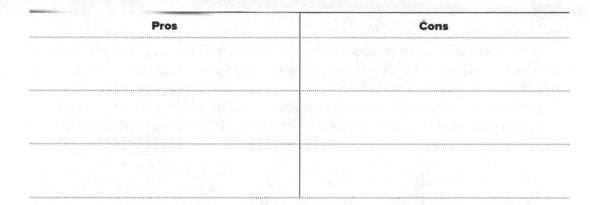

Pros	Cons

Hopefully, you identified some of the following points:

Question wording: Doing social science research can make you obsessive about wording. When writing questions like the one Cassandra wrote, you should think about *every word* in the question. Notice, for instance, that her question asks how <u>often</u> people read the newspaper, not how <u>much</u> they read it. So, someone who just glances at the front page headline each day might technically count as having "read" the newspaper every day; while someone who reads it in depth once a week would score lower. Think about the word <u>read</u> in her question. For one student, glancing at the headline might count as "reading," while for another student it might not; Cassandra should think about how her respondents may interpret the wording of her question. Perhaps most critically, Cassandra's question asks about <u>the newspaper</u>—a term that may imply *any* newspaper. But actually, she is only interested in the *Daily Centurion*. A critical error that researchers sometimes make is to imagine that their respondents are psychic!

> **Conceptual definitions.** If you don't know precisely what you mean by "*Centurion* reading," your measurement will not be clear. Before thinking about how to measure *Centurion* reading, Cassandra should have carefully defined what she meant by the term. For example:
>
> > *Centurion* reading is the number of minutes per day that a student spends reading or looking at pictures in the *Centurion* newspaper.
>
> This is called a **conceptual definition**—a verbal definition of what your variable *is*. A conceptual definition is a little like a dictionary definition. This definition should guide your measurement—if the conceptual definition says minutes per day, then you must measure reading in minutes per day. In other words, *your conceptual and operational definitions must match*—they must be consistent with one another.

Response options: In much social science measurement, respondents must select from a series of choices. The choices offered determine the data that you get, and sometimes the choices you offer can cause problems. In Cassandra's example, for instance, people who read the newspaper four times a week are stuck "between" two options (do they check "<u>almost every day</u>" or "<u>a couple of times a week</u>"?). That's not good—these people may just skip the question, or answer haphazardly, or just get pissed that they are not "represented" in the answer options.

The "never" option here also may be problematic: How many students on a university campus will literally *never* have read the campus newspaper? It isn't good to include options that apply to no one, so almost never or very rarely would probably be a better option here. Most importantly, if Cassandra really wants to know about *Centurion* reading in *minutes per day* (look back at the conceptual definition), she needs to ask about *that!* When writing this sort of question, you must think carefully about the response options you provide. We will explore how to write this kind of question much more later in the book.

FEMALE OR MALE (CHECK ONLY ONE OPTION)!?

Even when the response options for a particular question seem "obvious," they may need careful consideration. A few years ago, "male" and "female" seemed like the only and obvious options to a question asking people their gender (or "sex"). In recent years, we have become more aware of complexities in gender identity and the need to allow people more options than just male/female. The Human Rights Campaign (HRC) suggests wording like the following for asking about gender (and it is always worth checking with resources like the HRC for this sort of wording because opinions on what is appropriate change over time). This suggestion is for a workplace survey:

Our company does not discriminate on the basis of gender identity or expression. In order to track the effectiveness of our recruiting efforts and to ensure that we consider the needs of all our employees, please consider the following optional question. What is your gender?

☐ Female
☐ Male
☐ Nonbinary/third gender
☐ Prefer to self-describe _____
☐ Prefer not to say

Source: Human Rights Campaign

The people: Remember that Cassandra's editor asked her how much students are reading the newspaper. Presumably, the editor meant *students in general* or *average students*. Are students at the library "average" students? Probably not. Next, write *three* ways that students in the library may differ from students in general.

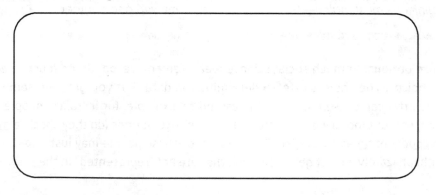

You probably guessed that students at the library might be more studious than students not at the library. Studious students might also be more serious and more likely to read the newspaper, so that difference really matters for the question the editor is asking. If Cassandra only asks students at the library, she might get an estimate of students' newspaper reading that is higher than it really is. Her estimate would be **biased**.

Students in the library might also be unusual in other ways. They might be older students (students who are parents might use the library as a refuge from their kids), or lower income students (if you can't afford broadband at home, the university library is a good place to do research), or history students (if the library has rare old books, perhaps you need to be in the library to study them—biology students are more likely to be in the lab). So the students in the library might not be the best way to go.

SUBJECTS/RESPONDENTS/PARTICIPANTS

The people in a study are variously called **respondents, subjects,** or **participants**. Those terms all mean the same thing. The group of *all* the respondents is called the **sample**, and the process of creating a sample (selecting the respondents) is called **sampling**. A sample that reflects a larger group of people is called a **representative sample.** The larger group of people is called a **population**. Cassandra's sample of students from the library is a **nonrepresentative** sample—it doesn't represent all students for the reasons described.

Cassandra's Final Plan

Cassandra's editor wants to know how much an average student reads the newspaper. Cassandra has now carefully defined what she (and the editor) mean by "reading the newspaper" (i.e., in the conceptual definition from earlier, it is <u>minutes per day</u> of reading or looking at the newspaper). Adopting this definition, Cassandra's measurement must be in minutes per day—her **operational definition** must match her **conceptual definition**. We also know that she wants to measure this variable with a group of students who are similar to the entire student body (not a group of particularly studious students, or students from only one major, etc.). She needs a **representative sample.**

To get a representative sample, Cassandra asks the campus registrar for a **random sample** of 50 student cell phone numbers. Random? That doesn't sound very scientific! Random actually has a very specific scientific meaning in this context. It means that every student on campus has an **equal chance** of being in Cassandra's sample of 50. This assures Cassandra that there can't be any **bias** toward more (or less) studious students, or one major over another, or any other characteristic. For communication researchers, random does *not* mean haphazard, hit or miss, or slipshod. To be truly random actually requires quite a bit of care—something we will return to later in the book.

Sampling error and bias. Samples can go wrong (fail to represent a population perfectly) because of two things: **bias** and **error**. A **biased** sample will *always* tend to feature a certain type of person. If you want a sample representing the entire U.S. population, you shouldn't sample outside an elementary school (you'll get ridiculous numbers of soccer moms and dads) or a movie theater (you'll get too many dating couples). On the other hand, *all* samples have **error**—error just means that the sample doesn't *perfectly* represent the population. Just due to chance factors, Cassandra's random sample of 50 cell phone numbers might turn out to contain a larger proportion of history majors than in the entire student population, or a smaller proportion. But it won't be **biased**—if you took a whole bunch of samples, on average, they'd have just the right number of history majors.

To get her data, Cassandra texts each student on the list and asks them to answer the following question:

In minutes, how much time did you spend yesterday reading the *Daily Centurion*?

_____ *minute(s) (please respond with a whole number; if you did not read the newspaper at all, respond with zero)*

Why do you think Cassandra asked specifically about <u>yesterday</u>? What are two pros and two cons of that strategy?

Pros	Cons

Asking about a very recent time period is a common strategy used by researchers. By asking about <u>yesterday</u>, Cassandra ensures that students are responding about a time period that they can fairly accurately recall. Our ability to remember what happened yesterday is much better than our ability to remember what happened 3 weeks ago. This strategy will mean Cassandra gets more accurate (valid) data.

The downside, of course, is that <u>yesterday</u> might not have been a normal day for some respondents. If it was a weekend day, or a day when they didn't have class, some respondents would report zero, even though on other days they read the newspaper a lot. Cassandra should send out the texts on a variety of days so as to capture students' reading across the entire week, not just on one day. It's OK if she captures a few students on unusual days—unusual days happen, so it's OK to measure them. Most students Cassandra measures will be captured on typical days because ... most days are typical (indeed, that's pretty much the definition of typical!).

Cassandra's strategy also relies on students responding accurately and indeed remembering accurately. The students' responses will not be perfect, obviously—they might misremember whether they spent 5 or 10 minutes with the newspaper. But they are unlikely to think they spent 2 hours with the newspaper when in fact they didn't look at it. This is what I mean by a "good enough" solution: Cassandra's data will reflect students' broad patterns of newspaper reading, even if they are not accurate to the nearest millisecond.

Assuming Cassandra's respondents answer her text, she will end up with 50 students' estimates of their previous day *Centurion* reading. Data! In the next chapter, you will see some things that Cassandra can do with these data.

> **Research ethics.** It is important to consider whether your research might have harmful effects before you do it. Of course, a researcher might not be the best judge of whether her research may be harmful, so most research institutions (universities as well as private research companies) have their own ethics boards, often called Institutional Review Boards (IRBs). These boards decide whether it's "OK" for the researcher to do a study based on a description submitted by the researcher. Throughout this book, we'll see some things a researcher might need to do to make sure they get the "thumbs up" from the IRB.

Writing the Report

Throughout the book, I'll be giving you examples of how to write reports of research. Gathering data is great, but it's typically not just for your own benefit. If you are working for a business, you will probably have to write a report for your boss about the data, and if you are an academic researcher, you will want to publish your findings. When you gather data, you need to explain what you *did* so that other people can judge what your findings *mean*. Report 1.1 is an example of what Cassandra might write to her editor to explain *how* she gathered her data. In the next chapter, you'll learn how she might report *what she discovered*.

> **REPORT 1.1 METHODS FOR MEASURING A VARIABLE**
>
> I randomly selected 50 Middle State students from a list of all students' phone numbers They were sent a question via text message asking them to report their readership of the campus newspaper Response rate was 100%

The sample was 70% female (26% male, 4% nonbinary/third gender) and was of typical college student age (*M* = 20 32 years, *SD* = 4 27) It was diverse in terms of race and ethnicity (62% white, 35% Latino/a/x, 28% black/African American, 14% Asian American, 6% Native American; numbers do not total to 100% because respondents could select more than one option)

Newspaper readership was assessed with a single question that asked the students to report in minutes how much time they spent "yesterday reading the *Daily Centurion*"

NOTES: The "*SD*" in this report represents standard deviation, a statistic you will learn more about in the next chapter. Typically, when reporting scientific research, you let your reader know basic information about your sample like the demographic information described here. This helps us understand the nature of the sample, even if you are not examining those factors in any detail. Most questionnaires, therefore, include questions about this demographic information. When doing research on any sample, reporting the response rate is also important (see the end of the first paragraph). This tells your reader how many of the people you *asked* to participate actually *did* participate. A response rate of 100% is, as I'm sure you can imagine, very rare!

QUALITATIVE, QUANTITATIVE, AND NONSCIENTIFIC QUESTIONS

Research involving numbers is called **quantitative** research—quantitative research involves counting, or rating, or scoring things. In contrast, some research is **qualitative**. Qualitative research explores questions that can't be fully answered with numbers. An important question like "*Why* do people read the newspaper?" doesn't have a purely numerical answer. Finally, some questions can't be answered with quantitative *or* qualitative information. If you want to figure out whether God exists, whether the death penalty is morally right or wrong, or *Star Wars* vs. *Star Trek,* you need the help of a philosophy or a film theory. Those are not *scientific* questions. This entire book is about questions that can be answered using facts about the world: **empirical questions** or **scientific questions** Empirical questions can be answered with quantitative or qualitative information. The book will deal first with quantitative questions and then discuss qualitative questions later.

Other Applications

You've been working through a fairly standard research problem in this chapter. Cassandra was trying to measure a single variable (time spent reading the newspaper) with a well-defined population (her school's student body). A strategy like hers would be useful with lots of other research questions involving measuring how much time people spend on specific tasks. Can you think of a couple of communication activities that you might be interested in measuring in a similar way?

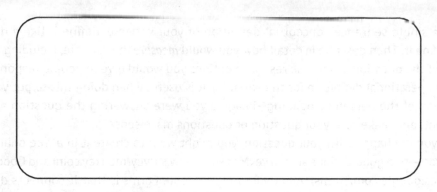

I would use a strategy like Cassandra's if my research involved finding out things like the following:

- In an organization, how much time do employees spend checking and responding to e-mail?
- On basketball teams, how much time do players spend talking to one another about rebounding?
- In marriages, how much time do the spouses spend talking to each other face-to-face? How much time do they spend texting each other?
- In college classes, how much time do students spend checking their cell phones?

The strategy might not work as well in other contexts. If you were interested in how much time preschool children spend playing with tablet computers, you would need to ask the parents or teachers, not the kids. Young children (and some other groups) can't respond to typical self-report measures because of reading ability, and young children also have a fairly loose idea of time. If you were interested in how much time prisoners were spending planning their escapes, using a cell phone or e-mail would not be a good idea, both because prisoners have limited access to electronic devices and because those devices *identify* the prisoners. When asking about sensitive information, you need to ensure respondent **anonymity,** both to get accurate responses and to protect your respondents. If you were studying the prisoners, you might use an anonymous paper and pencil questionnaire that is put in a locked drop box with many other responses.

Your Turn

Each chapter in this book has a "Your Turn" section for you to practice what you've learned in the chapter and to develop a real research project over the course of the book.

For this first chapter, pick one of the variables you thought of in the last response box (or another variable if you have since thought of something else that is more interesting to you). If you are having trouble thinking of a variable, consider aspects of people's communication in relationships, or their uses of media or technology, or communication phenomena that happen in their workplaces. Pick something that you find interesting.

Write a single sentence conceptual definition of your variable: define it like a dictionary would define it. Then describe in detail how you would *measure* the variable, including the exact wording of the question(s), and the response options you would give to people responding (i.e., create an operational definition for the variable). It is useful when doing this to put yourself in the position of the person responding—imagine you were answering the question as a naïve respondent, and make sure your question or questions make sense.

When you are happy with your question, you might want to create it in a free online survey creation tool—two good options are SurveyMonkey (www.survey-monkey.com) and Google Forms (www.docs.google.com/forms). An advantage of Google Forms is that it connects directly to Google Sheets, so if you actually collect data, you can move it easily from Forms to Sheets to do your analysis. A Google Forms version of Cassandra's question is at this link: http://bit.ly/2gtVclL.

Write your question down and have a friend respond to it to make sure it works. Ask your friend if s/he had any trouble understanding your question. Remember this information for the next chapter!

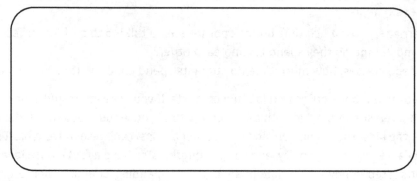

Wrap Up

This chapter has introduced some important concepts that you will use throughout the book. You may want to review the "key words" that follow to make sure that all the terms look familiar and that you understand the basics of each. More broadly, the chapter introduced the research process—how to go from a question to a plan for answering the question using observations of the world.

If you get nothing else from this chapter, remember the following:

1. You need to carefully define any variable that you want to measure (a conceptual definition).
2. Your measurement technique (operational definition) should be consistent with your conceptual definition.
3. Doing a research study is a process of making choices—choices about your sample, and your conceptual/operational definitions, and your research technique. Often, there is no "best" choice, but there *are* better and worse choices; the rest of this book is about helping you make good choices.

Doing the Research

Measuring Multiple Variables

Jake Harwood

Cassandra's first foray into research turned out pretty well, and so her editor has given her a new assignment. The newspaper is doing some market research to understand more about the demographics of their readers: advertisers are easier to recruit if you can tell them more about the audience they will reach. Cassandra's editor has asked her to investigate this issue. She'll be exploring a number of characteristics of the readers, but here we are just going to focus on one: the political orientation of *Centurion* readers.

When you start a research project, it can be very helpful to state a question in clear and specific form to guide your research. This question provides clarity for your reader, and indeed for *you*, about the goals of the project and what we all might know when the project is done. This type of question is called a research question (RQ). Here's Cassandra's question:

> RQ1: Is there an association between political ideology and readership of the *Daily Centurion*?

An alternative to an RQ is a hypothesis. A hypothesis states an explicit prediction about what the research project is expected to find. For instance, Cassandra may have a suspicion that liberals read the paper more than conservatives, and so she might hypothesize the following:

> H1: Students with more liberal political ideology will read the *Daily Centurion* more frequently than students with a more conservative political ideology.

Underlying the RQ and the hypothesis is the same fundamental question concerning an association between two variables. A lot of social science research begins at this level: Is variable A associated with Variable B? What are the two variables that Cassandra is examining?

If you decided that she is studying (a) newspaper readership and (b) political ideology, then you are following along.

What is the difference between an RQ and a hypothesis? As you can see from the earlier examples, a hypothesis is a <u>statement</u> that makes a <u>prediction</u>. To formally state a hypothesis, you have to go out on a limb and make a claim about your data before you have actually collected it. Notice that the earlier example (H1) includes a *direction* for the association: It says liberals will read the paper *more than* conservatives. It is possible to write a hypothesis that doesn't include the direction of the association—this is (appropriately!) called a nondirectional hypothesis:

H2: Political ideology will be associated with *Daily Centurion* readership.

Notice how this hypothesis makes a prediction (that ideology and readership are associated) but doesn't say in what direction (maybe liberals read the paper more, or maybe conservatives read it more). A directional hypothesis is good if you have a clear prediction for what you expect to find. If you just expect to find "something" but are not sure what, a nondirectional hypothesis or an RQ is a better choice. An RQ is (of course) a question: It *asks* whether something is true rather than specifically predicting it.

One final note on language. When you have an RQ, your research is then aiming to *answer* the question. When you have a hypothesis, the research will aim to *test* the hypothesis. You can't test a question or answer a hypothesis. The rest of the chapter is going to focus on how Cassandra can test her directional hypothesis:

H1: Students with a more liberal political ideology will read the *Daily Centurion* more frequently than students with a more conservative political ideology.

How to Test a Hypothesis

As you may guess, you test a hypothesis by doing research. One common mistake people make is trying to test a hypothesis simply by *asking people whether they think the hypothesis is true*. For Cassandra's H1, she might be tempted to go out and just ask people, "Do you think that liberals read the newspaper more than conservatives?" Provide one clear explanation of why that might be a bad way to test the hypothesis:

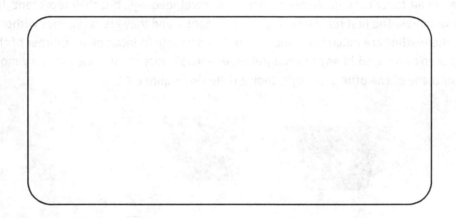

Think about a pharmaceutical company testing a new type of flu vaccine. Would they test it by asking people whether they *think* the vaccine will stop people from getting the flu? No! They would study people who receive the vaccine and people who don't receive the vaccine, and see whether the people who've been vaccinated actually get the flu less. The same is true for social science hypothesis testing. When a hypothesis makes a prediction about the association between two variables, the researcher measures how people score on both those variables and looks to see whether the predicted association is present. Let's explore the idea of measurement a little more.

Conceptualizing and Operationalizing a Variable: Levels of Measurement

Cassandra is fortunate in that she already knows how to measure one of her variables (newspaper readership)—Chapter 1 described the process of developing that measurement in some detail. All she needs to do now is figure out how to measure political ideology.

In Chapter 1, Cassandra learned the importance of defining her variables conceptually before trying to figure out how to measure them. That becomes even more important with a more complex variable like political ideology. People can mean a lot of different things when they talk about political ideology. Consider just the following three definitions:

1. Political party: Your political ideology is the political party to which you belong: Democrat, Republican, Green, Libertarian, Communist, Socialist, Modern Whig (yes, there's really a Modern Whig party), etc.
2. Ordered political category: Your political ideology is defined by whether you call yourself liberal, moderate, or conservative.
3. Political continuum: Your political ideology is your position on a scale from extremely liberal to extremely conservative.

These are all fairly reasonable definitions of political ideology, but they represent different types of variables. The first represents a set of categories, and they are categories without much order to them—they are much like a set of "bins," and people fit into one or another of the bins. The bins aren't arranged in any meaningful order—people just fit into one category more than they fit into any of the others. It might look a little like Figure 6.4.1.

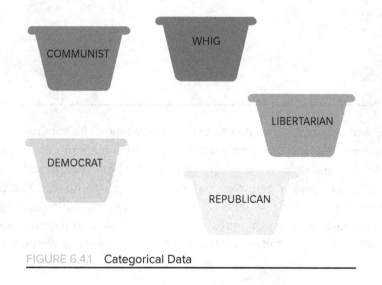

FIGURE 6.4.1   Categorical Data

This type of variable is called a **categorical** variable. Categorical variables are defined by a number of categories that are not arranged in any meaningful order. Other examples include religion (if you are Buddhist, Muslim, Catholic, Jewish, atheist, etc.) or nationality (whether you are American, Mexican, Nigerian, Pakistani, etc.). Of course, categorical variables can get complicated if someone falls into multiple categories—someone with dual citizenship, for instance. But for now, we'll keep things simple and imagine that everyone fits neatly into one and only one bin.

The second definition just involves three bins, and now the bins do have some sort of order to them: the "moderate" bin clearly fits in between the other two. See Figure 6.4.2.

This kind of variable is called an **ordinal** variable. The word "ordinal" comes from the idea that these bins (categories) have an *order* to them—they make sense in one order but not in other orders. A lot of measures of socioeconomic status are ordinal (lower class, middle class, upper class), as are measures of university class standing (freshman, sophomore, junior, senior). One

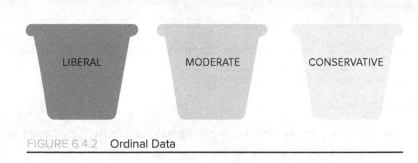

FIGURE 6.4.2   Ordinal Data

common characteristic of ordinal measures is that there are a very limited number of bins, and there is a lot of variation within the bins. For instance, at the University of Arizona, you are a sophomore if you have anywhere between 30 and 59 credit hours. If all I know about a student is that she is a sophomore, I am still missing a lot of information about how far advanced she is in her studies.

The third definition involves lots more bins—and they are arranged in a long line from one extreme to the other. See Figure 6.4.3.

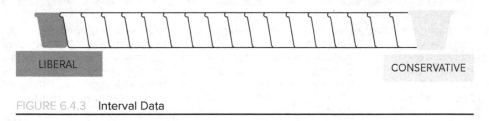

FIGURE 6.4.3   Interval Data

This type of measure is called an **interval** variable. The measurement of someone's degree of liberalism/conservatism is much more detailed, and the people who fall into the same bin will be very similar to each other. This is more like measuring academic progress using "credit hours completed" rather than class standing. Most variables that involve some sort of "score" are interval-level variables (your height, your SAT results). In the social sciences, a lot of measures of traits and attitudes are also measured this way (e.g., how extraverted you are, how high your self-esteem is, how much you love your spouse).

Take a moment to check your understanding of the different levels of measurement. Which of the following are categorical-, ordinal-, or interval-level variables?

Biological sex _____

Time taken to run 100 meters _____

Type of computer operating system (Mac OS, Windows, Linux)

_____

How you feel today (unhappy, meh, happy) ———————————————————————

Your level of support for increased defense spending (very low, low, medium, high, very high) ————————————————————————

In order, those examples are

- categorical (assuming we are just dealing with male and female, those are just two categories with no order associated with them),
- interval (time is a continuous scale),
- categorical (again, operating systems are just types of things with no order),
- ordinal, and
- ordinal. (However, it's worth noting with this one that there's no strict rule for how many options (bins) it takes for an ordinal scale to become an interval scale. If you weren't absolutely sure whether to call the last one ordinal or interval, then you are in good company—experienced researchers might treat it both ways depending on the circumstances.)

Understanding whether your variable is measured at the categorical, ordinal, or interval level is crucial to knowing what sorts of statistics you can use. You can only calculate a mean with interval-level data: It makes no sense to ask what the "average religion" is in a group of people. On the other hand, you can certainly calculate a mode with categorical-level data (the most common religious affiliation in a particular group of people). The following represents which measures of central tendency are appropriate with which types of data:

Level of Measurement	Measure of Central Tendency
Interval data	Mean, median, and mode
Ordinal data	Median and mode
Categorical data	Mode

The fact that you can't calculate a mean with categorical data, for instance, also means that you can't calculate a standard deviation or a z-score. A lot of statistics in the social sciences are based on means, standard deviations, and z-scores; if you have a choice, it can be very helpful to try to measure things at the interval level so you can use those statistics.

Before Cassandra can start testing her hypothesis, she needs to decide on a *conceptual* definition of political ideology (remember ...). Based on her hypothesis (which asks about people who are "more liberal" or "more conservative") she decides that it is most appropriate to use an interval-level conceptualization of political ideology. However, she knows she is dealing with busy undergraduates and that she doesn't have any compensation to offer them for helping her, so she wants to use a measure that will be really quick for the students to fill out.

Cassandra knows that other people have probably measured political ideology, so she starts looking through scientific research articles to see how they measured it. In her college library, she finds an article called "The Secret Lives of Liberals and Conservatives" (Carney, Jost, Gosling, & Potter, 2008). In it, the researchers measured political ideology with the following item:

On the following scale, rate your own political views:

1	2	3	4	5	6	7	8	9

Extremely
Conservative

Moderate

Extremely
Liberal

This looks perfect for Cassandra's needs, but she wants to make sure it is a good measure. First, she asks around about the journal the measure is published in (*Political Psychology*), and her professors tell her it's a good journal. Second, she reads the article she found it in and notices that the authors say that the measure has "good **test-retest reliability**" (p. 818). Test-retest reliability means that if someone fills the measure out at two points in time, it tends to give similar results. Somebody responding to this measure and saying that they are a "2" (very conservative) will not come back the next week and tell you that they are a "9" (extremely liberal). Test-retest reliability is one way to tell that a measurement instrument is OK to use. Imagine taking your temperature, and it says you are at 98.6 degrees, and then you come back 10 minutes later, and it says you are at 104. That would be poor test-retest reliability, and (unless you have suddenly become very sick very quickly!), you should buy a new thermometer!

By using an existing measurement instrument, Cassandra can be relatively sure that it is good quality and will measure what she needs. What is the level of measurement of this measure of political ideology—is it categorical, ordinal, or interval?

This is definitely not a categorical measure, and the best answer here is that it is an interval-level measure. Researchers might argue about whether it's an ordinal measure—and it wouldn't be wrong to say that it's ordinal.

Cassandra is ready to gather her data—she has measurement tools to assess both of her variables. [F]or simplicity, let's imagine she again uses 50 people. [T]he sample will be asked how much they read the newspaper, and now they will also be asked to report their political ideology using the question shown earlier. Cassandra will then have all the information she needs to test her hypothesis. [,,,]

Cassandra's Curiosity, Causality, and Scientific Theory

Through her data collection, Cassandra will learn the demographic profile of *Centurion* readers—which was her goal. She will be able to tell her editor whether there is an *association* between newspaper reading and political ideology. Her editor, in turn, will be able to tell advertisers what sort of readership they will reach if they advertise in the *Centurion*. This research project will meet the immediate needs of the paper.

In the course of gathering the data, Cassandra may get curious about *why* these two variables are associated. If liberals in fact read the newspaper more than conservatives, why might that be? Try to think of some different explanations for the association between these variables and write at least two of them here:

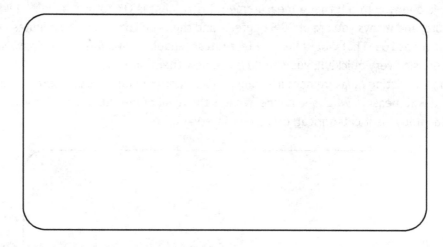

You probably thought of ideas like the following:

- Something about the newspaper causes liberals to read it more (e.g., that the paper is biased toward liberal viewpoints).
- Something about liberals makes them read the newspaper more (e.g., liberals are more interested in politics)
- An *effect* of reading the newspaper (i.e., reading the newspaper is *causing* people to become more liberal)
- Some other factor that causes the association between liberalism and news reading to happen (e.g., if liberals tend to enroll in easier majors, maybe they just have more time available to lounge around catching up on the news)

In a number of cases, these are causal (**cause-and-effect**) relationships: they describe how one variable (e.g., liberalism) causes changes in another (e.g., newspaper reading).

Causal Relationships Between Independent and Dependent Variables

You may have heard the phrase "correlation does not equal causality." Just because you observe that two variables are associated does not mean that one of them is causing the other. The association between the two variables is a **fact**. The interpretation of that fact can vary quite dramatically. Cassandra has found some *support* for all of the earlier bullet points, but she is a long way from *proving* any of them. When we do research, we need to understand the difference between what our data definitively say, as opposed to things that the data "suggest." Sometimes (as in the bulleted list), it can be quite fun to think up lots of possible reasons why two variables might be associated with one another.

Problems in knowing whether one variable *causes* another are inherent in **cross-sectional** survey research designs like Cassandra's. A cross-sectional design involves measuring a group of people on whatever variables you are interested in at one point in time. One key requirement in demonstrating causality is **time order:** a cause needs to occur *before* an effect. If I think that high quality social support causes improved mental health, I need to study whether mental health improves *after* people receive social support. This is one reason why cross-sectional research designs have trouble demonstrating causality. You can't show time order if you measure everything at the same time.

An additional requirement for cause-and-effect relations is a clear **mechanism** by which the effect happens—*how* A influences B shouldn't be a mystery. Can you think of a mechanism leading from social support to better mental health? How does it happen?

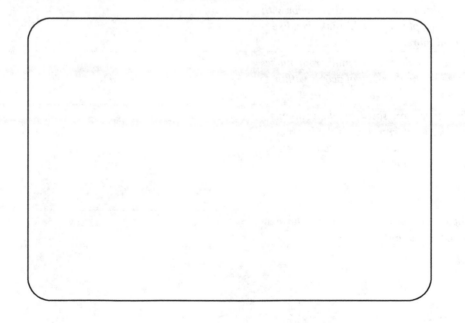

Sensible explanations for social support improving mental health might include the following:

a) Social support provides useful information to people (e.g., about seeking medical help for a mental health issue—which would improve mental health).
b) Social support provides logistical help (e.g., watching someone's kids so he or she can get a break from caregiving or catch up on schoolwork—this would reduce stress, which would improve mental health).
c) Social support provides emotional assistance (e.g., letting people talk through their problems and sympathizing with them, which would make them feel that they have a supportive "ear" when they need it, which improves mental health).

If you see that two variables are associated but have no sensible explanation for *why*, you are limited in your ability to claim that one causes the other.

While we are talking about cause-and-effect relationships, it's worth learning a couple of new terms. If variable X causes changes in variable Y, then X is called the **independent variable**—the variable that *does the causing*. Variable Y is called the **dependent variable**—the variable that is affected by X.

$$X \rightarrow Y$$
Independent variable $\rightarrow$ Dependent variable

Identify the independent and dependent variables for each of the following RQs (answers are on the next page):

	Independent Variable	Dependent Variable
Does engaging in synchronized behavior with someone (e.g., playing catch) make you like that person more?		
Is the quality of decision a small group makes influenced by the diversity of people within that group?		
Are physicians more satisfied when patients look up health information on the Internet before a visit or when patients do not look up health information?		
Does playing "racing" video games make people more likely to drive aggressively?		
Do people who consume more snacks have a higher body mass index?		

Answers:

	Independent Variable	**Dependent Variable**
Does engaging in synchronized behavior with someone (e.g., playing catch) make you like that person more than if you don't do the synchronized behavior?	Engaging in synchronized behavior versus not	Liking for the other person
Is the quality of a small group's decision influenced by the diversity of people within that group?	Diversity of group	Quality of decision made by group
Are physicians more satisfied when patients look up health information on the Internet before a visit, or when patients do not look up health information?	Looking up health information (versus not)	Physician satisfaction
Does playing "racing" video games make people more likely to drive aggressively?	Playing racing video games (versus not) or maybe the number of games you play	Aggressive driving
Do people who consume more snacks have a higher body mass index?	Snack consumption*	Body mass index

*This is probably the most obvious ordering—eating snacks makes you overweight However, the way the question is worded doesn't actually specify that order, so it wouldn't be wrong to infer the reverse for this one—it's plausible that being overweight may cause you to eat more snacks for some reason When trying to identify independent and dependent variables, look for language like "causes," "influences," or "makes" (as in X *makes* you do Y) but also think logically about what might plausibly influence what

Theory

Cassandra's project is aiming to answer a very specific question for a very specific purpose: to address her editor's desire to describe the readership of the paper. To that extent, her research project is not particularly theoretical. However, theory is central to most communication research. Researchers are not trying to answer one specific question in one specific context, but instead are trying to understand something more general about human communication. Theory helps us frame questions at that more general level. Indeed, even Cassandra's project can be understood as theoretically interesting, as hinted at in the previous section on causation. Once Cassandra gets interested in *why* the two variables are associated, she is starting to get interested in theory.

Here are some theoretical ideas that may be informed by Cassandra's research:

- Liberals are more interested in current affairs than conservatives.
- Newspapers are biased toward a liberal point of view.
- Liberals read more than conservatives.
- Liberals are lazier or less ambitious than conservatives.

Each of these represents an idea with broader implications for our social worlds than Cassandra's rather narrow question. If Cassandra wanted her work to become part of a broader theoretical discussion, she would need to decide which "angle" she wanted to take on her data. Then she should look at previous research and theory about her particular angle, understanding not only the claim but also the *processes* underlying that claim. A theory involves a detailed explanation of an entire process, not just a bullet point.

For example, if Cassandra is interested in the idea that the media have a liberal bias, that might lead her to some analysis of the *content* of her newspaper: does it actually lean liberal in terms of the stories it covers or the tone of the editorials? Using careful scientific procedures [...], she could examine media bias as an empirical question. She might also discuss with her editor whether they could increase conservative readership by increasing the number of conservative editorials in the paper. Again, this is an empirical question that could be investigated by manipulating the content of the paper over time and measuring how much the readership changed. Notice here that there are practical implications of theories. If your theory suggests liberal bias in the media, your scientific research should incorporate an examination of the content of the paper, and your practical solutions might involve adjusting the content. Alternatively, if your theory suggests that conservatives are just less interested in current affairs, you might be more interested in scientific research that measures interest in those issues among liberals and conservatives, and perhaps practical interventions designed to increase involvement in politics across the political spectrum.

Figure 6.4.4 illustrates the place of theory in the research process. Theory serves two fundamental functions. First, a theory can generate RQs or hypotheses—as in the earlier examples, a theory provides ideas for what observations of the world need to be done to test the theory.

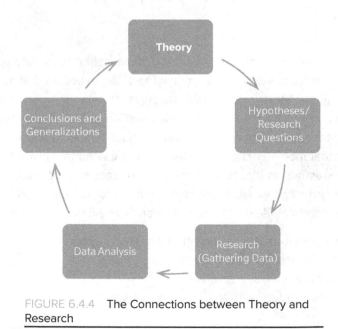

FIGURE 6.4.4 **The Connections between Theory and Research**

Second, a theory is a "repository" for research. Once a research study (or a series of studies) is complete, the results from those studies will contribute either to building new theories or adjusting existing theories. Cassandra was really just interested in her specific readers and her newspaper. But her research findings could become part of a much broader discussion about who reads newspapers and why, with implications for understanding what makes someone "liberal" or "conservative," and what counts as "news." Those are important questions that have implications beyond any specific study: That's what theory is.

Writing the Report

[...]A lot of Cassandra's description of her methods for the current project would closely resemble what she did in her first study. The only addition would be the description of how she measured the political ideology question.

> **NOTES:** It is important that if you use a measure taken from someone else's research that you cite the source—note how Carney et al. (2008) is cited in the section on measurement of political ideology. It's also important to describe the potential scores a measure can have and what high scores mean. On the political ideology measure, for instance, the description makes it clear that the scale can range from 1 to 9, and higher scores indicate more liberal ideologies, lower scores indicate more conservative.

REPORT 3.1 METHODS FOR MEASURING MULTIPLE VARIABLES

I randomly selected 50 Middle State students from a list of all students' phone numbers They were sent a link via text message asking them to respond to a brief questionnaire Response rate was 100%.

The sample was 70% female, 26% male, and 4% nonbinary/third gender, and was of typical college student age (M = 20 32 years, SD = 4 27) It was diverse in terms of race and ethnicity (62% white, 35% Latino/a/x, 28% black/

African American, 14% Asian American, 6% Native American; numbers do not total to 100% because respondents could select more than one option).

Newspaper readership was assessed with a single question, asking the student to report in minutes how much time they spent "yesterday reading the *Daily Centurion?*"

Political ideology was assessed with a single question, asking for the respondents' political views on a 9-point scale (1 = extremely conservative, 9 = extremely liberal; item from Carney et al, 2008).

Other Applications

Many research situations use the issues raised in this chapter: situations where the researcher is interested in the association between two interval-level variables. An advertising researcher interested in whether a campaign has been effective might measure how much people were exposed to the campaign and their feelings about the product. A relationships expert might be interested in whether the number of times couples say they love each other is associated with the longevity of their relationship. A political communication researcher might be interested in whether people who talk about politics more with their families also tend to vote more regularly. All those questions could be answered using the kinds of methods described in this chapter. Can you think of something that a new technology researcher might be interested in that could be addressed using a strategy like what was described in this chapter? Write an RQ and try to identify the independent and dependent variables.

RQ	Independent Variable	Dependent Variable

There are infinite questions that you may have thought of here. Is the number of texts sent during class associated with class grades? Is time spent using social media associated with low self-esteem? Does frequently checking your phone correlate with your attention span? Perhaps you thought of one of those ideas!

Your Turn

[...] For this chapter's activity, add another variable to your questionnaire. [C]onsider what other things might be associated with it. For instance, if you were interested in how much people watch sports programs on television, you might think about whether viewing sports is associated with actively playing sports. **Important:** For this second variable to work [...], you should try to think of a variable you can measure at the **interval level**.

Once you have picked your variable, think about how you might measure it. To help you with this, you might do some library research to find out whether someone else has already measured the variable and simply copy their measurement. Alternatively, you can create your own questionnaire if you want. Think about the things you learned [...] in terms of how to write your question or questions if you are going to write the questionnaire yourself. Create a questionnaire (pencil and paper, or online) so you know exactly how you might ask the questions of a set of respondents. Write a report [...] to describe for an audience how your variable is measured.

Wrap Up

In this chapter, you have read about a more extensive research project involving measuring two variables to examine the association between them. Most social science research projects involve at least two variables, as researchers attempt to understand how different social phenomena are associated with each other. You have learned the difference between categorical, ordinal, and interval levels of measurement, and the importance of understanding level of measurement before you start calculating statistics. You have also learned why it's a good idea to use an existing measurement tool when one is available rather than trying to create your own—don't reinvent the wheel! Finally, you should have started to get an idea of how theory and research interrelate. Most academic communication research aims to answer general questions about the world, not just a specific question in a single specific context. Applied research may be more oriented toward getting a single question answered for a single purpose ("did our advertising campaign work?"); however, applied research may also have theoretical implications.

If you get nothing else from this chapter, remember the following:

1. To answer any RQ about two variables, you must measure both variables (not just ask people if they think the two things are associated).
2. Understanding the level of measurement of a variable (categorical, ordinal, interval) is critical to knowing how to measure it and analyze those measurements.
3. Correlation is not causality—showing that two things are associated may be an important step in understanding a causal relationship but be cautious in making a causal claim from a correlation.

Annotated Bibliography

Carney, D. R., Jost, J. T., Gosling, S. D., & Potter, J. (2008). The secret lives of liberals and conservatives: Personality profiles, interaction styles, and the things they leave behind. *Political Psychology, 29*(6), 807–840. https://doi.org/10.1111/j.1467-9221.2008.00668.x

CHAPTER 6

Conclusion

Research in criminal justice and the social sciences relies on approaches that are qualitative, quantitative, or a combination of both of the above. The utilization of experimental research designs is rare in criminal justice research, and investigators often rely on alternative designs such as descriptive, historical, cross-sectional, longitudinal, or case studies to gather information to answer research questions/hypotheses. The articles in this chapter invite readers to apply course information to specific research questions and explore various measurement options and data-gathering techniques for measuring a single variable or exploring relationships between multiple variables.

Chapter 6 Reflection Questions

1. Define and differentiate between idiographic and nomothetic causal explanations.
2. What are the three criteria for causality?
3. Define and differentiate between experimental and quasi-experimental research.
4. List and describe the four levels of measurement. Provide your own criminal justice–related example of each.
5. What are the issues to consider in selecting a research design?
6. Summarize the types of research design (descriptive, historical, cross-sectional, longitudinal—trend, cohort, panel—and case study).
7. How do cross-sectional and longitudinal research designs differ from one another?
8. Complete the "Your Turn" exercises on pages 169 and 184.

Building Your Research Proposal

Chapter 6: Define the Concepts, Create the Measures, Design a Method

1. Summarize the key findings from the articles in your literature review (chapter 5). Provide a rationale for the importance of the research you are proposing.
2. Restate the research question or hypothesis you proposed and identify theoretical connections.
3. Define the concepts in your question or hypothesis. Identify the concepts that require measurement.
4. Create the measures. How could you operationalize these concepts? What levels of measurement would apply to each?
5. Assess the validity and reliability of your measures (chapter 3).
6. Design a method. What research approach do you propose to use to answer your question or hypothesis?
7. Who/what is your sample? How will you decide who will participate, or what source will you use to collect this data?
8. Identify any ethical considerations/issues that may relate to your study.

Data Collection

Introduction

The articles within this chapter outline a variety of methods and resources researchers can use to collect data (or information) to address research questions or hypotheses. Researchers may choose to collect their own original data (called primary data) via the administration of surveys/questionnaires, interviews, or focus groups, or through observing behavior or program activities. In the first article, "Collecting Primary Data," Walliman presents various data-collection methods available to researchers interested in gathering primary data, defines and discusses probability and non-probability sampling procedures (to be used if your study involves a large group of subjects), and provides direction in deciding which method of primary data collection may be best suited for a research study.

In the second selection, Withrow defines nonreactive research strategies as those that "tap into something that already exists—an everyday behavior, a scientific database, a written document—to answer a research question or test a research hypothesis." The author focuses this discussion on three major types of nonreactive research methods: field research, secondary analysis, and content analysis. Criminal justice researchers routinely utilize and analyze secondary data, or information that was originally collected for a different purpose. For example, police departments routinely gather data on arrests, criminal activity, officer performance, and citizen complaints, data that may be used by researchers to answer many different questions or test hypotheses. Examples secondary data sources that are publicly available include newspaper articles, social media, the FBI's National Incident Based Reporting System (NIBRS), and the National Crime Victimization Survey (NCVS). Researchers may be able to gain access to an agency's private data via the formation of relationships or partnerships with and approval from organizations (such as police departments, courts/legal entities, and correctional agencies) and IRBs. Definitions and concrete examples for how various types of nonreactive research methods are used in criminal justice research are discussed and benefits and limitations associated with these methods are presented.

Collecting Primary Data

Nicholas Walliman

Although we are surrounded by data, in fact, bombarded with them every day from the TV, posters, radio, newspapers, magazines and books, it is not so straightforward to collect the correct data for your purposes. It needs a plan of action that identifies what data you need, where the necessary data are to be found and what are the most effective and appropriate methods of collecting those data. You will need to consider whether to get information from people, in single or large numbers, or whether to observe and/or measure things or phenomena. You may need to do several of these things. For example, in sport you may need to examine not only people, but also their attitudes and fitness and the equipment they use; in commerce, you may be looking at both the product and the production system as well as marketing, sales and distribution—the people and the processes.

There are several basic methods used to collect primary data; here are the main ones:

- asking questions
- conducting interviews
- observing without getting involved
- immersing oneself in a situation
- doing experiments
- manipulating models.

Different disciplines use one or several of these methods to collect data, and customize them to cater for their needs. For example, experiments in social research might be conducted in a natural setting well away from a laboratory, while chemical research might require tightly controlled conditions in order to be successful.

Before we explore the different methods of data collection, we need to consider the issue of selecting who to question or what to examine when faced with a large number of cases.

Sampling

If you want to get information about a large group of individual people or things, for example, students or cars, it is normally impossible to get all of them to answer your questions or to examine all the things—it would take much too long and be far too expensive. The solution is to ask or examine some of them and hope that the data you get are **representative** (or typical) of all the rest. If the data you collect really are the same as you would get from the rest, then you can draw conclusions from those answers which you can relate to the whole group. This process of selecting just a small group of cases from out of a large group is called **sampling**.

In other situations, you may want to examine the dynamics within different groups rather than individuals, for instance the social interactions within different neighbourhoods or the processes within different production systems. Here, the individual cases will be groups rather than single people or the things that are members of the group. Again, if you want to draw conclusions about all the cases, you will need to select a few typical ones for detailed study, called **case studies**, using a sampling method. However, in some situations all the cases may be unique, for example different ethnic groups, so it is not possible to find a representative sample. What you can do then is take a comparative approach by selecting several very different cases, e.g. those showing extreme characteristics, those at each end of the spectrum and perhaps one that is somewhere in the middle and compare their characteristics. Alternatively, choose an 'exemplifying' or 'critical' case, one that will provide a good setting for answering the research questions. Results from individual groups might then be compared rather than making generalizations about all the groups. Both quantitative and qualitative methods are appropriate for case study designs, and multiple methods of data collection are often applied.

When doing a survey, the question inevitably arises: how representative is the sample of the whole population? In other words, how similar are characteristics of the small group of cases that are chosen for the survey to those of all the cases in the whole group? When we talk about **population** in research, it does not necessarily mean a number of people; it is a collective term used to describe the total quantity of things (or cases) of the type which are the subject of your study. So, a population can consist of certain types of objects, organizations, people or even events. Within this population, there will probably be only certain groups that will be of interest to your study; for instance, of all school buildings only those in cities, or of all limited companies, only small to medium-sized companies. This selected category is your **sampling frame**. It is from this sampling frame that the sample is selected, as shown in Figure 7.1.1.

Difficulties are encountered if the characteristics of the population are not known, or if it is not possible to reach sectors of it. Non-representative samples cannot be used to make accurate generalizations about the population. Populations can have the following characteristics:

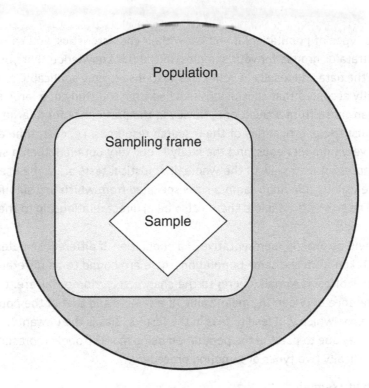

FIGURE 7.1.1   Sampling Frame in Relation to Population and Sample

- **homogeneous**—all cases are similar, e.g. bottles of beer on a production line. It does not matter which cases you select for your sample, as they all have the same characteristics. The larger sample you have, the more chance you will have of finding deviant cases, e.g. in this case it could be bottles not properly filled with beer;
- **stratified**—contain strata or layers, e.g. people with different levels of income: low, medium, high. You can select some cases from each stratum so that you can compare them in some way, e.g. proportion of income spent on accommodation;
- **proportional stratified**—contains strata of known proportions, e.g. percentages of different nationalities of students in a university. To get the right balance in your sample, you select the number of cases in the same proportion as they appear in the population, e.g. to ensure that you get a representative response to questions about the average time students spend exercising;
- **grouped by type**—contains distinctive groups, e.g. of apartment buildings—towers, slabs, villas, tenement blocks. Choose the same number of cases from each type to compare their experiences, e.g. the amount of noise disturbance from neighbours;
- **grouped by location**—different groups according to where they are, e.g. animals in different habitats—desert, equatorial forest, savannah, tundra. Again, choose some cases from each location to compare their habits, e.g. feeding.

With all these types of population, if you know their characteristics, you can choose to select only certain strata or groups for your samples, in the full knowledge that you are leaving out the others, so the data and results of your investigations are only applicable to the chosen ones.

It is generally accepted that conclusions reached from the study of a large sample are more convincing than those from a small one. However, the preference for a large sample must be balanced against the practicalities of the research resources, i.e. cost, time and effort. If the population is very homogeneous, and the study is not very detailed, then a small sample will give a fairly representative view of the whole. If statistical tests are to be used to analyse the data, there are usually minimum sample sizes specified from which any significant results can be obtained. The size of the sample should also be in direct relationship to the number of variables to be studied.

No sample will be exactly representative of a population. If different samples, using identical methods, are taken from the same population, there are bound to be differences in the mean (average) values of each sample owing to the chance selection of different individuals. The measured difference between the mean value of a sample and that of the population is called the **sampling error**, which will lead to bias in the results. **Bias** is the unwanted distortion of the results of a survey due to parts of the population being more strongly represented than others.

There are basically two types of sampling procedure:

1. probability sampling
2. non-probability sampling.

Probability sampling techniques give the most reliable representation of the whole population, while non-probability techniques, relying on the judgement of the researcher or on accident, cannot generally be used to make generalizations about the whole population.

Probability Sampling

This is based on using random methods to select the sample. Populations are not always quite as uniform or one-dimensional as, say, a particular type of component in a production run, so simple random selection methods are not always appropriate. The select procedure should aim to guarantee that each element (person, group, class, type, etc.) has an equal chance of being selected and that every possible combination of the elements also has an equal chance of being selected. Therefore, the first question to be asked is about the nature of the population. Is it homogeneous or are there distinctly different classes of cases within it, and, if so, how are they distributed within the population (e.g. are they grouped in different locations, found at different levels in a hierarchy or all mixed up together)? Specific techniques are used for selecting representative samples from populations of the different characteristics, such as simple random sampling, stratified sampling, cluster sampling, etc.

Non-Probability Sampling

Non-probability sampling is based on selection by non-random means. This can be useful for certain studies, for example, for quick surveys or where it is difficult to get access to the whole population, but it provides only a weak basis for generalization. There are a variety of techniques that can be used, such as **accidental sampling**, **quota sampling** and **snowball technique**.

Data Collection Methods

The following sections explore the different methods of primary data collection and briefly describe how they might be applied.

Asking Questions—Questionnaires

Asking questions is an obvious method of collecting both quantitative and qualitative information from people. Questionnaires are a particularly suitable tool for gaining quantitative data, but they can also be used for qualitative data. This method of data collection is usually called a **survey**. Using a questionnaire enables you to organize the questions and receive replies without having to talk to every respondent. As a method of data collection, the questionnaire is a very flexible tool which has the advantages of having a structured format, being easy and convenient for respondents, and being cheap and quick to administer to a large number of cases covering large geographical areas. There is also no personal influence of the researcher, and embarrassing questions can be asked with a fair chance of getting a true reply. However, questionnaires do require a lot of time and skill to design and develop. They need to be short and simple to follow, so complex question structures are not possible. Not everyone is able to complete questionnaires.

There are three methods of delivering questionnaires, personally, by post or through the Internet. The advantages of personal delivery are that respondents can be helped to overcome difficulties with the questions, and can be persuaded and reminded in order to ensure a high response rate. Obviously, there are problems both in time and geographical location that limit the scope and extent to which this method of delivery can be used. Postal questionnaires are used when many responses are sought, particularly when they are in different locations. The correct address for each respondent is required and postal costs must also be taken into account.

The rate of response for postal questionnaires is difficult to predict or control and they are very prone to low **response rates**, particularly if there is no system of follow-up. It is important that you get a good response rate if you have selected a representative sample. In this case, a poor response rate reduces the reliability of the sample being a true representation of the population. Including a stamped addressed return envelope will help, as will writing a clear and compact covering letter to explain why it is important that the recipient completes and returns the questionnaire and to give assurance about confidentiality. An attractive design, clear instructions for answering questions, and a short length that only requires a few minutes to complete will encourage people to take part. Follow-up reminders normally prompt a number of additional responses.

Internet questionnaires are the cheapest and least time-consuming method of delivery. Although it is easy to get blanket coverage by random delivery, response rates tend to be very low and it is difficult to know how representative the sample will be. For more structured deliveries, email addresses are required to pinpoint responses from the chosen sample. Followup reminders are easily administered.

There are basically two question types:

1. **closed format questions**—the respondent must choose from a set of given answers. These tend to be quick to answer, easy to code and require no special writing skills from the respondent. However, they do limit the range of possible answers. The simplest is a bivariate question—with a yes/no answer or just two other kinds of option. Be sure that there are no additional possible options to confuse matters. For a question on gender, male/female used to be all inclusive, but now should you add transgender? When giving any choice of answers, the point remains the same: no categories should be left out, e.g. when asking about party political affiliation, make sure all the political parties are given as options. If this is impossible, add a 'remainders' answer such as 'don't know' or 'other'. You can go further than simple categorization by asking a question that involves ranking.

    example—here are important qualities a prime minister should possess. Number them 1–5 in order of importance—1 being the most important:
    Honesty, Humour, Intelligence, Consistency, Experience.
    Closed format questions are used to gain quantitative data. Because the answers are predefined, the different responses can be counted and used for statistical analysis;

2. **open format questions**—the respondent is free to answer with their own content and style. These tend to permit freedom of expression and allow the respondents to qualify their responses. This freedom leads to a lack of bias but the answers are more open to researcher interpretation. They are also more demanding and time-consuming for respondents and more difficult to code.

    example—What are the most important qualities a prime minister should possess?
    Open questions are used to gain qualitative data. You cannot predict what data the answers will contain, so they will be difficult to accurately categorize and count. Instead they can provide a rich source of data about individual people's opinions, feelings, attitudes, etc.

There are several precautions to take to ensure that the questions can be accurately answered. Avoid asking double questions—impossible to answer both in one answer! Similarly, do not ask questions that are ambiguous by using words that can be interpreted in several ways, e.g. 'your relatives'—to which level of remoteness is intended, or 'dinner'—which can mean a midday meal or evening meal depending on how posh you are! Keep questions short, as no one wants to spend time working out what you mean. Be precise to make sure the respondent knows what you are asking about, e.g. 'What is your standard of living?' will prompt various interpretations of what you mean: level of income, housing conditions, work/home balance, social status, etc. Other types of questions to avoid are leading questions, those including negatives and those using difficult to understand technical terms or acronyms.

It is common practice to pre-test the questionnaire on a small number of people before it is used in earnest. This is called a **pilot study**. Requested feedback from the respondents includes checking for confusion about the reason for the survey, difficulty in understanding the questions, ambiguous wording, complex multiple questions, and inappropriate or incomplete choice of answers. These can then be corrected before the main survey is commenced.

It is important that you get a good response rate, particularly if you have selected a representative sample. In this case, a poor response reduces the reliability of being a true representation of the population. Postal and Internet questionnaire surveys are particularly prone to low response rates, but there are some precautions you can take to maximize returns.

There are many guides that provide standard templates for questionnaires, information on setting them up, how to design them for ease of analysis of the responses, ways to deliver and collect them, and ways to maximize response rates. When I Googled 'questionnaire design', I got over eleven million results! In order to simplify matters for you, I have suggested a few guides at the end of this chapter, some of them aimed at a particular discipline. Online questionnaire programs (such as Survey Monkey, eSurveysPro, SurveyExpression) have free options and are easy to use; they provide templates and basic analysis of the responses as part of their program, saving you much time and effort. You can also export the data as a spreadsheet for further analysis.

Questionnaires are commonly used in disciplines that are concerned with people, particularly as part of society. Research in social sciences, politics, business, healthcare, etc. often needs to gain the opinions, feelings and reactions of a large number of people and this most easily done with a survey. When the government wants to get answers from everyone in the population, then this kind of survey is called a census.

Accounts and Diaries

Asking people to relate their account of a situation or getting them to keep diaries is perhaps the most open form of questionnaire. These qualitative data collection methods are used to find information on people's actions and feelings by asking them to give their own interpretation, or account, of what they experience.

Accounts can consist of a variety of data sources: people's spoken explanations, behaviour (such as gestures), personal records of experiences and conversations, letters and personal diaries. If the accounts are authentic, there should be no reason why they cannot be used as an argued explanation of people's actions.

> For example: Trainee nurses are asked to keep a diary of all their activities during a week-long work experience session in a hospital. They are asked to record what they have done in each hour of their working day, and make comments on what they have learned at the end of each day.

Since the information must come directly from the respondents, you must take care to avoid leading questions, excessive guidance and other factors which may cause distortion. You can check the authenticity of the accounts by cross-checking with other people involved in the events, examining the physical records of the events (e.g. papers, documents, etc.) and checking with the respondents during the account gathering process. You will need to transform the collected accounts into working documents that can be coded and analysed.

Diaries are written accounts that usually record events over time. They can take several forms. The most structured form is a response to a series of questions posed by the researcher, prompting the diarist to limit responses to the issues raised by the questions. Both quantitative and qualitative data can be collected this way. Less restricted but still focused in purpose is the log book approach, in which the diarist records the sequence of a specific activity over time, recording tasks undertaken, timing, and possibly reflections about these. The least structured is a diary that is written without any guidance. This is the often the case with personal diaries in the form of historic documents used by historians, but can also be used in social studies as a very open form of gaining contemporary information on attitudes and opinions about life and events.

Conducting Interviews

While questionnaire surveys are relatively easy to organize, they do have certain limitations, particularly in the lack of flexibility of response. Interviews are more suitable for questions that require probing to obtain adequate information.

The use of interviews to question samples of people is a very flexible tool with a wide range of applications. Three types of interview are often mentioned:

1. **structured interview**—standardized questions read out by the interviewer according to an interview schedule. Answers may be closed format;
2. **unstructured interview**—a flexible format, usually based on a question guide but where the format remains your choice; you can allow the interview to 'ramble' to get insights into the attitudes of the interviewee. You can probe deeper into interesting aspects, perhaps revealing issues you had not suspected. No closed format questions;
3. **semi-structured interview**—one that contains structured and unstructured sections with standardized and open-type questions. You can therefore cover standard issues uniformly (such as personal details and basic attitudes) and then expand into more qualitative issues in a flexible way.

Though suitable for quantitative data collection, interviews are particularly useful when qualitative data are required. Interviews can be used for subjects, both general or specific in nature, and even, with the correct preparation, for very sensitive topics. They can be one-off or repeated several times over a period to track developments. As the interviewer and observer, you are in a good position to judge the quality of the responses, to notice if a question has not been properly understood and to encourage the respondent to be full in his/her answers.

Face-to-face interviews can be carried out in a variety of situations: in the home, at work, outdoors, on the move (e.g. while travelling), and they can be used to interview people both singly and in groups. Using visual signs, such as nods, smiles, etc. helps you to get good responses. How you record the responses is a matter of your choice and that of your interviewees. Taking notes can be difficult and is a skill worth practising, as you will be writing at the same time as listening and posing the questions. Making an audio or video recording is easy, but may not be liked by your interviewee. If you rely on your memory, make sure to make notes immediately after the interview, as details are quickly forgotten and you can confuse responses from one interviewee with another.

Focus groups can be seen as a type of group interview, but one that tends to concentrate in depth on a particular theme or topic with an element of interaction. The group is often made up of people who have experience or knowledge about the subject of research, or those that have a particular interest in it, e.g. consumers or customers. You need to be careful to manage the group to allow all the members to provide input.

Telephone interviews avoid the necessity of travelling to the respondents and can therefore be carried out more quickly than face to face. However, you cannot use visual aids to explain questions, and there are no visual clues. For interviewing very busy people, it is best to pre-arrange a suitable time to ring—modern communications technology is making it more and more difficult to talk with an actual person on the phone!

Interviewing by video is now a convenient option that provides a richer experience than contact by telephone. Popular free programs such as Skype, ooVoo, Ekiga, goober, VoxOx, Jitsi and Google Hangouts enable you to see while you talk, and even exchange documents. Group conferences are also possible. Video interviews will take rather more time to arrange than a simple telephone contact, and they are more prone to technical quirks, but they are almost as good as a face-to-face experience, and of course save travelling.

Interviews can be audio recorded in many instances in order to retain a full, uninterpreted record of what was said, but get permission first! However, to analyse the data, you will have to listen to the recording again and possibly transcribe it—a lengthy process if done in full. Recorded and transcribed interviews do not rely on memory and you can repeatedly check what was said. The raw data are also available for different analysis by others.

With every kind of interview, it pays to be well prepared to ensure that you ask all the questions you want to, and to help to keep the interview on track. Figure 7.1.2 is an example of an interview schedule used by Adi Walker in his PhD study about management of international aid organizations. It is carefully structured on the themes to be covered, and equipped with codes to make storage and retrieval for analysis easy. To save space, I have reduced the width of the notes column, which was big enough for Adi to make his notes straight into the schedule. There were also some opening questions to ensure that the interviewee was well informed about the nature of the study and reason for interview, and assurances about anonymity as outlined in the introductory letter.

Observing Without Getting Involved

This is a method of gathering data through **observation** rather than asking questions. The aim is to take a detached view of the phenomena, and be 'invisible', either in fact or in effect (i.e. by being ignored by people or animals). When studying humans or animals, this detachment assumes an absence of involvement in the group even if the subjects are aware that the observation is taking place. Observation can be used for recording data about events and activities, and the nature or conditions of objects, such as buildings or artefacts. This latter type of observation is

Interview code	Respondent code		Respondent name	IHDO	Date / /
Aspect	Theme	Specific/Lead Questions		Notes	Code
Intuition	2.1 Intuition for success	2.1.1 Do you agree with a survey findings that intuition is necessary for successful leadership?			IS1
	2.2 Intuition in practice	2.2.1 In which situations or specific contacts do you feel it is acceptable or relevant for leaders to use intuition in decision-making?			IP1
		2.2.2 In which type of circumference do you think that using intuition appropriate or relevant?			IP2
		2.2.3 What do you think are teachers that influence your leader to use intuition in his/her work?			IP3
		2.2.4 Can you describe any recent positive and/or negative outcomes from your experiences of your leader using intuition in his/her role?			IP4
	2.3 Developing and measuring intuition	2.3.1 How do you think intuition could be developed in leaders: what specific skills, knowledge, experience and attribute, and which approaches are required?			ID1
		2.3.2 How do you think intuition could be measured in leader's performance appraisals?			ID2
Versatility	3.1 Versatility for success	3.1.1 Do you agree with the survey findings that versatility in necessary for successful leadership?			VS1
	3.2 Versatility in practice	3.2.1 Which contacts or situations specifically demand that your leader be versatile?			VP2
Characteristics and competences	4.1 Organisational perspective	4.1.1 Does your organisation have its own set of core leadership characteristics and competences?			COO1
		4.1.2 If so how is this applied to promote and develop successful leadership?			COO2
		4.1.3 Does your organisation have and use any kind of bottom up leadership feedback mechanism?			COO3
		4.14 How effective is this in developing the characteristics and competences of your leader(s)?			COO4
	4.2 Characteristics and competences in practice	4.2.1 The two significantly and unanimously highest rated successful leadership attributes (from 63) were integrity and trustwarthiness. Why do you think this is?			COP1
		4.2.2 Overall, female leaders placed significantly more importance on leadership characteristics for success then their male counterparts, which both sexes were quite balanced when it comes to competences. How would you interpret these findings?			COP2
		4.2.3 Cross, inter and intra-cultural competences are highlighted as factors that affect successful leadership, in which way and to what extent are they promoted and developed in your organisation and/or by your own leader?			COP3
Influences	5.1 Nurturing key success factors	5.1.1 Leader's action logic (strategic approach to facing challenges) alongside their own competences and characteristics are seen as the main influencing factors on success. How are they nurtured and manifest in your context here?			INS1
	5.2 Cultural dimensions	5.2.1 The culture of the organisation, the leader, the team, and the local contact all influence successful leadership. How do these cultural dimensions affect (either positively or negatively) leadership here?			INC1

	6.1 Definitions	6.1.1 What is your understanding of the differences between leadership roles, functions and tasks?		LD1
	6.2 Perceptions of terms and different organisations	6.2.1 Followers see the leadership role as more successful in the hands of an individual leader, against leaders themselves who see this is more as a shared responsibility, what do you think this is?		LP1
Locus of leadership		6.2.2 Humantarian, transitional (mixed), and development organizations differed significantly in their options about where leadership tasks are most successfully handled. Why do you think this is?		LP2
	6.3 Collective vs. individual leadership	6.3.1 What are your opinions about the pros and cons (successfulness) of collective and individual leadership?		LO1
	7.1 Definition	7.1.1 What does professionalism signify for you?		PD1
	7.2 Professionalism in practice	7.2.1 Continuous self-development was rated as the highest element of professionalism that contributes to successful leadership. How is this manifest in your own contact (organisation, country, your leader)?		PP1
Professionalism		7.2.2 Humanitarian, transitional (mixed), and development organisations differed significantly in their options about the importance of certified entry to the aid sector. Why do you think this is? What are your own options?		PP2
	7.3 Professionalism in a future aid sector	7.3.1 Survey respondents stated that professionalism itself needs to be adapted for the sector. What for you should 'aid sector professionalism' look like?		PF1
		7.3.2 How could this 'aid sector professionalism' be applied to result in more successful leadership?		PP2
	8.1 Communication protocols	8.1.1 Would you like a transcript of this focus group discussion to appear prior to its further use?		C1
		8.1.2 Would you like a copy of the Doofocal thesis once it is published?		C2
		8.1.3 May I quote you in my research publications? If so, by name, pseudonym or anohymously?		C3
Wrap up		8.1.4 If I may quote you, what in your organisations PR protocol for this?		C4
		8.1.5 May I contact you again if I need to clearify something? At which email address?		C5
	8.2 FDG participants questions	8.2.1 Thank you! And now do you have any questions or other ideas or thoughts you would like to share with me?		Q1

FIGURE 7.1.2   Interview Schedule
Source: Adi Walker, PhD thesis draft.

often referred to as a survey (not to be confused with a questionnaire survey), and can range from a preliminary visual survey to a detailed survey using a range of instruments for measurement.

Observation is a basic data collecting activity for many branches of research, particularly the natural and technical sciences; for example, observing the results of experiments, the behaviour of models, the appearance of materials, plants and animals. It is also useful in the social sciences where people and their activities are studied. Using observation, you can record how people react to questions, and whether they act differently from what they say or intend. They can sometimes demonstrate their understanding of a process better by their actions than by verbally explaining their knowledge. Observation can be used to record both quantitative and qualitative data.

Observation is not limited to the visual sense. Any of the senses—e.g. smell, touch, hearing—can be involved, and these need not be restricted to the range perceptible by the human senses. You can use a microscope or telescope to extend the capacity of the eye, just as a moisture meter can increase sensitivity to the feeling of dampness. Instruments have been developed in every discipline to extend the observational limits of the human senses.

> For example: A researcher studying primary education methods records every hour how the space is being used in an infants' open-plan classroom. This is done by describing and sketching the location of the activities on a plan drawing of the room, listing the equipment used and the number of children engaged in each activity.

Observations of objects can be a quick and efficient method of gaining preliminary knowledge or making a preliminary assessment of their state or condition. For example, after an earthquake, a quick visual assessment of the amount and type of damage to buildings can be made before a detailed survey is undertaken. On the other hand, observation can be very time-consuming and difficult when the activity observed is not constant (i.e. you can waste a lot of time waiting for things to happen, or so much happens at once that it is impossible for you to observe it all and record it). Instrumentation can sometimes be devised to overcome the problem of infrequent or spasmodic activity, e.g. automatic cameras and other sensors.

Events and objects are usually complicated, so it is necessary that you identify the variables that are to be studied, and to concentrate on these. It is important that you devise a simple and efficient method of recording the information accurately, particularly when recording frequent or fast-moving events. It may not be possible for you to spend hours and days doing observations, so explore the possibility of observing in periods of time, e.g. one hour in the morning, afternoon and evening, or short periods of time (ten minutes) every hour throughout one day, etc. This is a form of sampling, so it is important to use suitable timing to ensure that you achieve a full impression of the activities. Use instrumentation where and when appropriate; those that make an automatic record of their measurements are to be preferred in many situations.

Immersing Yourself in a Situation

This is a process of gathering primary data that not only involves observation, but also **experience** in every sense of the word. It is based on the techniques devised by anthropologists to study the social life and cultural practices of communities by immersing themselves in the day-to-day life of their subjects.

Obviously, the observations must be carried out in the natural setting. You try to 'fit in' as much as possible to see and understand the situation from the viewpoints of the group being studied. At its most extreme, the subjects of the study will not be aware that they are being observed by you. Covert methods can be used to disguise your role of observer.

For example: A researcher wants to find out what the group dynamics are amongst homeless people living on the streets in a large city. He/she poses as a homeless person and joins them in their habitual locations at night, and makes notes on the observations about relationships between the people each day.

In anthropological studies, data are usually collected in phases over an extended period of time. Frequent behaviours, events, etc. tend to be focused on to permit the development of understanding of their significance. Although mostly associated with qualitative approaches, there is no reason why quantitative data are not relevant.

There are a variety of issues that can make the data you collect unreliable or distorted. One commonly mentioned feature is that the behaviour of people might change due to the fact of being knowingly observed. This might not even be a conscious reaction, but could be significant nonetheless. Often it takes time for participants to get used to having an observer around, and they will normalize their behavior after a time. As an observer, you are also exposed to influences that might affect your recording of events. You might have preconceptions that lead you to seek out particular patterns, your memory of events can be inaccurate if you delay recording the data, and you may be influenced by the personalities of those you are observing, e.g. those that are particularly dominant or helpful, or those that are shy and unresponsive. Awareness of these factors will enable you to avoid or minimize them.

Doing Experiments

You can collect data about processes by devising experiments. An **experiment** aims to isolate a specific event so that it can be investigated without disturbance from its surroundings. Experiments are primarily aimed at gaining data about causes and effects—to find out what happens if you make a change, why and when it happens, and how.

Experiments are used in many different subject areas, whether these are primarily to do with how things (objects, substances, systems, etc.) interact with each other, or how people interact with things, and even how people interact with other people. Although experiments are commonly associated with work in laboratories where it is easiest to impose control, you can carry them out in almost any other location. It might not even be possible to move the event to be studied into the laboratory, or doing so might unduly influence the outcome of the experiment. For example, some events in nature or social occurrences are so rooted in their context that they cannot be transferred to the laboratory. The design of experiments and models depends very much on the type of event investigated, the sort of variables involved, and the level of accuracy and reliability aimed at practical issues such as time and resources available.

The first step you must take is to identify the essential factors that create the event so that all others can be eliminated or neutralized, something that may be difficult if the context is complicated and you do not know what all the variables are and how they act or are being acted upon. Data are generated when you isolate and manipulate one or more variables that supply the causes (independent variables) and observe the effects of this manipulation on variables that are affected by the causes (dependent variables).

It is important to check that the assumptions you make, on which you base your experiment, are valid. You can do this by introducing a control group, an identical set-up that runs parallel to your experiment, but in which you do not manipulate the independent variables. A common example of this is the use of placebo pills for one group of patients when gauging the effect of a drug on another group. The condition of the patients taking the placebos acts as a 'baseline' against which to measure the effects of the drug on the condition of the other patients.

Non-Reactive Research Methods

Brian L. Withrow

[...] Reactivity occurs when research subjects change their behavior because they become aware that they are being watched or measured. To overcome this common threat to external validity, researchers may want to observe and measure the behavior of their research subjects in a natural setting. 'Natural setting' does not mean in the woods. It means observing how people behave normally in social situations.

To capture human behavior in natural settings, researchers have developed numerous non-reactive research methodologies. Non-reactive research is a collection of research methods that unobtrusively gather information from research subjects, that is, without their knowledge. Because the research subjects are unaware that they are being observed, they are less likely to change their behavior. Of course there are certain ethical considerations in this research method, but when done carefully, non-reactive research methods can add to the body of knowledge. We will start with an example from my personal research experience.

MAKING RESEARCH REAL 7.2.1—WHO BUYS GASOLINE HERE?

I am always hungry after teaching evening classes. I know that by the time I get home, everyone in the house will be asleep and, with a family as large as mine, there will not be leftovers from supper. So I often stop at a convenience store for a late night snack and sometimes a tank of gasoline. I have two choices of convenience stores: one near the university and another near my house. Both are part of the same chain and they are nearly identical in what they sell and how they are arranged.

Several years ago, while filling my tank at the store near the university, I noticed that the "Pay Inside Cash" button was noticeably worn while the "Pay Outside Credit/Debit" buttons were nearly unused. That evening, I looked at several of the other pumps and found that almost all of the "Pay Inside Cash" buttons were noticeably worn.

The following weekend, my family and I took a trip to the country. On the way, we stopped at the other convenience store, the one nearest my house. The wear on these buttons was the exact opposite from my previous observations at the other store. The "Pay Outside Credit/Debit" buttons were noticeably worn while the "Pay Inside Cash" buttons appeared to be unused. I deduced that customers at the store nearest the university were more likely to pay cash for their gasoline, whereas the customers at the store near my house paid mostly with credit and debit cards.

Never one to let a good observation go to waste, I shared my observations with my research methods students. They arrived at these hypotheses:

- The customers who shop at the store nearest the university are poor and therefore less likely to have access to debit and credit cards.
- The customers who shop at the store nearest my house are well off and therefore more likely to have access to debit and credit cards.

To test their hypotheses, I called the corporate office and spoke to a very nice person in Customer Relations. I informed him of my observations and of my students' hypotheses. He looked into it and called me back in a few days. It seems that we were right. The differences between the customers that frequent these two locations are quite profound, as we can see from the table below.

	Store Near the University	Store Near My House
Tobacco sales	A higher percentage of single cigarette package and single cigar sales.	Fewer overall tobacco sales, but a higher percentage of carton cigarette and expensive cigar sales.
Beer and wine	A higher percentage of single can beer and less expensive wine sales. More malt liquor and wine cooler products.	A higher percentage of six-pack and case beer sales. More premium beer and higher priced wines.
Staffing	Higher levels of staffing because cash customers have to enter the store to complete their gasoline purchase.	Lower levels of staffing because credit/debit customers are not required to enter the store to purchase gasoline.

One might assume that the store nearest my house is the more profitable of the two. After all, this store serves a clientele that has more income for discretionary spending. But according to the customer relations person at the corporate headquarters, the store near the university is more profitable overall. As it turns out, convenience stores earn very little profit on gasoline sales. Most of their profit comes from inside sales, like the snacks I purchase on my way home from class. Customers who purchase gasoline at the pump (with a credit or debit card) are less likely to enter the store, and therefore less likely to make an additional inside purchase. Customers who pay with cash must enter the store and are more likely to make an additional purchase.

The findings from my informal research were based on a non-reactive measure. The research subjects (gasoline purchasers) were not aware that their behaviors had been observed when I first noticed the worn buttons on the gasoline pumps. I was 'observing' their behavior without their knowledge and drawing conclusions from my observations. In this chapter, I will discuss how researchers collect information without the knowledge of research subjects and use this information to understand various human behaviors and social phenomena.

Getting to the Point 7.2.1—Non-reactive research is a collection of research methods that gather information from research subjects without their knowledge. Because the research subjects are unaware that they are being observed, they are less likely to change their behaviors. These techniques are effective for observing behavior in a natural setting.

Non-Reactive Research Methods Basics

Again, non-reactive research is any research process that allows a researcher to gather information on research subjects without their express knowledge or permission. These methods are often described by the kinds of data that they produce. For example, one way to observe human behavior indirectly is to study the physical traces that are left behind. Physical traces are sources of evidence that are based on products of past behavior. There are two ways of measuring physical traces: accretion and erosion. **An accretion measure** determines behavior by evaluating the things people possess. For example, a careful observation of the contents of a trashcan might reveal a research subject's eating, spending, and/or social habits. An **erosion measure** determines behavior by evaluating how things are used by people. For example, a worn grassy area caused by pedestrian traffic might suggest the need for an additional sidewalk. Likewise, the worn buttons on a gasoline pump might suggest something about the clientele of convenience stores.

Other non-reactive techniques seek to capture data, but to capture it in an unobtrusive way. The most prominent technique in this regard is **unobtrusive observation**, which is simply observing behavior without being noticed. For example, a researcher might be interested in observing how people protect themselves against possible criminal acts by observing individuals in a crowded bus station. In this context, individuals will not likely know that they are being observed and will act as they normally do. A researcher could count the number of times that individuals touch belongings with both hands; they could observe how many people are reading, talking, or looking around; they could determine how long people stand in one place before moving. All of these data are captured through simple, unobtrusive observation.

Finally, a researcher may look to retrieve **archival data**, which are data that have already been collected and made available by an individual, group, or organization. Archival data might include publicly available records, such as U.S. Census data. Archival data may also be available through private organizations. For example, a researcher may look at newspaper archives to study how newspaper coverage of homicide has changed over time.

Getting to the Point 7.2.2—Non-reactive research methodologies have in common their ability to collect information from and about human beings without their knowledge. These methods can include evaluating the things people possess (accretion measures), studying how things are used (erosion measures), observing how individuals or groups behave (unobtrusive observation), and analyzing information collected and made available by someone else (archival data).

Types Of Non-Reactive Methods

There are three major types of non-reactive methods: field research, secondary analysis, and content analysis. In field research, the researcher observes behavior(s) in a natural setting. For example, we might observe drug addicts to better understand their behavior. Below is another example of field research in criminal justice practice.

MAKING RESEARCH REAL 7.2.2—FIELD RESEARCH IN CRIMINAL JUSTICE

Joe Robinson, Captain of the Patrol Division of a large metropolitan police department, received a call from Margie Mathonican, the President of the Brook Haven Neighborhood Association. Margie was angry about a growing incidence of newspaper thefts in her neighborhood.

"At first it was just one or two of us every other week or so. Now, half of us don't get a paper most of the time. The newspaper company swears they deliver but somebody keeps stealing them," she explained to Captain Robinson. In the overall scope of issues Captain Robinson deals with on a daily basis, newspaper theft, even serial newspaper theft, is certainly not the most important thing to him. But Ms. Mathonican's neighborhood is populated primarily by retired residents. Many of them have lived there for decades. These sorts of minor incivilities tend to bother these residents and cause them to be fearful. He assured Ms. Mathonican that he would have somebody look into it.

Later that day the Captain met with the patrol command staff. He asked the lieutenant and sergeant who supervised the patrol beat that included the Brook Haven Neighborhood to "look into the newspaper thefts." Eventually the order worked its way to Officer Malcolm Adcock, who is the beat manager for the Brook Haven Neighborhood area.

Officer Adcock spoke with Ms. Mathonican and several of the other residents about the newspaper thefts. There seemed to be no pattern within the thefts other than that they were increasing in overall frequency. Together the residents and Officer Adcock decided to increase patrols during the time between when the newspapers were delivered (around 4:00 am) and when most residents retrieved them from their driveways (around 8:00 am). It did not work. Newspaper thefts increased.

Exasperated, Officer Adcock asked the sergeant to approve overtime money so that he could ask the officers to do some stakeouts around the neighborhood. The sergeant agreed, but "only for a couple of nights." At 3:30 am on a Thursday, seven patrol officers sat in unmarked vehicles in strategic locations throughout the Brook Haven Neighborhood. Thirty minutes later the newspaper delivery man drove through the neighborhood throwing papers from the window of his car.

At 4:15 am one of the officers heard the front door to a house across from him open and shut. He observed a young Labrador Retriever emerge from the house and trot to the front yard of the house across the street. After urinating on a tree the dog picked up the neighbor's paper and dropped it into the storm drain in the curb. The dog repeated this process at several houses and then ran between two houses to the adjacent street. The officer at that street observed the dog retrieve newspapers from front yards and drop them in the storm drain on that street. In all the dog retrieved seven papers and dropped all of them into the storm drain before the dog's owner emerged from the house and whistled. The dog returned to his house and the owner petted him as they went back into the house.

The officers who had observed the dog shone their flashlights down into the storm drains. Sure enough there were dozens of newspapers in them still wrapped in plastic bags. In fact, the storm drains were so full that they had to call the Wastewater Department to come clear them.

Officer Adcock interviewed the dog's owner. He concluded that the newspaper thefts began at about the same time the owner had enough confidence in the puppy to allow it to 'do its business' without supervision. The owner had no idea that the dog was stealing newspapers. The problem was solved when the owner agreed to supervise the dog during its early morning constitutional.

This is an example of field research. It involved the unobtrusive observation of behavior in its natural setting. The fact that the 'culprit' in this case was a dog rather than a human being does not change the nature of this research methodology.

Another unobtrusive method is **secondary analysis**. Here, the researcher analyzes previously collected or archival data. Sometimes the data are collected for the purpose of another research project. Sometimes the data are collected and made public for scholars and practitioners to analyze as they see fit. In either case, a researcher would obtain the data set and analyze all or parts of it. For example, we might use census data to understand the changing demographic characteristics of high crime areas. Here is another example of secondary analysis.

MAKING RESEARCH REAL 7.2.3—SECONDARY ANALYSIS IN CRIMINAL JUSTICE

Janice Armstrong, Warden at the Southern City State Penitentiary, is not at all pleased with a recent proposal from the state legislature to triple bunk prison cells. The state is experiencing severe budget constraints and cannot find enough money to build new or expand existing prisons. Warden Armstrong is worried that increasing the prison population at her facility will lead to more violence among inmates and put her correctional officers at risk.

Warden Armstrong decides to investigate her concerns further. She asks her assistant to gather two pieces of information. First she wants to know the inmate population of the Southern City State Penitentiary each year for the past 20 years. This information resides in the annual reports they submit to the state corrections board. Second, she wants to know the number of correctional officers who were injured on the job through physical confrontation with inmates during the same period. This information resides with the penitentiary's safety officer who keeps these sorts of statistics. Warden Armstrong's assistant provides her with the information and, just as she suspects, as the inmate population increased, the number of officers injured from inmate confrontations also increased. She uses the results of her secondary analysis to argue against an increase in the inmate population at her prison.

A third and final type of non-reactive method is **content analysis**. In a content analysis, the researcher analyzes existing textual information to study human behavior or conditions. For example, we might study the blog posts and website content of a known terroristic organization to predict a future act of terror. Below is another example of content analysis.

MAKING RESEARCH REAL 7.2.4—CONTENT ANALYSIS IN CRIMINAL JUSTICE

Ann Krause, a new Assistant Professor of Technical Writing at State College, is interested in learning more about how police officers communicate in writing. She wants to be able to assist police officers in training with their technical writing skills. To learn more, she decides to conduct a content analysis of existing reports written by police officers.

Professor Krause gathers a sample of 100 case reports from a local police department. She analyzes these reports and identifies the common words and phrases within them. Using this information, she develops a training program to teach police officers how to be more precise in their report writing.

The Benefits and Limitations of Non-Reactive Research Methods

Non-reactive research methods are highly effective in many research situations, such as when a researcher fears that subjects may change their behavior when they know they are being observed. In this and other cases, researchers must find ways to observe behavior covertly. For example, if we want to understand how prostitutes recognize and approach potential clients, it would be best to observe them without their knowledge, lest they act differently or not at all for fear of criminal prosecution. In a previous chapter, we referred to this as reactivity, which is a major threat to internal validity.

Non-reactive methods are also ideal when the researcher wants to observe behavior in its natural setting. It would be very difficult, maybe impossible, for a researcher to recreate certain situations (e.g., an urban riot) in order to observe certain behaviors or phenomena. In this case, going to the field to observe behavior may be the best option. Finally, in some instances, the data that would be helpful for answering a researcher's question may have already been collected by another researcher. For example, if a researcher wanted to compare the crime rate with the unemployment rate, he or she would find both pieces of information already available. Why collect data that has already been collected? Table 7.2.1 summarizes these uses of non-reactive research.

TABLE 7.2.1   The Uses of Non-Reactive Research

- When research subjects are likely to change their behavior after learning that they are being observed
- When the researcher wants to observe behavior in its natural setting and/or as it naturally occurs
- When the data has been previously collected by a different individual, group, or organization

Getting to the Point 7.2.3—Non-reactive research techniques are most effective when research subjects are likely to change their behavior when they know they are being observed, when the researcher wants to observe behavior in its natural setting, and/or when the data the researcher needs is already available.

There are some research situations that do not lend themselves to using a non-reactive technique. First, non-reactive methods are not effective when a researcher wants to understand the motivations, attitudes, and beliefs underlying some behavior. For example, a person may behave courteously toward members of another race, but still hold deep racial prejudices. Simply observing her behavior would not provide insight into her underlying prejudice. Second, there may be ethical issues that prevent the use of non-reactive methods. Behaviors observed in public places are generally considered 'fair game' since the research subject has no expectation of privacy. But in other cases, the research subject may have a right to privacy, which would prevent the use of non-reactive techniques. For example, a researcher could not join a support group of individuals whose loved ones had been murdered in order to study the group without their knowledge. This would be a major breach of research ethics. Finally, and perhaps obviously, non-reactive research involving secondary analysis is not possible when the data simply do not exist.

Validity is often a concern in non-reactive research. Internal validity has to do with whether the researcher's measures accurately portray what is occurring. The internal validity of a non-reactive study is sometimes threatened by a researcher's inability to fully understand the meaning of observed behaviors or by a misinterpretation of the observations themselves. In either case the observations may not actually measure what the researcher alleges they measure. External validity is also a common problem in non-reactive research. Non-reactive research often involves observations of very small populations or geographical areas. It is likely that these sample sizes and the manner in which the sample is selected do not produce a truly representative sample of the overall population. So, any conclusions drawn from non-reactive research may not necessarily be generalizable to a larger population or other similar populations. Table 7.2.2 reviews the circumstances in which non-reactive research would not be appropriate.

TABLE 7.2.2   The Limitations of Non-Reactive Research

- Ineffective for studying the internal motivations, beliefs, and attitudes that underlie some behavior
- Potentially unethical if it involves breaching research subjects' right to or expectation of privacy
- Impossible in cases where secondary or archival data do not already exist or are unavailable
- Non-reactive studies are often hampered by internal and external validity problems

Getting to the Point 7.2.4—Non-reactive research methods are not particularly effective when a researcher needs to understand underlying motivations and belief systems, when research subjects have a right to or expectation of privacy, and when secondary or archival data do not exist.

The Non-Reactive Research Process

As in the previous two chapters, we will take a look at the actual research process to understand non-reactive methods in greater depth. Following the steps of the research process [...], we will review the process by which a researcher might conduct field research, secondary analysis, and content analysis. To illustrate the process further, I will highlight one research study that involved a content analysis. We begin with a general introduction of this case study.

DEVELOPING THE METHOD 7.2.1—A CASE STUDY IN NON-REACTIVE RESEARCH (ECONOMIC CONDITIONS AND IDEOLOGIES OF CRIME IN THE MEDIA: A CONTENT ANALYSIS OF CRIME NEWS)

Several years ago, when my children were young, my wife announced, "From now on, we are not going to watch the evening news! It's too violent." She was right. We were living in a large city at the time and it seemed like the evening news was filled with stories about murder, rape, assault, robbery, and other violent acts. "If it bleeds, it leads" is a common saying in news rooms. In short, crime 'sells.'

The tendency of media outlets to focus on crime and violence has the unfortunate effect of creating false perceptions regarding crime. After a few weeks of watching the evening news, one might think that crime is both common and getting worse. But the statistics indicate that crime is both uncommon and decreasing. In fact, between 2001 and 2012, violent crimes have decreased 13.2 percent.

To better understand media portrayals of crime, Melissa Hickman Barlow, David E. Barlow, and Theodore G. Chiricos set out to conduct a content analysis of media content on crime. They wanted to know whether economic conditions had an effect on how the media portrayed crime. In 1995, they published their research in the scholarly journal *Crime and Delinquency* under the title "Economic Conditions and Ideologies of Crime in the Media: A Content Analysis of Crime News." Their research is an excellent example of content analysis and non-reactive methods in general.

Ask a Research Question

Remember that the method chosen by a researcher should be determined by the research question. Some research questions are best answered by surveys, while others are best answered through experimental methods. Generally speaking, a non-reactive technique should be used when the researcher's presence would affect the research subject's behavior, when the researcher wants to observe behavior in a natural setting, and/or when the data that can answer a research question already exists. Before deciding to use a non-reactive method, however, we have to be certain that we can ethically observe behavior covertly or that we can logistically obtain access to existing data.

A good example of a research question for which a non-reactive method is well suited is: *"What is the average speed of vehicular traffic on a particular residential street?"* Calculating the average speed of vehicular traffic on a residential street would require the use of speed detection equipment, such as RADAR. If RADAR were mounted on an unmarked car parked on the shoulder or on a stationary object near the roadway, most drivers would be unaware that their speeds were being measured. Therefore, they would be unlikely to change their driving speed. The result would be a more accurate measure of vehicular speed on this particular street.

Non-reactive methods are seldom able to document causal relationships and therefore are less commonly used in explanatory research. Indeed, most non-reactive research is of an exploratory or descriptive nature. Exploratory research seeks to document emerging social trends. More often than not, the best way to learn of these trends is to observe them in their natural setting. Descriptive research seeks to describe an existing social process or phenomenon. Again, the best way to describe a social process or phenomenon would be to study it as it occurs naturally. Some examples of exploratory and descriptive research questions for which non-reactive methods are well suited are as follows:

- *How do residents of high-crime neighborhoods carry themselves in public so as to prevent physical confrontations?*
- *What marketing techniques do male and female escorts use when advertising their services in magazines?*
- *Are low-income neighborhoods a major target for sub-prime lenders in the housing industry?*

DEVELOPING THE METHOD 7.2.2—ASKING A RESEARCH QUESTION IN NON-REACTIVE RESEARCH

Barlow et al. (1995) state that their study is exploratory, which would be appropriate for a content analysis. However, the authors propose that political and economic conditions might help *explain* how the media portrays crime. Thus, it appears that there are pieces of this study that are explanatory in nature. In their own words, they wanted to know "whether media accounts misrepresent crime in ways that support dominant class interest and whether misrepresentation changes in relation to conditions in the political economy" (Barlow et al., 1995: 6). In other words, they are asking whether the media reports on the crimes that most of us want to read about because of what is happening at the time both politically or economically.

Getting to the Point 7.2.5—Most non-reactive research is exploratory or descriptive in nature. Because it is often difficult to measure the underlying cause of behavior using a non-reactive research method, non-reactive methods are less often used in explanatory research.

Conduct a Literature Review

One of the things a researcher will look for in a literature review is how previous researchers defined the concepts that they are investigating. This is especially true in non-reactive research. For example, a researcher interested in bullying behavior may choose to observe school children during recess at a local elementary school. But before going to the field, the researcher must first define 'bullying behavior.' This is not as easy as it seems. The threat of physical violence would likely fall within the definition of bullying behavior. But what about ridicule, verbal insults, or peer pressure? As a researcher, you are free to develop your own conceptual definitions and operational measures. But if a previous researcher has developed a workable definition, you may want to use it in your own research.

Reviewing the research of previous researchers who conducted projects similar to yours may also reveal imaginative ways to gain access to certain populations and/or ways of avoiding detection. The mistakes of previous researchers can be instructive, as well. You may recall [...] the discussion of Laud Humphreys' *Tearoom Trade*. Humphreys covertly observed the homosexual behavior of 'publically heterosexual' men and then, posing as a census taker, contacted these men's families afterward to gather additional information. Had the identities of these men been revealed, it could have resulted in considerable personal and legal harm to them. As a result of this case, researchers using non-reactive methods are careful to protect the privacy of research subjects.

DEVELOPING THE METHOD 7.2.3—CONDUCTING A LITERATURE REVIEW IN NON-REACTIVE RESEARCH

In their review of the literature, Barlow et al. (1995) discovered a rather robust research history. They found numerous sources that confirmed what we all suspected: "crime news distorts and/or frames crime and crime control in ways that support institutions of power and authority" (Barlow et al., 1995: 3). In short, there are political and economic interests involved in how crime is portrayed in society. Though the literature suggested that media reports on crime painted a distorted picture of crime, previous research had not determined how these distortions changed with changing political and economic conditions. So, the researchers decided to proceed with their study.

Getting to the Point 7.2.6—Reviewing the research methods and mistakes of previous researchers who used non-reactive research techniques may help define concepts, access certain populations, and avoid detection in non-reactive research.

Refine the Research Question

In non-reactive methods intended to produce exploratory or descriptive information, traditional hypotheses that predict relationships between variables are not usually required. Instead, you may simply want to pose research questions and/or general statements about what you expect to find in the study. In non-reactive methods intended to produce explanatory information, hypotheses are more appropriate. Here are some examples:

> *Ha: The presence of a marked patrol car on an interstate highway reduces speed among vehicles.*

In this case, the researcher would attempt to determine whether the presence of a patrol car leads to a reduction in speed. This would involve non-reactive field research with a speed detector. Here is a hypothesis for explanatory research using secondary data analysis:

Ha: Specified training programs improve the efficiency of police detectives.

To explore this hypothesis, the researcher might investigate the relationship between the amount of training (measured in hours) and the "efficiency of police detectives," measured as the percentage of criminal cases that result in arrest. This would involve the analysis of training records and Uniform Crime Report data. Here is one more sample hypothesis you might find in a content analysis:

Ha: As media coverage of domestic violence increases, public support for stiffer penalties against domestic violence perpetrators increases.

To respond to this hypothesis, the researcher might conduct a content analysis of media coverage regarding domestic violence over time and compare these findings to public opinion polls regarding domestic violence penalties.

DEVELOPING THE METHOD 7.2.4—REFINING THE RESEARCH QUESTION IN NON-REACTIVE RESEARCH

Barlow et al. (1995) predicted that newspaper coverage of violent crime would not only overstate the problem of violent crime, but that coverage would be most intense during times of unemployment and economic stagnation. Thus, they presented two sets of hypotheses at the outset of their article. The first set of hypotheses focuses on the depiction of violent crime in news articles:

Hypothesis 1: The proportion of news articles that are about crimes of violence is significantly larger than the percentage of violent crimes known to the police.
Hypothesis 2: The proportion of news articles on crimes of violence is greater during high-unemployment years than during low-unemployment years.

Hypothesis 3: The proportion of news articles on crimes of violence is greater during periods of economic stagnation than during periods of economic expansion.

The researchers' second set of hypotheses focused on the "characteristics and images of offenders within crime news articles" (Barlow et al., 1995: 10):

Hypothesis 4: A significantly larger proportion of non-White offenders are depicted in the news articles than the proportion of non-White offenders who are actually arrested.

Hypothesis 5: When the social class of the offender is mentioned, the largest proportion of social class descriptions is in the lower class category.

Hypothesis 6: The proportion of negative images of offenders is greater during high-unemployment years than during low-unemployment years.

Hypothesis 7: The proportion of negative images of offenders is greater during periods of economic stagnation than during periods of economic expansion.

In general, the researchers predicted that newspaper coverage would highlight the non-White and lower class characteristics of criminal offenders during times of unemployment and economic stagnation. That is, the media would focus *disproportionately* on non-White, lower class criminal offenders during economically difficult times.

Getting to the Point 7.2.7—In non-reactive research that is exploratory or descriptive in nature, researchers may simply pose research questions and/or general statements about what they expect to find in the study. In non-reactive research that is explanatory in nature, researchers will develop more formal hypotheses.

Define the Concepts and Create the Measures

The process by which a researcher using a non-reactive method develops conceptual definitions is not particularly different from in other types of research. A researcher interested in studying the frequency and intensity of sports violence, for example, might attend numerous sporting events and record instances of sports violence at these events. But before going 'into the field,' he or she would have to define the concept of 'sports violence.' Would it include any aggressive behavior, or just aggressive behavior that exceeds the usual level of competition for the sport? Would it include unusually aggressive behavior between participants in the sporting event, or would it also include aggressive behavior between spectators as well? These questions would have to be answered before proceeding with the field observations.

The challenge in the case of non-reactive research lies in ensuring the validity and reliability of non-reactive measures. Using the above example, it may not be clear whether an instance of aggressive behavior fits our researcher's particular definition of 'sports violence.' This confusion would be even more problematic if there were multiple observers. What if one field observer identified a particular aggressive act as an incidence of 'sports violence,' but another did not? To avoid this problem, researchers may spend considerable time training their research team on what to look for during their observations. For more complicated observations, the researcher may want to assign two to four researchers to observe the same behaviors and then compare their independent conclusions. If all of the researchers reach the same conclusion, they may conclude with more confidence that the measurement strategy is reliable. This is known as **inter-rater reliability** [...].

DEVELOPING THE METHOD 7.2.5—DEFINING CONCEPTS AND CREATING MEASURES IN NON-REACTIVE RESEARCH

Barlow et al. (1995) propose that two elements of crime reporting will vary by economic conditions: (1) the *type* of crime that is reported, and (2) the *characteristics* of offenders that are highlighted. In essence, they define the concept of 'media coverage of crime' in two parts.

To measure the type of crime reported by the media, the researchers differentiated between two types of crime: violent and non-violent. Thus, when the researchers analyzed media content, they coded the content as focusing on violent or non-violent crimes. To measure the characteristics of offenders that are highlighted, the researchers included the following variables: age (under 30 or 30+), race (White or Non-White), gender (Male or Female), social status (Lower,

Middle, or Upper), employment (Unemployed, Blue-collar, or White-collar), marital status (Married or Not married), family history (Positive or Negative), education (High school + or Less than high school), friends (Has friends or Is isolated) and religion (Religious or Not religious). It is likely that the researchers selected these variables because their review of the literature suggested that factors like age, race, and gender influence whether and how criminals are depicted in the media.

The authors conceptualized 'economic conditions' in two ways: (1) the level of unemployment, and (2) the level of economic stagnation. The authors do not explicitly define what they mean by 'high' or 'low' unemployment. Instead, they decided to analyze media coverage during the year 1953, when there was a relatively low unemployment rate (2.9 percent), and 1958, when there was a comparatively high unemployment rate (6.8 percent). Likewise, the authors do not define what they mean by 'economic stagnation' and 'economic expansion.' Again, they decided to analyze media content during years that are popularly known to be periods of economic stagnation. Those years were 1975, 1979, and 1982, during which the unemployment rates were 8.5, 5.8, and 9.7 percent respectively (Barlow et al., 1995: 6).

Getting to the Point 7.2.8—For the most part, the actual process of conceptualization and operationalization is the same in non-reactive research as it is in other research methods.

Design a Method

The principal characteristic of a non-reactive research method is its ability to gather information without the knowledge of the research subjects. In field research, a researcher covertly observes behavior in its natural setting. He or she may also participate in the behavior(s) covertly. In a way, covert observation and participation are like an undercover police investigation, wherein suspects have no idea that their behavior is being observed. The objective of these investigations is to determine whether or not a crime is being committed and, if so, who is culpable. The officers have a hypothesis (i.e., a probable cause) and a conceptual definition of the behaviors they are interested in observing (i.e., criminal violations of the law). Likewise, covert observers should have a very clear idea of what they should be looking for and what observations to make.

Field researchers may consider conducting a pilot or trial run before commencing field research. This involves going into the field, observing, and recording behavior for a short time period to determine whether the method will actually capture the kind of information they need to answer their research question. If it does not, the researcher should revisit earlier steps involving conceptualization, measurement, and design.

Just as in an uncover surveillance operation, it is important to know when to end a field research project. To begin, research is expensive. The more time in the field, the more funds have to be expended for salary, transportation, meals, lodging, and other expenses. Research, especially in the field of criminal justice, can also be dangerous. Having an exit strategy to ensure a researcher will be able to safely disengage is essential. In this regard, researchers should also develop contingencies for events that might interrupt the research process, create ethical problems in research, and/or reveal the researcher's presence. For example, a field researcher observing teenage drinking behaviors may encounter an inebriated research subject about to drive away from the research scene. Should the researcher let the drunken teenager drive?

These and other ethical problems threaten the continuation of the research, not to mention the liability of the researcher and his or her sponsoring agency.

> **Getting to the Point 7.2.9**—Non-reactive field research involves covert observation of and, in some cases, covert participation in the behavior that a researcher is interested in studying. In this method, it is important to prepare for all possible contingencies that may arise in the field and all possible threats to researchers' safety.

Another type of non-reactive data collection is secondary analysis, which is used when the data a researcher is seeking already exists. In a sense, the use of secondary data is not a data or information-gathering method. The data or information has already been gathered. Instead, the researcher searches for available data sets and evaluates whether the data set is useful to his or her research project. There is no shortage of available data sources. Often, researchers who accept federal funding must agree to file their data in an archive managed by the sponsoring government agency. For example, the Bureau of Justice Statistics, part of the U.S. Department of Justice, maintains archival data sets submitted by previous researchers. The Inter-University Consortium for Political and Social Research also maintains an archive of more than 500,000 files of social science research. These files include data on education, crime, substance abuse, and terrorism (ICPSR, 2011).

A researcher using secondary data must ensure that the data set is both relevant and responsive to his or her research question. For example, data collected by a researcher who studied bullies in 1975 would not likely be useful to a contemporary researcher studying cyber bullying. Even if the data are relevant to a researcher's topic, it might not be responsive to his or her specific research question or hypothesis. For example, if a researcher wants to know the average property damage (in dollars) caused by high-speed vehicular pursuits, previously collected data that merely indicated whether or not a high-speed vehicular pursuit resulted in property damage would not suffice. Note that because the data are already available, pretesting and preliminary analyses are not as critical for researchers using secondary analysis. Assuming the available data is responsive to your research question, it does not make sense to conduct a preliminary analysis.

When using two or more data sets, researchers should make sure that there is congruence between the definitions used in each of the data sources. For example, a researcher studying crime cross-nationally should ascertain how each national data set defines crime and ensure congruence between these definitions. Murder in one nation, for instance, may be considered manslaughter in another.

> **Getting to the Point 7.2.10**—The use of secondary data is appealing to most researchers because of its availability and low cost. However, the secondary data must be responsive to the researcher's data needs and research question(s).

Content analysis is a third non-reactive research method. In this technique, a researcher uses previously recorded or written information to study human behavior or conditions. Content analysis is a non-reactive technique because the research subjects are unaware that their behaviors are being observed. In fact, the 'research subjects' may not even be people. For example, television programmers are often criticized for the amount of violence depicted in prime time television programs, especially those programs aired during the 'family hour.' Using a content analysis technique, a researcher might measure the level of violence in these programs. In this case, the 'research subjects' are the television programs.

The most important step in designing a content analysis is to create strong conceptual definitions and operational measures for the phenomena that are being studied. For example, if a researcher wants to develop a list of active terrorist organizations using the internet as a data source, he or she would have to begin with a clear definition of what constitutes a 'terrorist organization.' Failure to clearly define concepts and measure variables will result in not knowing what to look for when data collection commences. In this case, a researcher might define a 'terrorist organization' as a group of two or more individuals who commit violent acts that target innocent civilians for religious, political, or ideological reasons. Using this definition, he or she might go to the internet and look for groups that meet these criteria.

As with field work, it is often a good idea to try out the measures of a content analysis informally to see how they would work when data collection begins in earnest. Pilot tests and trial runs are especially useful when multiple researchers are involved. Differences in how researchers interpret and code data affect both the validity (accuracy) and reliability (consistency) of the information. Using the previous example on terroristic organizations, one researcher may define a group as a terrorist organization, whereas another researcher might not. To reduce such threats to validity, researchers might consider conducting a series of training exercises wherein the researchers and research assistants become familiar with the conceptual definitions and operational measures.

> **Getting to the Point 7.2.11**—The most important step in designing a content analysis is to create strong conceptual definitions and operational measures for the phenomena that are being studied. In some cases, this may involve training research assistants.

DEVELOPING THE METHOD 7.2.6—DESIGNING A METHOD IN NON-REACTIVE RESEARCH

To study media coverage of crime at different periods of time, Barlow et al. (1995) decided to study articles appearing in *Time* magazine. The researchers chose *Time* because it was a widely circulated news magazine and "the best available representative of mainstream media as an influence on and reflection of popular consciousness concerning contemporary social issues" (Barlow et al., 1995: 6). In short, the authors suspected that the magazine might reflect changing public opinion and cultural mores.

An additional consideration for selecting *Time* was that the magazine had a long publication history, making it a suitable source of longitudinal information on changing portrayals of crime. Their selection of this publication enabled the authors to examine "the content of crime news articles ... at different points in the postwar period" and to analyze "media representation of crime in relation to changes and developments in the political economy" (Barlow et al., 1995: 6).

Collect the Data

Again, there is no real data collection that occurs in secondary analysis since the data have already been collected. But for researchers conducting field research and content analysis, data collection can be, and often is, just as rigorous as conducting an experiment or administering a survey. Researchers conducting field research and content analysis often use pre-formatted tables to record information, just as they do in survey research. These are commonly called **coding sheets**. For example, in a content analysis, a researcher might develop a coding sheet to collect data on the frequency and intensity of violent acts depicted on major television networks during the so-called 'family hour' (8–9 pm). The coding sheet might look something like Figure 7.2.1.

Program viewed: _____

Television channel: _____

Date: _____

Day of the week: _____

Researcher: _____

	Mild violence									**Graphic violence**
	1	**2**	**3**	**4**	**5**	**6**	**7**	**8**	**9**	**10**
Time^1										
Time^2										
Time^3										
Time^4										
Time^5										
Notes:										

FIGURE 7.2.1   A Coding Sheet for a Content Analysis of Violence on Television

Each individual row on the coding sheet in Figure 7.2.1 would represent one instance of violence observed on television. Using the scale provided, the researcher would rate the intensity of violence from 1 (mild violence) to 10 (graphic violence). Using the data from this form, the analyst would enter the results into a database. The program's name, television channel, date, day of week, and the name of the research assistant would be entered. Next, the number and intensity of each violent act would be recorded. Using these data, the researcher could develop additional variables to determine overall violence levels for each television program. Recording the research assistant's name and the date would enable the head researcher to reconcile coding mistakes and omissions.

The use of a coding sheet has two important advantages. First, it provides an efficient way to record observations and information. Field researchers or research assistants merely have to glance at the sheet to remember what they are looking for and well-designed tables and blanks provide a space for them to pencil in their observations or data. Second, data sheets provide a concise way to compare the notes made independently by multiple researchers. Such comparisons greatly enhance the reliability of the measure because areas of disagreement can be resolved prior to the analysis.

> **Getting to the Point 7.2.12** – Coding sheets provide researchers with an effective and efficient mechanism for recording information in content analyses and field observations.

There are some additional considerations that apply when taking field notes. The most accurate way to record observations in the field is to videotape them. Unfortunately, the overt presence of a camera might cause research subjects to change their behavior. In this sense, the field research would no longer be non-reactive. When possible, researchers can use a video recorder covertly, but they may do so only in public settings where individuals have no right to or expectation of privacy. The same applies to an audio recording. Since hiding video and audio recorders usually poses ethical challenges, many field researchers opt simply to make notes of their observations on paper or a laptop computer while they are observing in the field. This method of recording observations is less accurate, but also less likely to cause a change in the subjects' behavior. The final recording option is for the researcher to make notes after leaving the field, away from the presence of the research subjects. This option is the least reactive, but also the least accurate. Ultimately, researchers must find the appropriate balance between accuracy and obtrusiveness.

> **Getting to the Point 7.2.13**—Recording observations is a central part of field research. Video- and audio-taping observations are the most accurate recording methods, but they are also the most reactive and, in some cases, they are also unethical. Recording observations on paper or a laptop are the least accurate, but also the least reactive. Researchers must find the appropriate balance between accuracy and obtrusiveness.

DEVELOPING THE METHOD 7.2.7—COLLECTING DATA IN NON-REACTIVE RESEARCH

During the years on which their analysis focused (1953, 1958, 1975, 1979, and 1982), Barlow et al. (1995) chose articles that were "completely or substantially about crime, criminals, or criminal justice." Only articles that were at least one column in length were chosen. A total of 175 articles met these criteria. Technically speaking, this would be a purposive sample. Only the articles on crime appearing during the years they chose were included in their analysis. The researchers in this case did not use a random sample presumably because no sampling frame existed. In this case, the researchers would have had to identify every article on crime ever published in a written and widely circulated American news source during the selected years. Though this was arguably possible, it was not feasible or efficient. Instead, the researchers chose a representative news source to study media portrayals of crime. Though their sampling strategy was not random, it provided important insight into human behavior.

Once the articles were identified, the researchers turned their attention to conducting the actual content analysis. To do this, they read each article and collected information related to the variables in which they were interested. First, the researcher differentiated between articles about violent and non-violent crime, which was relatively straightforward. Collecting information about the characteristics of the offenders was a bit more problematic. Few articles included information on each of the 10 variables in which the researchers were interested. For example, very few of the articles included information about the offenders' education, relationships with friends, religion, or marital status. In short, their analysis did not yield information about every variable related to the characteristics of the offender.

Although they did not report this detail in their article, it is likely that Barlow et al. (1995) used coding sheets as they read each of the articles. These coding sheets probably contained a list of each variable along with its attributes. As they read the article, the researchers likely made notes on these coding sheets to facilitate subsequent data entry and further analysis. For example, if the article contained a reference to the offender's college degree, the researcher would place a check mark beside the attribute 'High school +' under the education variable.

It is also likely that the researchers read through a few of the articles at first to see if their data collection procedure would work, though, again, they do not report this. For example, if none of the articles contained information about the offender's religion, it would be futile to include this variable in the analysis. If, on the other hand, most of the articles contained information about the offender that they had previously not considered important (e.g., history of drug use), they might have considered adding this variable to their analysis.

Analyze the Data

Secondary analysis is typically of a quantitative nature, though this is not always the case. Criminal justice researchers, for example, might analyze quantitative data from the National Crime Victimization Survey to study longitudinal trends in certain types of criminal victimization. Many quantitative analyses using secondary data use sophisticated statistical techniques, in addition to basic descriptive statistics. Some data sets, however, lend themselves to qualitative research. During the 1930s, for example, interviews were conducted with surviving ex-slaves as part of the Federal Writers' Project. In this case, a researcher might conduct a qualitative data analysis of the interview material to understand how African Americans experienced a life in bondage.

The analysis of field observations and content materials is typically qualitative in nature, but, again, this is not always the case. Researchers might be interested in studying how pedestrians act when approached by panhandlers. In this instance, they might describe different pedestrian responses and/or explore how the race, gender, and age of the panhandler influence pedestrian responses. These descriptive and exploratory accounts would be more subjective and qualitative.

It is also possible to conduct quantitative analyses of data gathered through field observations and content analysis. In our hypothetical research scenario involving a content analysis of violence on primetime television, for example, information on the frequency and intensity of violence on television was collected in numerical form. Likewise, field observations of bullying behavior on a school playground could involve the calculation of frequency and intensity of bullying behaviors.

DEVELOPING THE METHOD 7.2.8—ANALYZING DATA IN NON-REACTIVE RESEARCH

Barlow et al. (1995) did not include information in their article about how they prepared the information for analysis or how they actually analyzed the content of the articles. It is likely that they entered the information from the coding sheets into a computer program like Excel or SPSS for subsequent analysis. This assumption is based on their use of tabular data within the text of their article.

In terms of their analysis strategy, the authors relied on a statistical technique called chi square analysis, in which they compared percentages. [...] For example, they compared the percentage of articles that focused on violent crime during periods of high unemployment with the percentage of articles that focused on violent crime during periods of low unemployment.

Getting to the Point 7.2.14—The analysis of secondary data, field observations, and content material can be qualitative or quantitative. The type of analysis depends on the research question and the type of data that are available.

Interpret the Results

At this stage of the research process, researchers evaluate their research question or hypothesis using the findings of their research. It is often the case in non-reactive research that there is room for multiple interpretations. Secondary data analysis, for example, might have produced strange and interesting findings that neither support nor refute a research hypothesis. In the case of field work, where researchers often enter the field with research questions rather than strict hypotheses, interpretations of the data can be more subjective. In either case, it is always a good idea to entertain various interpretations of the data and to be up front about the limitations of the data and study design.

DEVELOPING THE METHOD 7.2.9—INTERPRETING THE RESULTS IN NON-REACTIVE RESEARCH

Overall, Barlow et al. (1995) found what we already suspected: crime news is not at all representative of actual crime trends. In other words, the media does not do a very good job of creating an accurate or representative picture of crime. These researchers were somewhat successful in developing a connection between economic conditions and the types of crime stories reported in the media. However, the causal connection between economic conditions and crime reporting is really not known. For example, there is really no way to determine whether the economic conditions existing at the time actually influenced the editorial decision to report on a particular type of crime. These types of causal connections are often difficult in non-reactive research.

Though insightful, this particular study was not without its flaws. Some of these were pointed out by the researchers. First, one could argue that the sample of articles is not representative of the overall media. Other news outlets reported on crime during this period and may have taken a different position from the editors at *Time*. Second, the articles included in the analysis were from five years within a 29-year time frame. *Time*'s editorial philosophy and idea of what was newsworthy may have changed numerous times during this time frame. Finally, though the authors show some relationship between economic conditions and distorted depictions of crime, their analysis did not allow them to substantiate why this might be the case.

Getting to the Point 7.2.15—The data or information produced by many non-reactive research techniques often can be interpreted in multiple ways. As such, researchers using these techniques should entertain various interpretations. They should also be up front about the limitations of their study.

Communicate the Findings

Again, if researchers want to engage members of the scholarly community, they should publish their findings in an academic journal or through a university press. If, however, researchers want to appeal to a broader audience, they should publish their findings in a trade journal or other mass media outlet.

In terms of the actual content of the material published, non-reactive research methods may use tables, charts, and graphs if the analysis is quantitative in nature. If the analysis is qualitative in nature, the findings might be written up more as a 'story.' For example, a content analysis of violence in video games might produce quantifiable results like the frequency or intensity of violent acts within the video game. But telling the story of how adolescents behave before, during, and after playing violent video games might also be part of the report.

DEVELOPING THE METHOD 7.2.10—COMMUNICATING THE RESULTS OF NON-REACTIVE RESEARCH

Barlow et al. (1995) chose to publish their results in a peer-reviewed academic journal. They are university scholars and as such benefit from the publication of their results in this medium. Publishing their research in an academic journal also enhances the scientific value of their major finding that the media provides a distorted portrayal of crime. There has been much debate over media bias between traditional media outlets like ABC, NBC, and CBS and cable news outlets like Fox News, CNN, and MSNBC. Presenting research on this subject in a respected academic journal removes it from the usual muckraking that happens between media providers and contributes actual evidence to the debate around media bias.

Getting to the Point 7.2.16—Researchers may use tables, charts, and graphs to communicate the results of their non-reactive research if the analysis is quantitative in nature. Alternatively, if the analysis is qualitative in nature, they may tell a 'story' using quotes, examples and descriptions.

Final Thoughts

Non-reactive research taps into something that already exists–an everyday behavior, a scientific database, a written document–to answer a research question or test a research hypothesis. Let me illustrate with one final example. I have a reputation for being a bit frugal. In fact, you might even call me a tightwad. I analyze each dollar I spend to be sure I am getting the best deal. As our children reached driving age, I noticed that our automobile insurance premiums rose rather substantially. So I made an appointment with my friendly insurance representative.

As it turns out, we were getting a pretty good deal. We had numerous discounts for safe driving, driver training, and having multiple cars insured by the same company. We even got a discount because our children made good grades. During my conversation with the insurance agent, the agent made a curious comment: "Your rates are also lower because your credit rating is high." Apparently, people with poor credit tend to be poor drivers. The relationship is not causal. But there is enough of a correlation between the two variables that insurance companies in some states establish insurance premiums based in part on an individual's credit history. In this case, and many others, information collected for one purpose may be used for an entirely different purpose. And this is not unlike non-reactive research. The key is to make sure the use of existing information answers the research question and is ethical.

References

Barlow, M.H., Barlow, D.E., and Chiricos, T.G. (1995). Economic conditions and ideologies of crime in the media: A content analysis of crime news. *Crime and Delinquency, 44*, 3–19.

ICPSR (Interuniversity Consortium for Political and Social Research) (2011). Retrieved from www.icpsr.org (accessed March 2013).

Conclusion

This chapter presented information regarding various methods that can be used to answer a research question or test a hypothesis. Researchers may elect to collect primary data via methods such as interviews, surveys, or focus groups, or utilize data/information that already exists via nonreactive methods such as secondary data analysis or content analysis. Following is a list of examples of secondary data sources of criminal justice–related data. There are several benefits and limitations associated with utilizing each method. Choosing the best option for a study depends on several factors, including the type of data needed to address a research question or hypothesis, availability of data/sources, and researcher capabilities and preferences for specific data analytic techniques.

Secondary Sources of Criminal Justice–Related Data

Center for Victim Research: https://victimresearch.org/
The Violence Project, Mass Shooter Database:
https://www.theviolenceproject.org/mass-shooter-database/
National Archive of Criminal Justice Data: https://ojjdp.ojp.gov/archived-data
National Criminal Justice Reference Service: https://www.ncjrs.gov/
National Incident-Based Reporting System: https://www.fbi.gov/services/cjis/ucr/nibrs
The Bureau of Justice Statistics: https://www.bjs.gov/
National Crime Victimization Survey: https://www.bjs.gov/index.cfm?ty=dcdetail&iid=245
Office of Juvenile Justice and Delinquency Prevention: https://ojjdp.ojp.gov/statistics

Sourcebook of Criminal Justice Statistics: http://www.albany.edu/sourcebook/
Uniform Crime Reports: http://www.fbi.gov/about-us/cjis/ucr/ucr

Chapter 7 Reflection Questions

1. Identify and describe the various methods that can be used for collecting primary data. What are the advantages and disadvantages of each method?
2. Differentiate between closed and open questions. What are the advantages and disadvantages of each?
3. List and describe the three major types of nonreactive methods researchers use. What are the benefits and limitations of utilizing these methods?
4. Visit the webpage for The Violence Project:
   https://www.theviolenceproject.org/mass-shooter-database/

Explore the website, gain access to the Mass Shooter Database, and address each of the following: (1) Who/what agency collected this data? (2) What research methods were used to gather this data (surveys, official agency data, etc.)? (3) Which population/sample was used? (4) List five research questions that could be answered from this source of information.

5. Repeat the exercise in question 4 using any of the other sources of secondary data referenced.
6. Imagine that you are preparing to administer a survey to residents in your city concerning citizen encounters with the police. Write a series of questions that include four of the open and closed question designs and use Survey Monkey (www.surveymonkey.com) to administer your survey. Collect and present responses from at least ten friends/classmates.

Executing the Research

Chapter 7 Exercise: Collect the Data (or Identify Sources of Data)

1. Restate your research question or hypothesis.
2. Identify at least one primary and one secondary data source you could use to answer the research question or hypothesis you developed in earlier exercises. For your secondary references, be sure to provide a specific data source and link. Which source(s) do you propose to use within your study?
3. Identify your measures. How are they operationalized within your source of secondary data? How could you operationalize them in your primary research?

4. Which source of data do you feel would be the best suited to answer your question or hypothesis? Why? Identify which primary **and/or** secondary source you will use (or propose to use) in your study. (Note: You can choose one or a combination of both.)

5. Prepare to collect the data. If your primary source involves conducting an interview or survey, develop those questions or that instrument. Identify the population you will interview or survey and specify how you will choose a sample from this population. How many subjects will you interview or survey? If you are completing a research proposal only, stop here. If you are executing your research project at this time, complete the next step.

6. Collect the data (be sure that you consult with your institution's IRB prior to obtaining any nonpublic or sensitive data). Only complete this step if you are carrying out the search at this time.

Data Analysis

Introduction

The data analysis process may commence after the information has been collected. The type of analysis employed is dependent on the type of data collected. A researcher must first consider whether the data collected is qualitative (categorical or text), quantitative (numeric), or a combination of both. This chapter presents information about the techniques that can be used to analyze both types of data. Although not discussed in this chapter, it is important to recognize that many social scientists use statistical computer program packages for analyzing data. A computer software package called SPSS (Statistical Software Package for the Social Sciences) is commonly used to analyze categorical and quantitative data, and a qualitative computer software package called Nvivo can be used by social science researchers to analyze qualitative data. Advances in technology, such as Artificial Intelligence (AI), Machine Learning (ML) and Natural Language Processing (NLP) are also available and increasingly being utilized as tools for data analysis in the social and behavioral sciences.

As you read this chapter, pay careful attention to different types of analysis, including univariate (examining the dispersion of characteristics of one variable) and bivariate statistics (examining whether there is a relationship between two variables). Presenting information on multivariate statistical analysis (i.e., regression) is beyond the scope of this text.

Descriptive Statistics for Quantitative and Qualitative Research

Lawrence T. Orcher

The function of descriptive statistics is to summarize data. Statistics that summarize, such as averages and percentages, help researchers understand and communicate data.

While statistical analysis is much more closely associated with quantitative research than with qualitative research, both qualitative and quantitative researchers often use descriptive statistics to describe demographic data (i.e., background data) such as data on age, income, and educational status of participants in their research. For instance, both quantitative and qualitative researchers might report the average age of the participants and the percentage who graduated from high school.

For the analysis of the main data generated by their studies, however, qualitative researchers use judgmental methods [...], while quantitative researchers use statistical methods [...]

The coverage of statistical methods in this chapter and the following ones is highly selective. In this chapter, only descriptive statistics that are widely used by beginning researchers are presented. It is assumed that students reading this book have taken or will take a statistics course in which the computation of statistics is covered. Hence, computational procedures are described in this chapter only when a discussion of computations will help in understanding the meaning of the statistics being discussed.

Describing Nominal Data

Nominal data refers to data that consist of names or labels that contain words, not numbers. For instance, when researchers ask participants to name their country of birth, they will reply with names such as the United States, Mexico, and Canada. The most straightforward way to analyze nominal data is to calculate percentages.

A *percentage* indicates the number of participants per 100 that have some trait or characteristic. Thus, if there are 1,000 participants and 800 said that they were born in the United States, a researcher could report that "80% were born in the United States."

Example 8.1.1 illustrates the use of percentages in describing demographics in a *qualitative* study. Note that not only are percentages reported, but the underlying numbers of cases (i.e., *n*) are also provided in the example. Reporting the *n* associated with each percentage, often in parentheses as shown in the example, is widely recommended by statisticians.

> **Example 8.1.1**
> *Percentages used to describe demographics in a qualitative study*
> With regard to religion, 38% identified as "Catholic," 33% identified as "Protestant Christian" (e.g., Evangelical, Pentecostal, etc.), and 24% identified as "other." Thirty-eight percent reported not finishing high school, 38% reported finishing high school or GED, and 19% reported having and college degree. In terms of annual income, 57% of both men and women reported earning $25,000 a year and 76.2% reported having insurance coverage in Massachusetts (e.g., Mass Health Coverage).[1]

To examine the relationship between two nominal variables, quantitative researchers build a two-way table called a *contingency table*, in which the rows are for one variable and the columns are for the other. Example 8.1.2 shows a contingency table in which the rows are for the nominal variable called "gender," and the columns are for the nominal variable called "level of agreement" with some proposition. The percentages in the example show a relationship between the two variables, such that women are much more likely to strongly agree than men, while men are much more likely to strongly disagree than women.

> **Example 8.1.2**
> *A contingency table for the relationship between gender and level of agreement (two nominal variables)*

	Strongly Agree	Agree	Disagree	Strongly Disagree
Men ($n = 50$)	10.0% ($n = 5$)	20.0% ($n = 10$)	30.0% ($n = 15$)	40.0% ($n = 20$)
Women ($n = 200$)	60.0% ($n = 120$)	25.0% ($n = 50$)	12.5% ($n = 25$)	2.5% ($n = 5$)

---

1   Moreno, O., & Cardemil, E. (2013). Religiosity and mental health services: An exploratory study of help seeking among Latinos. *Journal of Latina/o Psychology*, 1, 53–67. doi: 10.1037/a0031376

Describing Ordinal Data

Ordinal data put participants in *rank order* from high to low. For instance, a researcher could ask a teacher to rank order his or her students based on their reading comprehension skills by giving a rank of "1" to the most skilled student, a rank of "2" to the next most skilled, and so on. While it is simple to have participants ranked, rank orders convey little information. For instance, suppose Jennifer is ranked "1" in reading comprehension while Jake is ranked "2." These ranks indicate only that Jennifer is somewhat higher than Jake, but they do not indicate how much higher she is. For instance, the ranks of "1" and "2" could be obtained if Jennifer is only very slightly higher than Jake, but they could also be obtained if Jennifer is much higher than Jake.[2]

Because ordinal data provide such limited information, researchers tend to avoid collecting such data. If collection of ordinal data is unavoidable for some reason, the data can be summarized with the *median* and *interquartile range*, which are descriptive statistics covered later in this chapter.

Describing Ratio and Interval Data

Ratio data have three characteristics. First, they tell "how much" of a characteristic each participant has. For instance, if a researcher measures a participant's height and finds that it is 72 inches, the researcher knows that the participant has 72 units of a characteristic called height. Second, in ratio data, all units represent the same amount of the characteristic. For instance, each of the 72 inches that the participant has is the same amount of height as each other inch. Put another way, the difference between 60 and 61 inches represents the same difference in height as any other two adjoining values such as between 70 and 71 inches.[3] Third, ratio data have a true, absolute zero point. For instance, on a tape measure, researchers know where the zero point is, and it is meaningful because it truly represents "nothing," or in this example, it truly represents "no height."

Interval data have the first two characteristics of ratio data. For instance, scores on objective tests indicate how much skill examinees have (not just their rank orders), and it is reasonable to assume that the differences represented by adjoining test scores are all equal. For instance, getting 10 right instead of 9 right on a multiple-choice test is about the same amount of difference as getting 20 right instead of 19 right.

---

2   The obvious alternative to ranking students on the basis of their reading comprehension skills is to administer an objective test of reading comprehension that yields scores. The scores would tell "how much" skill each student has and thereby indicate how much superior Jennifer is to Jake (e.g., 1 point superior would indicate little superiority). Objective achievement tests yield *interval data*, which is the next topic in this chapter.

3   Note that ordinal data discussed earlier do not have this characteristic. For instance, the amount of difference represented by ranks of 1 and 2 might be small while the difference represented by ranks of 2 and 3 might be large.

Unlike ratio data, interval data do not have a true zero. For instance, if a participant gets zero correct on a multiple-choice vocabulary test, this result indicates that he or she has no knowledge of the vocabulary on that test. It does not indicate that the participant has absolutely zero knowledge of any vocabulary. Hence, a zero on an objective test such as a multiple-choice vocabulary test is arbitrary (not absolute) because the zero point depends on what particular items were written and their difficulty.

While the distinction between ratio and interval data is useful for some mathematical purposes, both types of data are analyzed in the same way using the statistics described in the rest of this chapter in the social and behavioral sciences.

The Mean and Median

By far, the most commonly used descriptive statistic for summarizing ratio and interval data is the *mean*, which is a particular type of average. Computationally, it is the average obtained by summing all the scores and dividing by the number of scores. Examples 8.1.3 and 8.1.4 show the use of the mean to describe some demographic data that might be reported in a report on either quantitative or qualitative research. One of the symbols for the mean (i.e., *M*) is shown in Example 8.1.4. The upper-case *M* should be used if the data are for an entire population, while the lowercase *m* should be used if the data are for only a sample drawn from a population.[4]

> **Example 8.1.3**
> *Means used to describe demographics*
> The mean age of the participants was 17.4, and the mean number of years of schooling completed was 11.8.

> **Example·8.1.4**
> *Means used to describe demographics (with the symbol M)*
> The average female participant was younger (*M* = 34.5 years) than the average male (*M* = 38.2 years).

The mean has a major drawback for certain data sets. Specifically, if there are some extreme scores on one side of a distribution without extreme scores on the other side to balance them out, the mean may be pulled too far toward the side with the extreme scores to be representative of the typical participant. When the distribution of a set of scores is unbalanced in this way, the distribution is said to be *skewed*. Consider the scores in Example 8.1.5, in which the distribution is skewed to the right because there are two very high scores (350 and 400), which are very different from the others. The mean equals 60.4, which is higher than the scores for all but two of the 25 participants. Clearly, the mean has been pulled up by the two extreme cases, which resulted in an average that is unrepresentative of the typical case.

---

4   Note that all statistical symbols should be italicized to distinguish them from letters of the alphabet. For instance, "M" is a letter of the alphabet while "*M*" is the symbol for the mean.

Example 8.1.5
A skewed distribution of scores (mean pulled toward the high scores)
The mean number of times marijuana was reportedly smoked in the month before the 25 adolescents began treatment at a drug rehabilitation facility was 60.4.
Note: The raw scores used to compute the mean, which would not be reported in a research report are: 20, 20, 25, 26, 27, 28, 30, 31, 31, 32, 32, 32, 32, 34, 35, 35, 37, 37, 40, 40, 45, 46, 46, 350, 400.

When the mean is highly influenced by a small number of participants who are very different from most participants, there are two ways to handle the problem. First, the mean could be calculated both with and without the extreme cases with an explanation that the distribution is skewed, as illustrated in Example 8.1.6.

Example 8.1.6
Sample statement illustrating the use of the mean with a skewed distribution
The mean number of times marijuana was reportedly smoked in the month before adolescents began treatment at a drug rehabilitation facility was 60.4. Two of the 25 cases had extreme scores: 350 and 400, creating a skewed distribution. With these two cases removed in order to summarize the behavior of the vast majority of the cases, the mean is only 33.1.

An alternative to reporting the mean when a distribution is highly skewed is to report a different average: the *median*. The median is always the score that has 50% of the cases above it and 50% below it.[5] To obtain an approximate median, simply count up from the lowest score until half the cases are reached. The score at that point is the median. For the raw data in Example 8.1.5, approximately 50% of the cases are above and 50% are below a score of 32. Thus, the median is 32, which seems reasonably representative of the typical case since 23 of the 25 participants had scores ranging from 20 to 46. Note that the median is an alternative to the mean for describing skewed distributions because it is insensitive (i.e., not pulled in one direction or the other) to small numbers of extreme scores.

The Standard Deviation and Interquartile Range
The mean and median are averages that indicate the typical score for interval and ratio data. While an average is a key feature of any set of scores, it does not provide a thorough description because it does not indicate the amount by which the scores vary. To understand this, consider the following two sets of scores, which differ greatly in their variation.

Scores for Group A: 100, 100, 100
M for Group A = 100.0
Scores for Group B: 0, 100, 200
M for Group B = 100.0

---

5   Note that the mean of 60.4 in Example 8.1.5 has 23 cases below it and 2 cases above it. This illustrates that the mean does not always have half above and half below.

Both sets of scores have an average of 100.0. However, the two sets of scores are quite different. Specifically, Group A's scores have no variation because they are all the same. The scores for Group B, in contrast, are much more varied, ranging from 0 to 200. Because variation is an important characteristic of a set of scores, statisticians have developed descriptive statistics called *measures of variation*,[6] which describe how variable a set of scores is. The two that are most frequently used are described next.

The *standard deviation* is the statistic that is almost always used to describe variation when the mean has been used as the average. To get a general understanding of the standard deviation, consider the three sets of scores in Example 8.1.7 on the next page. All three sets have a mean of 10.00. However, for Set X, the standard deviation equals 0.00 because all the scores are the same (i.e., they have no variation). Set Y has greater differences among the scores than Set X, which is reflected by a standard deviation of 1.49. In contrast, Set Z has the most variation (i.e., larger differences among the scores), which is reflected by a standard deviation of 7.45. Thus, the general rule is the more variation, the larger the standard deviation will be. According to most statistics textbooks, the symbols for the standard deviation are S when describing a whole population or s when describing a sample from a population. In reports published in journals, researchers often use SD or sd for populations and samples, respectively.

Example 8.1.7
Standard deviations for three sets of scores that have the same mean but differ in their variation
Set X: 10, 10, 10, 10, 10, 10, 10, 10, 10 (no variation among scores)
　　SD for Set X = 0.00
Set Y: 8, 8, 9, 9, 10, 11, 11, 12, 12 (modest variation)
　　SD for Set Y = 1.49
Set Z: 0, 0, 5, 5, 10, 15, 15, 20, 20 (more variation)
　　SD for Set Z = 7.45

The standard deviation was designed specifically to describe what is known as the *normal distribution* (also known as the *bell-shaped curve*), which is shown in Figure 8.1.1. This type of distribution is widely found in nature. Specifically, most of the cases are near the middle, and it

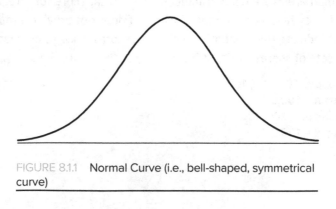

FIGURE 8.1.1　Normal Curve (i.e., bell-shaped, symmetrical curve)

6　*Averages* are sometimes called *measures of central tendency*.

is symmetrical, with fewer cases to the left (where there are lower scores) and to the right (where there are higher scores). Because it is symmetrical (not skewed), the mean is an appropriate average for such a distribution.

Suppose a researcher calculated a mean and standard deviation for a normal distribution and obtained $M = 40.00$ and $SD = 10.00$. These results would indicate that a score of 40 is in the middle of the distribution and that by going out 10 points on each side of the mean (to scores of 30 and 50), about 68% of the cases would be included. This is illustrated in Figure 8.1.2.

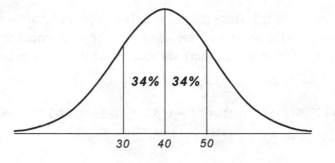

FIGURE 8.1.2   Normal Curve with a Mean of 40.0 and a Standard Deviation of 10.0 Points

The inclusion of 68% within a standard deviation unit of the mean is always true as long as distribution is normal. Put another way, when a researcher calculates the mean and standard deviation of a normal distribution, he or she is calculating the number of points that one must go out on both sides of the mean to gather up about 68% of the cases. Consider Example 8.1.8 in which two normal distributions with different amounts of variation are described.

> **Example 8.1.8**
> *Statistics and interpretations for two normal distributions of scores*
>
> **Statement in a research report for Study A**: "The mean equals 70.0, and the standard deviation equals 5.0."
>
> **Statement in a research report for Study B**: "The mean equals 70.0, and the standard deviation equals 20.0."
>
> **Interpretation by an individual who read both reports**: "The middle of both distributions is the same at a score of 70, while the distribution in Study B is much more variable than the distribution in Study A. In Study B, a researcher needs to go out 20 points from the mean (to 50 and 90) to gather up the middle 68% of the cases. In Study A, the researcher needs to go out only 5 points from the mean (to 65 and 75) to gather up 68% of the cases."

Just as the mean is unduly influenced by highly skewed distributions (with some extreme scores on one side but not the other), the standard deviation is, also. Thus, for a highly skewed distribution another measure of variability known as the *interquartile range* should be used instead of the standard deviation. The definition of the interquartile range is the range of the middle 50% of the scores. To understand this, consider these scores:

   5, 10, 11, 12, 15, 16, 17, 20

Ignoring the bottom 25% of the scores (the bottom two scores) and the top 25%, the middle 50% is left, as shown here:

   ~~5, 10,~~ 11, 12, 15, 16, ~~17, 20~~

The range of the middle 50% is 5 points (16 –11 = 5). Thus, the interquartile range is 5 points.[7]

   To see that the interquartile range is a measure of variation (differences among scores), consider this set of scores, which has much more variability than the previous set.

   0, 10, 14, 20, 35, 44, 55, 60

Ignoring the bottom 25% of the scores and the top 25%, the middle 50% is left, as shown here:

   ~~0, 10,~~ 14, 20, 35, 44, ~~55, 60~~

The difference between 44 and 14 is 30 points, so the interquartile range is 30, which is much higher than the simple range of 5 for the entire set of scores.

   Now consider a highly skewed set of scores, with a score of 476, which is much higher than the rest of the scores.

   0, 10, 14, 35, 40, 44, 55, 476

If the mean and standard deviation were calculated for this set of scores, they would be greatly pulled up by the extreme score of 476, which skews the distribution. However, because the top (and bottom) 25% of the scores are ignored in the calculation of the interquartile range, it is a good measure of variability for such a highly skewed distribution. Ignoring the bottom 25% of the scores and the top 25%, the middle 50% is left, as shown here:

   ~~0, 10,~~ 14, 35, 40, 44, ~~55, 476~~

Because the difference between 44 and 14 is 30, the interquartile range is 30 points, which was calculated without using the very high score of 476 that skewed the distribution.

   Consider Example 8.1.9 in which two normal distributions with different amounts of variation are described.

Example 8.1.9

Statistics and interpretations for median and interquartile range

---

7   A more precise method of calculation, typically covered in statistics courses, is needed to calculate the precise interquartile range when there are tie scores at the points that identify the middle 50%. For instance, if there were three individuals with a score of 11 and four individuals with a score of 16, the method shown here would yield only an approximate answer.

Statement in a research report for Study X: "The median equals 25.0, and the interquartile range equals 2.0."

Statement in a research report for Study Y: "The median equals 25.0, and the interquartile range equals 10.0."

Interpretation by individual who read both reports: "In both studies the typical score is 25 with 50% of the cases above a score of 25 and 50% of the cases below a score of 25. However, the scores in Study Y are much more variable than the scores in Study X. In Study Y, one needs to go out 10 points on each side of the median to gather up the middle 50% of the scores, while in Study X, one needs to go out only 2 points on each side of the median to gather up the middle 50% of the scores."

A reminder: When analyzing interval and ratio data, if the distribution is not highly skewed, the mean and standard deviation should be used. When there is an obvious skew, the descriptive statistics that should be used are the median and the interquartile range.

Correlational Statistics for Quantitative Research

Lawrence T. Orcher

Basic correlational methods allow researchers to examine and describe relationships between pairs of scores for a group of participants. For instance, consider the two sets of scores in Table 8.2.1. They are correlated because individuals who are high in geography are also high in history. For instance, Allison has the highest geography score, and she also has the highest history score. At the same time, Wilber has the lowest geography score, and he also has the lowest history score. This type of relationship (with highs associated with highs *and* lows associated with lows) is known as a *direct relationship* (also known as a *positive relationship*).

TABLE 8.2.1   Scores on Geography Knowledge and History Knowledge Tests

Participant	Geography Score	History Score
Allison	10	12
Fernando	9	10
Betty	4	9
Brian	5	8
Wilber	3	6

While there is a direct relationship between geography and history in Table 8.2.1, it is not perfect because there are exceptions to the direct trend. For instance, Brian has a higher score than Betty in geography, but he has a lower score than Betty in history. In other words, the two sets of scores do not put the individuals in the exact same rank order.

Lawrence T. Orcher, "Correlational Statistics for Quantitative Research," *Conducting Research: Social and Behavioral Science Methods*, pp. 167–170. Copyright © 2016 by Taylor & Francis Group. Reprinted with permission.

A statistic known as a *correlation coefficient* provides a precise number to express the strength of a relationship. A correlation coefficient can range from 1.00 for a direct relationship with no exceptions (i.e., a perfect, direct relationship) to 0.00 for the complete absence of a relationship (i.e., no pattern). For the scores in Table 8.2.1, the value of the correlation coefficient is 0.90, which is close to a perfect 1.00 and thus, is very strong.

A correlation coefficient has a negative value when the relationship between two sets of scores is inverse. In an *inverse relationship* (also known as a *negative relationship*), those who score high on one variable tend to score low on another variable. For instance, consider the scores in Table 8.2.2 for the variables called "self-concept" and "depression." Those who are near the top of the group in self-concept (such as Joey with a score of 10) are near the bottom of the group on depression (such as Joey with a score of 2). At the same time, those who are near the bottom of the group on self-concept (such as Mike) tend to be near the top of the group on depression.

TABLE 8.2.2   Scores on Self-Concept and Depression

Participant	Self-Concept Score	Depression Score
Joey	10	2
Francine	8	1
Juanita	9	0
Brian	7	5
Wilber	7	6
June	6	8
Hector	4	8
Mildred	1	9
Mike	0	9

For inverse relationships, correlation coefficients can be as low as –1.00, which indicates a perfect, inverse relationship (with no exceptions to the trend). The relationship in Table 8.2.2 is not perfect because there are exceptions such as Mildred being higher than Mike on self-concept, while she is tied with Mike on depression. Still, the relationship is strong. Computing the correlation coefficient for these data yields a coefficient of –0.86.

While there are a number of different types of correlation coefficients, by far the most widely used is the *Pearson product-moment correlation coefficient*, developed by a statistician named Karl Pearson. The symbol for his statistic is a lower-case, italicized *r*. Often, it is simply called the Pearson *r*.[1]

---

1   For all practical purposes, consumers of research can interpret all types of correlation coefficients in the same way that a Pearson *r* is interpreted.

In review, a correlation coefficient (such as the Pearson *r*) describes two characteristics of a relationship. First, it indicates whether a relationship is direct (indicated by a positive value of *r*) or inverse (indicated by a negative value of *r*). Second, a correlation coefficient indicates the strength of the trend. The relationships between the scores in Tables 8.2.1 and 8.2.2 are strong because are there only a few minor exceptions to the trends. Hence, the values of the Pearson *r* for them are near 1.00 (i.e., 0.90 and −0.86).

It is easier to spot a relationship when relationships are strong with only a few minor exceptions, such as in Tables 8.2.1 and 8.2.2. For instructional purposes, these relationships intentionally were made to be very strong. In practice, researchers often find weaker relationships. Example 8.2.1 shows some values of the Pearson *r* for direct (i.e., positive relationships) recently reported in published reports of research.

Example 8.2.1

Values of r for direct relationships recently reported in published research

For the relationship between satisfaction with life and social support, researchers reported a Pearson *r* of 0.39, indicating a weak tendency for those individuals who have *more* alcohol use disorders to experience *more* psychological distress.[2]

For the relationship between compulsive buying behavior and perceived social status associated with buying, researchers reported a Pearson *r* of 0.60, indicating a strong tendency for individuals who have *more* compulsive buying behavior to be *more* likely to perceive buying as an indicator of social status. (p. 307)[3]

For the relationship between self-esteem and ethnic identity among Hispanics, researchers reported a Pearson *r* of 0.30, indicating a weak tendency for those who have *more* self-esteem to also have *more* ethnic identity. For whites, however, the researchers reported a very weak relationship, with *r* equal to only 0.11. (p. 341)[4]

Example 8.2.2 shows some values of the Pearson *r* for inverse (i.e., negative relationships) recently reported in published reports of research.

Example 8.2.2

Values of r for inverse relationships recently reported in published research

2   Glaesmer, H., Grande, G., Braehler, E., & Roth, M. (2011). The German version of the Satisfaction With Life Scale (SWLS): Psychometric properties, validity, and population-based norms. *European Journal of Psychological Assessment, 27*(2), 127–132.
3   Yurchisin, J., & Johnson, K. K. P. (2004). Compulsive buying behavior and its relationship to perceived social status associated with buying, materialism, self-esteem, and apparel–product involvement. *Family and Consumer Sciences Research Journal, 32*, 291–314.
4   Negy, C., Shreve, T. L., Jensen, B. J., & Uddin, N. (2003). Ethnic identity, self-esteem, and ethnocentrism: A study of social identity versus multicultural theory of development. *Cultural Diversity and Ethnic Minority Psychology, 9*, 333–344.

For the relationship between marital satisfaction and depressive symptoms among women, researchers reported a Pearson r of −0.36, indicating a weak tendency for those who are *more* satisfied with their marriages to have *less* depression. (p. 310)[5]

For the relationship between satisfaction with life and depression, researchers reported a Pearson r of −0.44, indicating a moderately strong tendency for those who have *more* satisfaction with life to have *less* depression. (p. 130)[6]

For the relationship between GPA and frequency of bullying other students, researchers reported a Pearson r of −0.11, indicating a very weak tendency for those who have *higher* GPAs to engage in *less* bullying behavior. (p. 60)[7]

Describing the Strength of a Relationship

A value of a Pearson r that is very close to 1.00 (e.g., 0.95) would be described as a "very strong" direct or positive relationship. Likewise, a value of a Pearson r that is very close to −1.00 (e.g., −0.95) would be described as a "very strong" inverse or negative relationship.

In contrast, a positive value of a Pearson r that is very close to 0.00 (e.g., 0.15) would be described as a "very weak" direct or positive relationship. Likewise, a negative value of a Pearson r that is very close to 0.00 (e.g., −0.15) would be described as a "very weak" inverse or negative relationship.

Table 8.2.3 provides some descriptive labels for beginning researchers to use when interpreting correlation coefficients. Because there is no universally accepted set of descriptors, the descriptors in Table 8.2.3 are merely suggestive. They represent what this author has found to be typical descriptors for varying values of r based on extensive reading of published research reports.

TABLE 8.2.3　Suggested Descriptors for Various Values of the Pearson r

Value of r	Suggested Descriptor	Value of r	Suggested Descriptor
0.85 to 1.00	Very strong	−0.85 to −1.00	Very strong
0.60 to 0.84	Strong	−0.60 to −0.84	Strong
0.40 to 0.59	Moderately strong	−0.40 to −0.59	Moderately strong
0.20 to 0.39	Weak	−0.20 to −0.39	Weak
0.00 to 0.19	Very weak	−0.00 to −0.19	Very weak

5　Cano, A., & Vivian, D. (2003). Are life stressors associated with marital violence? *Journal of Family Psychology, 17,* 302–314.

6　Glaesmer, H., Grande, G., Braehler, E., & Roth, M. (2011) The German version of the Satisfaction with Life Scale (SWLS): Psychometric properties, validity, and population-based norms. *European Journal of Psychological Assessment, 27,* 127–132.

7　Chapell, M., Casey, D., De la Cruz, C., Ferrell, J., Forman, J., Lipkin, R., Newsham, M., Sterling, M., & Whittaker, S. (2004). Bullying in college by students and teachers. *Adolescence, 39,* 53–64.

Inferential Statistics for Quantitative Research

Lawrence T. Orcher

Inferential statistics are used by researchers who have sampled from a population. To understand the need for inferential statistics, first consider Example 8.3.1, in which researchers did not sample and thus, their results could not be in error due to sampling.

Example 8.3.1
A study with no sampling error

A team of researchers asked all 725 clients currently receiving services at a counseling center whether they would recommend the center to others. Forty-four percent of the clients answered "Yes." Because the researchers did not sample, their results were not subject to sampling errors. Thus, the researchers could state with confidence that at the time the survey was taken, only a minority (44%) would recommend the center.

Next, consider Example 8.3.2, in which the researchers sampled in order to have a more manageable number of participants in their study.

Example 8.3.2
A study with sampling error

A team of researchers drew a random sample of 225 of the 725 clients currently receiving services at a counseling center and asked the sample whether they would recommend the center to others. Forty-four percent of the clients answered "Yes." Because the researchers sampled, they realized that their results were subject to sampling errors and might not be accurate. More specifically, the researchers could not be sure whether only 44% of all 725 clients would recommend the center. This uncertainty existed because the researchers posed the question to only 225 of the 725 clients.

Margins of Error

The inferential statistic that is needed to aid in the interpretation of the results in Example 8.3.2 is a *margin of error*, which is based primarily on the number of participants. Specifically, the larger the sample of participants, the lower the margin of error will be. For the information in Example 19.2, the margin of error that will give the researcher 95% confidence is 6.5 percentage points.[1] In other words, the researchers can have 95% confidence that the true percentage in the population is within 6.5 percentage points of 44%. This means that they can be 95% confident that the percentage in the population who would recommend the center is somewhere between 37.5% (i.e., 44% minus 6.5%) and 50.5% (i.e., 44% plus 6.5%). In other words, an allowance of 6.5 percentage points should be made because of random sampling, which does not always produce precisely correct results.

A margin of error must have some degree of confidence associated with it. The 95% confidence level mentioned in the previous paragraph is probably the most commonly used. Standard statistical computer programs will also produce the 99% margin of error. As it turns out, for the data in Example 8.3.2, the 99% margin of error is 8.5 percentage points, meaning that the researchers can be 99% confident that the true percentage in the population who would recommend the center is somewhere between 35.5% and 52.5%. Notice that for a larger degree of confidence, a larger margin of error must be used. In this example, the margin is 6.5 percentage points for 95% while it is 8.5 percentage points for 99% confidence.

Standard statistical software will also produce margins of error for means. For instance, for a given sample, a mean might equal 44.0 and the 95% margin of error might equal 3.0 points. A researcher with such a result could be 95% certain that the true mean in the entire population is somewhere between 41.0 (i.e., 44.0 minus 3.0) and 47.0 (i.e., 44.0 plus 3.0).

The Null Hypothesis

The *null hypothesis* needs to be considered any time a researcher has sampled at random and finds a difference. Specifically, the null hypothesis states that a difference may have been created by errors caused by random sampling, These errors are simply called *sampling errors*.[2] Consider Example 8.3.3 in which there is a difference between percentages that might have been caused by sampling error.

> **Example 8.3.3**
> *A study with a difference that may have been caused by sampling error*

---

1   Margins of error are standard statistics that can be computed with any of the widely used statistical programs. The same is true of the other inferential statistics in this chapter.
2   Another way to state the proposition is that "there is no true difference." Statisticians define a "true difference" as the difference that would be obtained if an entire population and not a sample had been studied.

A team of researchers drew a random sample of 200 male students and a random sample of 200 female students and asked how they planned to vote on an issue that will be presented in an upcoming student body election. They obtained this result: 60% of the men and 40% of the women planned to vote "Yes." The researchers cannot be certain of the apparent "gender gap" because they sampled instead of polling the entire population. In this case, the null hypothesis says that the 20 percentage point difference between 60% and 40% was created by sampling error, which is the same as saying that there is no true difference between the populations of men and women; a difference exists in the study only because of random samples that are not representative. The null hypothesis for differences between percentages can be tested with the chi-square test, which is discussed below.

It is important to distinguish between "research hypotheses," which state what researchers predict they will find, and the "null hypothesis," which always asserts that the difference may have been created by sampling error. Thus, a research hypothesis is a judgmental hypothesis made by a researcher, while the null hypothesis is a statistical hypothesis that comes into play whenever random sampling has been used.

The Chi-Square Test

The *chi-square test* is a test of the null hypothesis involving differences among percentages. To understand it, consider again the results in Example 8.3.3. What could have created the 20-point difference in that example? From a statistical point of view, the answer is that there are two possible explanations:[3]

1. There is no difference in the population, but a difference was found in the sample due to random sampling, which created sampling error. This explanation is called the *null hypothesis*.
2. There is a difference between men and women in the population, and this difference has been reflected in the results obtained with the sample. This explanation is called the *alternative hypothesis* because it is an alternative to the null hypothesis.

The chi-square test establishes a probability that the null hypothesis is a correct hypothesis. For the example being considered, it establishes the probability that random error alone would produce a 60%–40% split, given a total sample size of 400. If the probability is sufficiently low, the null hypothesis can be rejected, leaving only the alternative hypothesis as a viable alternative. As it turns out, a standard statistical software program will indicate that for the data in the example being considered, the probability is less than 1 in 1,000. By almost all standards, this would be considered a very low probability. Because this is so low, the null hypothesis should be rejected because it is a very unlikely explanation for the 20-point difference.

---

3   From a nonstatistical point of view, it is also possible that the researcher deliberately or inadvertently created some type of bias such as by asking the question using different words with women than were used with men. Care in conducting a study can rule out such an explanation.

In the social and behavioral sciences, any probability of 5 or less in 100 is usually regarded as sufficiently low to reject the null hypothesis. Thus, for instance, if the probability that the null hypothesis is true is .05 in a given study, the null hypothesis would be rejected as probably being an incorrect hypothesis. In other terms, the decision is being made that the difference under consideration is probably not a chance (i.e., random) difference.

The .05, .01, and .001 levels are the most commonly reported in published research. However, any probability of .05 or less (such as .04, .03, .02, and so on) would lead to rejection of the null hypothesis by conventional standards.

When the null hypothesis for a specific difference (such as 40% versus 60%) has been rejected based on an inferential statistical test such as the chi-square test, researchers declare the difference to be *statistically significant*. In other words, saying that a difference is "statistically significant" is equivalent to saying that "the null hypothesis has been rejected as an explanation for the difference."

The symbol for chi-square is χ,^{2} and the symbol for probability is *p*. Example 8.3.4 shows a statement from a published research report using these symbols. Note that chi-square is not a descriptive statistic. Instead, it is an inferential statistic that was used to get the probability, which is the end result of a significance test. In other words, showing the value of chi-square is like showing the answer to a substep in a math problem. It is not presented for interpretation by consumers of research.

Example 8.3.4
Expression of statistical significance based on a chi-square test

Compared with males, light and nondrinkers, female heavy drinkers [HD] endorsed the highest percentage of lifetime depression rates [female HD = 33.3% male HD = 9.1%; χ^2 (5, 581) = 12.28, *p* = .031].[4] (p. 163)

For all inferential tests, including the chi-square test, degrees of freedom (*df*) must be calculated and used to obtain the probability. In Example 8.3.4, the numbers 5 and 581 are the degrees of freedom for this example. They are indicated by being in parentheses. Often, values of the degrees of freedom are indicated by using the symbol *df*, as in *df* = 5, 581. Regardless of the way the degrees of freedom are shown, showing them is similar to showing the answer to a substep in an arithmetic problem. It is not a value to be interpreted. Only the value of *p* leads to an interpretation.[5] In short, the only value of interest to the typical consumer of research for the results such as those in Example 8.3.4 is the probability level of *p* = .031, which is less than *p* = .05. When the value of *p* is low, *p* indicates that it is unlikely that the null hypothesis is true. If something is unlikely to be true, then we reject it.

---

4   Based on results reported in Cheng, A. W., Lee, C. S., & Iwamoto, D. K. (2012). Heavy drinking, poor mental health, and substance use among Asian Americans in the NLAAS: A gender-based comparison. *Asian-American Journal of Psychology, 3*, 160–167. doi: 10.1037/a0028306
5   Before computers, researchers had to calculate the values of chi-square and the degrees of freedom and use these two values when reading a probability table to get the probability for a particular difference.

The *t* Test

The *t* test is widely used to test the null hypotheses relating to means and correlation coefficients.

The *t* Test for Means

A major use of the *t* test is to obtain the probability that sampling error created the difference between two means (i.e., the probability that the null hypothesis is true for the difference between two means).[6]

Example 8.3.5 shows how the results of two *t* tests might be reported. Note that *p* >.05 means that "*p* is greater than .05" (odds are more than 5 in 100). By conventional standards, *p* must equal or be less than.05 for the null hypothesis to be rejected. Also note the use of *ns*, which is a standard abbreviation for "not significant."

> **Example 8.3.5**
> *Statement regarding statistical significance based on a t test for the difference between pairs of means*
>
> A national sample of 620 married and 531 single adults was surveyed. The difference in average number of minutes per day spent exercising (*m* = 7.1 for married and *m* = 8.1 for singles) was not statistically significant (*t* = .59, *p* > .05, *ns*), and, therefore, the null hypothesis was not rejected. In contrast, the difference between the averages in time spent in social activities (*m* = 46.7 for married and *m* = 69.0 for singles) was highly significant (*t* = 3.26, *p* < .001). Thus, the null hypothesis was rejected for this difference. (p. 267)[7]

The *t* test can be used for testing the difference between only one pair of means at a time. The use of ANOVA for testing one or more pairs in a single analysis is discussed later in this chapter.

The *t* Test for Correlation Coefficients

When a correlation coefficient is based on a sample from a population, the null hypothesis says that there is no true correlation (i.e., whatever degree of correlation that exists in the sample is not present in the population as a whole). For instance, the correlation coefficient in Example 8.3.6 was obtained with a national sample of 3,551 adults. The null hypothesis says that the *r* for this sample was created by the random sampling process and that in the population as a whole there is no relationship. Because the probability that this is true is less than 5 in 100, the null hypothesis was rejected by the researcher. Note that standard statistical software programs automatically report the associated value of *p* whenever a correlation coefficient is computed.

---

6   If there are two medians instead of two means to be compared, a *median test* can be used to determine statistical significance. This test is interpreted in the same way as a *t* test.
7   Loosely based on results reported in Lee, Y. G., & Bhargava, V. (2004). Leisure time: Do married and single individuals spend it differently? *Family and Consumer Sciences Research Journal, 32*, 254–274. Note that it is customary to report the standard deviations immediately after reporting the means.

Example 8.3.6
Statement regarding statistical significance of a correlation coefficient based on a t test

The correlation between perceiving their work to be meaningful and reporting that they have learning opportunities was direct, moderately strong, and statistically significant ($r = .53$, $p < .05$). **Thus, the null hypothesis that there is no true relationship** between these variables was rejected. (p. 407)[8]

Note that while the value of t is almost always reported when reporting on the significance of the difference between two means, it is customary to omit the value of t when reporting the significance of a correlation coefficient.

The *F* Test (ANOVA)

Frequently, researchers have more than two values of the mean whose significance needs to be determined in a single comparison. An extension of the t test known as an F test might be used in this case. The F test is conducted using a set of procedures known as Analysis of Variance (ANOVA). Like the t test, the F test is a test of the null hypothesis. It can be used to determine the significance of the set of differences among any number of means.

For instance, consider a research team that conducted an experiment in which three methods of reinforcing behavior were administered to first-grade students. Group A received verbal praise for raising their hands during lessons, Group B received token rewards for the same behavior, while Group C was designated as the control group, which received no special reinforcement. Suppose that the means in Table 8.3.1 were obtained. (p. 121)[9]

TABLE 8.3.1   Mean Number of Times Students Raised Their Hands during a Lesson

Group A (Verbal Praise)	Group B (Token Rewards)	Group C (Control)
$M = 6.00$	$M = 5.50$	$M = 2.33$

There are three differences associated with the means in Table 8.3.1. They are

1. Group A (6.00) has a higher mean than Group B (5.50),
2. Group A (6.00) has a higher mean than Group C (2.33), and
3. Group B (5.50) has a higher mean than Group C (2.33).

---

8   Loosely based on results reported in Voydanoff, V. (2004). The effects of work demands and resources on work-to-family conflict and facilitation. *Journal of Marriage and Family, 66*, 398–412. Note that it is customary to report the means and standard deviations for the two variables that were correlated before presenting the results of the significance test.

9   This example is based on one in Patten, M. L. (2012). *Understanding research methods: An overview of the essentials* (4th ed.). Glendale, CA: Pyrczak Publishing.

The null hypothesis says that the set of differences immediately above is the result of sampling error (i.e., there is no true difference). In effect, it says that the random sampling that was used to draw students for each of the three groups produced three groups of students that differed in their classroom behavior only by the luck of the draw (e.g., by chance, Group A consisted of students who tend to raise their hands more often).

The F test can be used to test the null hypothesis. As it turns out, the F test for the data in Table 8.3.1 yields a probability of less than .05 ($p < .05$). This means that it is unlikely that the set of three differences, as a whole, was created at random. Thus, the null hypothesis is rejected and the set of differences is declared to be statistically significant.

Note that the significant value of F only indicates that the set of differences as a whole probably has some nonrandom differences. To determine which specific pairs of means are significantly different from each other, another test known as a *multiple comparisons test* (based on the t test) should be used. A multiple comparisons test indicates the following:[10]

1. Group A is *not* significantly superior to Group B because p is greater than.05 ($p > .05$),
2. Group A is significantly superior to Group C because p is less than.05 ($p < .05$), and
3. Group B is significantly superior to Group C because p is less than.05 ($p < .05$).

The type of F test just considered is conducted using a set of procedures known as a *one-way ANOVA*, which can be found on any standard statistical software. Also, such software will automatically conduct multiple comparisons tests.[11]

Statistical versus Practical Significance

Statistical significance indicates only that whatever difference(s) is/are being considered is/are unlikely to have been created at random (by chance). Thus, a statistically significant difference is not necessarily of any practical significance.

A major consideration in determining practical significance is *cost in relation to benefit*. Suppose an experimental group achieves, on the average, a statistically significant five points more than a control group on a multiple-choice achievement test but that the treatment given to the experimental group costs substantially more than the conventional treatment in terms of time, money, and effort. These costs would call into question whether the benefit (five points) is great enough to justify the cost.

Another important consideration is whether statistically significant results suggest actions that are questionable from an ethical or legal standpoint. If so, this would limit practical significance.

---

10   There are a number of multiple comparisons tests that usually yield similar results. The one used for these comparisons is known as *Scheffé's test*. Multiple comparisons tests are also known as *post hoc tests*.
11   Such software will also perform more advanced analysis of variance procedures, which are beyond the scope of this book.

The third and final major consideration is *acceptability*. Actions suggested by a statistically significant result might be perfectly ethical and legal but be unacceptable to clients, students, teachers, social workers, and others who have a stake in whatever process is being examined. Objections by major stakeholders limit practical significance.

Looking Ahead to Data Analysis for Qualitative Research

Lawrence T. Orcher

The purpose of this chapter is to describe basic methods for analyzing qualitative data, which can be used when writing the Analysis section in a preliminary research proposal. Preparation of a research proposal is the topic of the next chapter.

Because most beginning researchers who choose the qualitative approach to research collect and analyze interview data, this chapter is written on the assumption that responses to interview questions will be analyzed. The principles and guidelines presented here, however, also apply to other types of data such as that generated by focus groups, participant observation, and nonparticipant observation.

The Intermingling of Data Collection and Data Analysis

In quantitative research, it is traditional to collect all data from all participants before beginning the data analysis, which is almost always done with statistical methods. In contrast, preliminary, informal data analysis is usually performed during the process of collecting the data in qualitative research. This is illustrated by three practices commonly employed by qualitative researchers. First, while collecting data, qualitative researchers often engage in *memo writing*, in which the interviewers make notes of their own reactions and interpretations of the data as they are being collected.[1] These memos are then considered later during the more formal data analysis.

---

1   Memo writing is also widely used during subsequent, more formal data analysis sessions in which researchers also make notes on their own reactions to the data, their changing interpretations, and the basis for their interpretations.

Second, as data are being collected, qualitative researchers reflect on it (a form of informal analysis) and use their reflections as a basis for modifying questions, formulating additional questions, and even changing the line of questioning in order to obtain more useful data.

Third, qualitative researchers often collect data from additional participants until they reach the point of *data saturation*. This refers to the failure of additional cases to add new information beyond what was collected from previous participants. The point of data saturation can be determined only by informal data analysis during the course of the interviews.

Selecting a General Approach to Data Analysis

To guide their data analysis, qualitative researchers usually select a general, overarching approach. Some approaches are well delineated with specific data-analytic techniques that guide the analysis. Others are more philosophical and provide only a general orientation within which specific analytic techniques (described later in this chapter) are applied. Two general approaches are described next. These descriptions are necessarily brief. (Each approach would require an entire book to describe it fully, much like an entire book would be necessary to fully describe basic statistical methods employed by quantitative researchers.)

The Grounded Theory Approach

Perhaps the most frequently used approach is *grounded theory*.[2] At first, the term "theory" in "grounded theory" can be a bit misleading because it does not refer to a theory of human behavior. Instead, it refers to an *inductive method* of analysis that can lead to theories of behavior. In the inductive approach, which is characteristic of all qualitative research, the results (including "theories") emerge through consideration and analysis of the data. In other words, qualitative researchers start with the data and develop theories based on the data (i.e., grounded in the data).

Put another way, qualitative researchers start with the "pieces" (such as the things the participants say about being abused by their spouses) and make generalizations from them (such as a psychological theory that accounts for why some spouses are abusive and others are not).[3]

The first step in the grounded theory approach is called *open coding*. In this step, segments of the transcripts of the interviews are examined for distinct, separate segments (such as ideas or experiences of the participants) and are "coded" by identifying them and giving each type a name. For instance, in a study of adolescent delinquents, each statement referring to overt aggression by the participants might be coded with a certain color highlighter. Subcategories should also be developed, when possible. For instance, "overt aggression" might have two

---

2   See the seminal work on this approach by Strauss & Corbin (1990) for more information.

3   In contrast, many quantitative researchers start with an existing theory or deduce a new one from existing information and collect data to test the theory. They typically do not examine the data they collect in order to develop completely new theories. Thus, quantitative researchers use a *deductive method*. Put another way, quantitative researchers start with a theory and gather "pieces" of information to test the theory.

subcategories: "overt aggression toward peers" and "overt aggression toward adults, including parents and teachers."[4] Preliminary notes on any overarching themes noticed in the data should also be made at this point.

The second step in the grounded theory approach to data analysis is called *axial coding*. At this stage, the transcripts of the interviews and any other data sources, such as memos written during data collection, are reexamined with the purpose of identifying relationships between the categories and themes identified during open coding. Some important types of relationships that might be noted are (1) temporal [X usually precedes Y in time], (2) causal [X caused participants to do Y],[5] (3) associational [X and Y usually or always occur at about the same time but are not believed to be causally connected], (4) valence [participants have stronger emotional reactions to X than to Y], and (5) spatial [X and Y occur in the same place *or* X and Y occur in different places].

In the final stages of the grounded theory approach to analysis, qualitative researchers develop a *core category*, which is the main overarching category under which the other categories and subcategories belong. They also attempt to describe the *process* that leads to the relationships identified in the previous stage of the analysis. A process description should describe how the categories work together (or in opposition to each other) in order to arrive at the conditions or behaviors contained in the core category. Such a process description can be illustrated with a diagram, a possibility illustrated later in this chapter.

Consensual Qualitative Approach

Hill's Consensual Qualitative Research approach (CQR), which emphasizes having several individuals participate in the analysis, has specific steps designed to lead to a consensus regarding the meaning and interpretation of the results.[6]

Example 8.4.1 shows a brief description of the consensual approach in a form that might be included in a brief preliminary proposal for research.

> **Example 8.4.1**
> *A brief description of the Consensual Qualitative Research approach to data analysis for a brief, preliminary research proposal*
>
> Hill et al.'s (1997) Consensual Qualitative Research approach (CQR) specifies a series of procedures to code the data across participant responses. First, the primary research team will follow these two steps for each case: (a) assign chunks of data to domains (or themes)

---

4   In keeping with the inductive approach, categories and subcategories should be suggested by the data during data analysis, not developed prior to analyzing the data. Categories and subcategories developed at this stage should be regarded as preliminary and subject to change during the remainder of the analysis.

5   Participants' claims that "X caused me to do Y" should be viewed with caution because participants sometimes are not sufficiently insightful into the causes of their behavior. Qualitative researchers need to look at the full context of the behavior and make judgments about the reasonableness of a causal connection.

6   For more information, see Hill, C. E. (Ed.). (2011). *Consensual qualitative research: A practical resource for investigating social science phenomena*. Washington, DC: American Psychological Association.

and (b) develop abstracts within domains based on core ideas (i.e., essence of participant responses). In each step, the primary team members will initially complete the tasks independently and work together to develop a consensus version of the product (i.e., one that is agreeable to everyone on the research team). Then, an auditor who will not be involved in the previous procedure will examine the domains and core ideas to ensure that the data were accurately represented. Any inaccuracies identified by the auditor will be reconsidered by the primary team for possible changes. Following the audit, the primary research team will follow these two steps: (a) identify categories (i.e., clusters of core ideas across cases) based on core ideas in each domain and (b) determine the frequency of categories across cases. Again, the primary research team initially will work independently and then work together to form consensus products in each of the two steps, and the auditor will examine the categories and their frequency to verify their accuracy.[7]

Specific Techniques for Analysis of Qualitative Data

Below are some commonly used techniques for analyzing qualitative data.

Enumeration

Enumeration is counting how many respondents mentioned each important construct (such as a feeling, behavior, or incident). Some researchers use the information in writing up their results, as illustrated in Example 8.4.2. Using terms such as "many," "some," and "a few" based on enumeration data makes it possible to discuss the results without cluttering them with specific numbers and percentages for each type of response.[8]

Example 8.4.2
Sample use of enumeration to guide in the description of the results

Enumeration data were used in the results section that follows. Specifically, the word "many" indicates that more than 50% of the participants gave a particular type of response, the term "some" indicates that between 25% and 50% did so, while the term "a few" indicates that less than 25% did so.

---

7   Based on Noonan, B. M., Gallor, S. M., Hensler-McGinnis, N. F., Fassinger, R. E., Wang, S., & Goodman, J. (2004). Challenge and success: A qualitative study of the career development of highly achieving women with physical and sensory disabilities. *Journal of Counseling Psychology, 51,* 68–80.

8   Another approach to enumeration is to count how many times a particular response is given regardless of how many participants gave it. For example, one participant might give the response five times during the interview, another participant might give it three times, and another might give it zero times. The total count for this example is eight. Counting how many times something is said could be reported in the results section of a research report along with how many participants said it, which would provide consumers of research with two types of information.

Selecting Quotations

It is very common to present quotations from participants to illustrate points made in the results section of a qualitative research report. Preliminary decisions should be made on which quotations to use during data analysis. Perhaps the most common criterion for the selection of quotations is that they are somehow "representative," which might be indicated by enumeration data discussed above (e.g., the more frequently something is said, the more likely that it is representative). Another criterion is the degree to which a quotation articulates main ideas in the results. For instance, many participants might report the same thing, but one might state it more clearly and forcefully. A third criterion is intensity. Statements made with strong words or higher-than-normal volume might indicate an emotional intensity associated with the statements. These might be more important in helping readers understand the results than less emotional statements.

Intercoder Agreement

When possible, it is desirable to have two or more researchers code the data (as in *open coding* described above under grounded theory). It is customary to have them consult with each other to determine the general approach (e.g., grounded theory, as described above) as well as the specific techniques that will be employed (e.g., enumeration, as described above). Having made these determinations, the researchers typically begin by working independently (i.e., working without consulting with each other) in coding the data. Then, they consult with each other to determine the extent to which their codes and interpretations are in agreement. If the researchers largely agree, this is evidence of the dependability of the results. Large areas of disagreement indicate that the data are subject to more than one good interpretation. The researchers might then work together to strive to reach a consensus on the results, which is an important feature of Consensual Qualitative Research described earlier. In the Results section of a research report, the extent to which there was initial agreement and the extent to which the researchers were able to arrive at a consensus should be discussed.

Diagramming

Having performed the analysis, qualitative researchers often diagram the results. This is done by placing the *core concept* (an overarching concept identified in the data analysis) in a box at the top and showing the array of related categories below it. Figure 8.4.1 shows an example for a hypothetical study of misbehavior in a first-grade classroom.

For instructional purposes, the drawing in Figure 8.4.1 was deliberately kept simple. When diagramming real data, as many boxes should be used as are needed to show the complete results. In addition to the types of boxes shown above, others could include boxes for (1) Intervening Conditions (such as reasons why some parents are more involved than others), (2) Associational (such as times of day when misbehavior occurs most often), and (3) Implications (such as training to make teachers more aware of social influences on misbehavior).

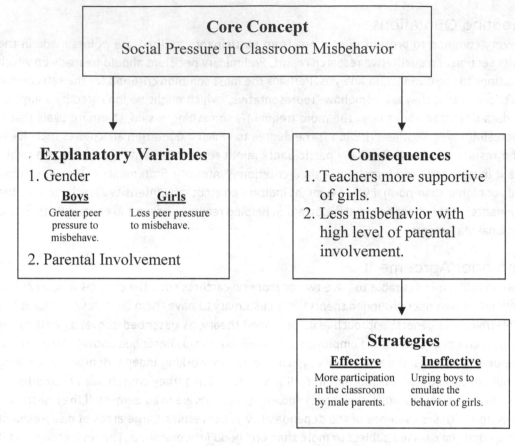

FIGURE 8.4.1   Diagram of the Results of a Hypothetical Qualitative Study

Peer Debriefing

Peer debriefing consists of having a qualified researcher who is not directly involved in the data collection or the analysis of the results consult with the researcher. This outsider should consider whether the theory and hypotheses emerging from the data are reasonable in light of how the data were collected and the contents of the transcripts of the interviews as well as any other materials, such as the researchers' memos. For a thesis or dissertation, one or more of the committee members might help with this activity. For those conducting a term project, if the instructor has too many students in a class, using another student for peer debriefing might be useful even though the student is not an experienced researcher.

Auditing

To use auditing, a researcher must keep detailed accounts of how the data were collected and the thought processes used while analyzing the data. Some of these accounts might be in the form of memos resulting from the process of "memo writing," mentioned earlier in this chapter. In preparation for auditing, journals, which are more extensive records of the research process than memos, might also be kept. Keeping accurate records as well as preserving the original raw data is known as creating an *audit trail*.

Auditing is similar to peer debriefing in that a qualified outsider is used for the activity. However, in peer debriefing, the outsider acts more as a consultant who is assisting the researcher. In auditing, the auditor is more like an outside financial auditor for a corporation. The auditor's role is not to participate in the research but to examine it near the end in the hope that he or she will be able to certify the appropriateness of the research methods and interpretations of the results.

Note that the use of auditing is described in Example 8.4.1 near the beginning of this chapter.

Member Checks

In "member checks," the term "member" refers to participants. When conducting member checks, participants are asked to meet again with the researcher to review the data and results. For instance, they can be asked to verify the accuracy of the transcriptions of the interviews, and they can be asked to comment on the adequacy of the interpretations of the data. When participants disagree with certain interpretations, the researcher should explore how they might be reformulated to take into account the participants' views.

Conducting thorough member checks can be quite time-consuming. As a consequence, qualitative researchers sometimes ask only a sample of the original participants to participate in this activity.

Identifying the Range of Responses

Even when all or almost all respondents provide similar accounts in terms of content, their responses can range in emotional tone (e.g., from mild to strong) as well as in frequency (e.g., an incident that frequently happened to some participants but seldom happened to others). Noting the range of responses when analyzing the data can assist in writing up the results, as illustrated in Example 8.4.3.

> **Example 8.4.3**
> *A sample statement noting the range of emotional responses*
>
> Among the subgroup that reported having cold, distant fathers, the emotional language used in describing their relationships with their fathers ranged from mild (such as "I was glad when he would spend a Sunday away from home") to very strong (such as "I felt so unloved that I hated to be near him").

Discrepant Case Analysis

During data analysis, it is important to note and consider discrepant cases. For instance, if almost all those who had cold, distant fathers report negative attitudes toward their fathers but a few are positive, those with the positive attitudes should be noted as discrepant cases. Researchers should consider whether there are other ways that might explain the discrepancy in which the minority differs from the majority. For instance, did the discrepant cases have fathers who were absent most of the time, did they have fathers who became more emotionally warm later in life, and so on. If the original data do not answer these types of questions, it might be useful to ask some of the discrepant cases to return for another interview.

Conclusion

This chapter presented information specific to the analysis of quantitative and qualitative data. The author carefully pointed out that "while statistical analysis is much more closely associated with quantitative research than qualitative research, both qualitative and quantitative researchers often use descriptive statistics to describe demographic data (i.e., background data) such as data on age, income, and educational status of participants in their research." The application exercise at the end of this chapter encourages the reader to think about which data analysis strategy/strategies may be used to analyze the data that have been collected or that the reader is proposing to collect. Will your data analysis plan include the analysis of qualitative data, quantitative data, or both, and what type of data analysis will your study require?

Chapter 8 Reflection Questions

1. What are descriptive statistics? When are they used?
2. What are correlational statistics? When are they used?
3. What are inferential statistics? When are they used?
4. What methods are used to analyze qualitative data? How do these methods differ from quantitative data analysis?

Executing the Research

Chapter 8 Exercise: Analyze the Data (or Consider How the Data Should Be Analyzed)

Reflect on the source of data best suited to answer your research question or hypothesis (question 2 in chapter 7's exercise).

1. Restate your research question or hypothesis.
2. Identify your variables. How will they be operationalized?
3. What is your data source? Be specific.
4. Based on the nature of this data and the variable(s) identified (qualitative, quantitative, or combination of both), what type of data analysis will your study require? Why?
5. Analyze the data. Use this data to answer your research question(s) or hypothesis.

Writing the Research Report

Introduction

Welcome to the final chapter! The selection for this chapter summarizes the process of writing research reports, provides guidance on preparing to write, and introduces the structure of the chapters and content that should be included within each section of the report: (1) introduction and statement of hypothesis or research question, (2) literature review, (3) methodology, (4) findings/results, and (5) discussion. The authors stress that writing a research report should not commence once the research has been completed but should begin at the start of the research process.

Writing Research Reports

Gerald J. Bayens and Cliff Roberson

Introduction

For some, the most difficult task involved in research is writing the report. One reason is because writing is time consuming. It entails the preparation of an initial draft, revising and editing, and then revising again. Another reason is that a researcher's writings must typically conform to a specific manuscript format associated with the field of study. This especially applies to students in academic institutions, and such requirements may create problems for a novice researcher who possesses little or no experience in writing an objective research report.

The difficulties associated with writing the research report can be eased if the researcher views report writing as a process that starts when the researcher begins generating ideas and simply makes notes. These notes evolve into outlines and eventually into a rough draft of the report. Initially, it is common to focus on the introduction, literature, and methodology chapters. After data collection has been completed, it is time for the remaining results and discussion chapters to be written. This chapter briefly explores the process of writing a research report and discusses some of the more important issues associated with this endeavor. We provide several guidelines for writing a research report and take a close look at each of its sections.

When to Begin Writing

The writing of the research report starts at the beginning of the research process. That is, the writing starts when the researcher begins making notes about the research study. The notes will serve as the foundation for the actual report. Typically, a researcher's first notes pertain to research ideas and possible hypotheses, potential resource materials for the literature review, and possible methodological approaches. This is particularly true if the researcher plans to write a **research prospectus** (the preliminary first half of a research report that includes the introduction, literature review, and methodology chapters). Opportunities to make notes and prepare draft writings occur throughout a research study as a researcher performs related tasks. Consider the following tasks relating to the composition of a research prospectus:

- When contemplating a title for the study, several titles can be proposed and discussed with fellow researchers or an academic supervisor.
- When a researcher begins gathering previous research documents related to the subject under study, it is a good idea to begin writing a preliminary draft of the literature review, which is commonly the second chapter of a research report. Likewise, an annotated bibliography can be started for later use on a reference list.
- When research is to be grounded on theory, it is important to formulate theoretical constructs. The need for theory-generating or theory-testing research to investigate a certain physical, psychological, or social problem is commonly part of the introductory chapter.
- When conceptual definitions are to be specified in a report, the researcher should keep account of the definitions found in the literature review. While it is acceptable to cite definitions previously offered by another researcher, it may be more appropriate to write definitions that better represent the general concepts of the study.
- When deciding on a methodology, a researcher should begin drafting ideas about sample size, design, procedures, and data analysis plans to be included in the methods chapter. It is likely that the methodology will be modified later because of necessary adjustments to the original data collection plans.

Preparatory Tips

The most successful researchers develop well-thought-out plans before they start writing. They prepare in advance and have a sense of what challenges may lie ahead. The following suggestions concern preparation for writing a research report:

- Think about the research topic and purpose. To prepare to write, review the topic statement and consider the purpose of the research.
- Identify your audience and consider how that will affect your paper. Never assume that the audience has prior knowledge of the topic. Know what style and tone of writing are required—informal, scholarly, first-person reporting, or dramatized.
- Review a copy of a "model" research report. Read other research reports that have been accepted to see how they were organized.

- Establish a process and stay focused. Writing the paper is the ultimate goal, but several tasks must be completed before the end product can be written. If you focus too quickly on what the results may show or the possible implications of your research, you may miss some of the important details that should have been covered earlier in the study.
- Use time management skills. Make good use of your time by establishing a schedule for your research writing and determine how much you will write. We suggest producing three to five rough draft pages during each writing session. After you establish a schedule of writing sessions, try to adhere to it.
- Designate a proofreader. Identify fellow researchers, academic supervisors, or others to read your preliminary writings and offer their reactions and ideas. Another person often has a fresh perspective and may say something that triggers new ideas. Furthermore, it is often difficult to identify corrections needed to one's own paper.

Components of Report

The customary sections of a research document include:

1. An introduction to the research problem
2. A thorough review of the existing literature on the subject
3. The methodological approach for collection and analyses of the data
4. Disclosure of the findings
5. Discussion of the findings
6. References

We discuss each of these sections as separate and distinct chapters of the research report.

Chapter 1: Introduction and Statement of Hypothesis
Introduction

The main purpose of the **introduction** is to provide an overview of the research problem or questions under inquiry. The format and content of the introduction depend upon a number of variables including the style of the discipline and the expectations of your academic supervisor. There are guidelines to keep in mind, however, when composing the initial chapter. In general, your introduction should:

- Catch the attention of your readers while introducing the topic.
- Provide relevant context for your topic and establish its importance.
- Clearly state the purpose or aim of the research.
- Provide conceptual definitions as necessary.
- Provide the theoretical context of the study.
- State the hypotheses or research questions.

Examine the following excerpts taken from the introduction sections of several research reports. Note how these paragraphs fulfill one or more of the general guidelines listed above.

Perhaps no problem in America is more serious than the unequal treatment of racial and ethnic groups by the institutions responsible for administering justice. Two of the professed values of the American judicial system are equal protection and fundamental fairness of the law; they may represent the central aim of our entire judicial system. With respect to these values, however, the professed and the operational have differed seriously at times.[1]

A number of different theories have been developed that attempt to explain the increased level of crime in society. Two of these theoretical perspectives—routine activities and social disorganization—tend to overlap and complement one another in their explanation of crime causation. The present study tests some of the basic premises of these two theories.[2]

In the abundant literature on occupational or workplace stress, various definitions and conceptualizations of stress have been used. Sometimes stress refers to the sources (i.e., stressors), though stress (or strain) more usually is viewed as an inner state reflected by anxiety or frustration, or as a response characterized by behaviors such as yelling or adrenaline flow (Ellison and Genz, 1983). In this paper, the sources of stress are called "causes" or "stressors." We indicate problematic occupational stress by self-reports that the informant is in an emotional state of stress, experiencing consequences unfavorable for physical or emotional wellbeing.[3]

Measuring the amount of force or the frequency with which police use either reasonable or excessive force is not the focus of this study. Nor is it the purpose of this study to examine when officers should use deadly force. Instead, by focusing on the various kinds of situations that officers face every day, this study seeks to develop insight into two major components that influence use of force outcomes. The first component concerns officers' perceptions of the threat level or risk inherent in a police-citizen encounter to either the respondent or others in the immediate area. The second component is to understand more fully how officers respond given the totality of the situation. The study also seeks to explain factors that contribute to variations in officers' collective responses concerning when and how much force is appropriate. Thus, this effort seeks to explain the factors that officers believe contribute to their estimation of the dangers inherent in police-citizen encounters.[4]

Statement of Hypothesis

A well-written **statement of hypothesis**, usually expressed in one sentence, is one of the most important sentences in the introduction. It states the position of the researcher, reflecting the full scope of a phenomenon that the researcher will go about proving or disproving.

When writing a hypothesis, be sure that it is not too broad to be defended within the scope of your paper. The hypothesis should be as specific as possible and devoid of confusing language. Also, a hypothesis should indicate what will actually be studied, not the value judgments of the researcher. A simple statement of the hypothesis includes the two variables under study and the type of relationship the researcher expects to demonstrate. If a report will cover more than one hypothesis, both should be stated clearly and distinctly.

In regard to where the hypothesis appears in the research report, it may initially emerge toward the end of the introduction chapter. However, it is important to restate the hypothesis in a paragraph toward the end of the literature review chapter. Doing so connects the statement of the hypothesis to the next (methodology) chapter that establishes the approach used to test the hypothesis. The following abstracts contain well-written statements of hypotheses. Note that the final example states two hypotheses.

> This study used quantitative data from Japan and the United States to test the hypothesis that the Japanese public has higher confidence in their police than does the American public.[5]
>
> The authors tested the hypothesis that greater enforcement of existing laws against carrying concealed weapons would reduce firearms violence in Kansas City, Missouri.[6]
>
> Using cost estimates for the homicide rate in a number of cities, this study tests the hypothesis that the war on illicit drugs has diverted police resources from other law enforcement activities, resulting in a higher rate of violent crimes than would otherwise have been the case.[7]
>
> This study tested the hypothesis that the presence of guns in the home, the type of gun, and the method of gun storage are associated with risk for adolescent suicide.[8]
>
> This study of gender differences in police physical abilities tested two hypotheses: (1) female applicants would fail the physical ability test more often than male applicants, and (2) the physical ability selection test administered by the police agency would not measure critical tasks.[9]

Chapter 2: Literature Review

Before addressing several issues relating to writing the literature review, it is important to reiterate that the **literature review** is the starting point for many research projects. During or after the development of a research topic, the researcher initiates a literature review to obtain a sense of the entire area of study. The review helps the researcher appreciate the previous contributions of others in the field, thereby identifying the major researchers in the discipline, and shows how other researchers present their studies and address the strengths, weaknesses, and significant contributions of previous studies. The key to writing a good literature review is to read books, periodicals, and other documents, and then isolate the materials that are most relevant to your area of study. While masses of literature may be relevant to your research, you must focus on the classics and contemporary literature directly linked to your subject.

Perhaps the best way to begin is to develop an outline of what is to be accomplished. First, consider the classics—historical research that established the framework for a particular area of study. One of the best ways to identify a classic is to note how many times certain studies are cited in other researchers' literature reviews. Consider how these historical research efforts connect to your own research and note the similarities with regard to theoretical framework, research agenda, and problem orientation. Next, organize all other relevant documents and specifically identify contemporary research documents that are most closely aligned to your own work because you will probably want to show trends and themes in the literature. Noting the contemporary literature last can be an excellent way of building up to your own study and establishing a need for such research. Typically, a literature review is presented chronologically or thematically. Next, identify the various ways that your study differs from the previous research. This necessarily means that you have identified the variables to be studied and established a research methodology. Finally, develop a standard method to summarize the previous research. At a minimum, the research problem, methodology, and findings of each study should be detailed.

When writing the literature review, your task is to educate readers on the extant literature relevant to your research question. It may be helpful to visualize this chapter in terms of a spiral or a coil. The outer edge of the spiral represents the foundational literature (Figure 9.1.1) generally associated to your topic. As you follow the coil inward toward the center, you begin to refine your review to include prior study areas more closely related to your topic. The center of the spiral addresses the area that contains your particular research question. The following sources can provide more information about literature reviews:

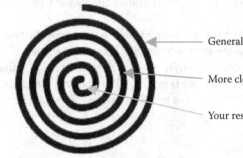

FIGURE 9.1.1 Spiral Concept of Literature Review.

- www.writing.utoronto.ca/advice/specific-types-of-writing/literature-review
- The literature review: a few tips on conducting it:
  - https://writingcenter.unc.edu/tips-and-tools/literature-reviews/
- American Psychological Association literature review samples

Chapter 3: Methodology

The **methodology** chapter gives a detailed explanation of the methods used to collect and analyze the data. It includes a description of the research environment, sampling design, procedures, and data analysis plan. The intent is to provide readers with enough detail to replicate the research.

Research Environment

Providing a background of the research location can be an important initial subsection of the methodology chapter. It is used primarily as a means of describing the research environment. It is especially important to provide background information if it has direct relevance to the nature of the research. The following example clearly describes the background and setting:

This research was conducted at a Midwest county adult detention facility, which made the transition from a traditional linear facility to a podular, direct supervision one. In 1965 the county built a 100-bed traditional linear jail and hired a jail staff of 28. In 1974 jail inmates filed a class action lawsuit in federal court alleging Eighth Amendment violations. As a result, a 220-bed podular direct supervision jail opened in March 1988 with a staff complement of 50, which included transfer of all 28 staff from the traditional jail. New staff had a minimum of 6 months' experience in the traditional jail before the facility was closed and all inmates and staff were transferred.[10]

Design

This subsection specifies the type of study conducted and describes the instrumentation (i.e., experimental design, survey questionnaires, records, etc.) used in the data collection effort. The following excerpt describes a research design:

> This exploratory study seeks to determine whether demographic characteristics explain variations in levels of occupational identification. Relationships between race, age, length of service, military experience, and educational attainment and occupational identification and levels of socialization among personnel in small or medium-sized departments are evaluated. The departmental characteristics, size, and population density were measured as to their impact on occupational identification and levels of socialization.
>
> A self-administered questionnaire was distributed to four sessions of a regional police academy. The underlying assumption guiding the research suggests that over-identification with an occupational subculture may not be an occupational universal, but may be mediated by various background characteristics. Levels of identification will be determined from responses to attitudinal items on the survey.
>
> The survey instrument is a modification of several empirically tested measures. The level of socialization measure is a modification of Chao, O'Leary-Kelly, Walz, Klein, and Gardner's (1994) organizational socializations scale. This scale evaluates items of organizational politics and organizational culture. For purposes of this study, factors that were task related were removed. This modification was necessary since original measures of task efficiency directed to specific tasks were not consistent or immediately identifiable to organizational members. Furthermore, in some instances, generic references were replaced by occupational-specific terminology.
>
> The survey consists of 37 questions in three areas: socialization levels, feelings of isolation, and organizational solidarity. The demographic variables measured are age, race, gender, military experience, educational level, and past law enforcement experience. Two departmental variables, department size and community population, are included. A total of eight independent variables are measured. On the perceptual section of the questionnaire, responses were scaled on a Likert scale. In the demographic section of the questionnaire, individuals were given open-ended questions that after review were categorized by the researcher.[11]

Sampling

This subsection provides information about study subjects; for example, details about the number of cases sampled and how individuals were chosen. It also describes response rates and other factors that set the limits on generalizability of the sample data.

Procedures

This subsection, often combined with sampling information, summarizes the procedures followed during the research. The aim is to disclose all steps taken to gather data. The following excerpt combines descriptions of sampling and procedures:

> The data for this study were collected in spring 1994 via a telephone survey of households in Knox County, Tennessee, which is home to the city of Knoxville and the University of Tennessee. The questionnaire was based on the instrument used in the 1990 FVS study (Boyle, 1992). The telephone interviews were conducted by experienced interviewers at the University of Tennessee's Social Science Research Institute using computer-assisted telephone interviewing software.
>
> The samples were drawn using random digit dialing. Of the 835 persons contacted, 400 agreed to be interviewed for an overall response rate of 48%. Although the response rate is slightly lower than desired for a telephone survey, we have two reasons for believing that it did not adversely affect the validity of our findings. First, our results replicate similar studies by Titus et al. (1995) and Boyle (1992) in that we found nearly identical victimization rates and similar patterns of correlation with demographic variables. Second, our sample is representative of the population from which it was drawn.[12]

Data Analysis

In the final subsection of the methodology chapter, the researcher explains processing of data after collection. Measures of qualitative data relate to the specific content analysis techniques used. When the data collected is quantitative, descriptive and inferential measures used are explained. The following is an example of a data analysis subsection:

> We conducted two separate analyses to assess the impact of gang membership on charging and sentencing decisions. First, we estimated logistic regression models to determine the net impact of gang membership on each of these decisions after controlling for other offender and offense attributes. Second, we estimated separate logistic models for gang and non-gang cases to evaluate whether offense and offender characteristics were considered equally important in both types of cases. We conducted formal tests of the interactive models' improvement of fit over a main effects model to assess whether estimating separate models for gang and non-gang cases was the more appropriate specification.[13]

Chapter 4: Findings or Results

After the methodology has been explained and the data analyzed, the **findings** may be disclosed. This chapter may also be called **results**; some researchers may prefer to combine the results and discussion sections within in one chapter.

Typically, the chapter on findings begins with descriptive statistics. Data are summarized in frequency distributions, measures of central tendency, measures of variability, and correlations. Tables and figures are used to present results visually. Often, most of the text explains what the visual presentations show. Next, the results of inferential statistical tests are presented. Again, narrative is used to explain visual displays such as correlations, matrices, diagrams, and other illustrations. The text shows how numerical values were derived and what they indicate. Listed below are suggestions for writing the findings chapter. These points apply when the findings are written as a unique chapter apart from the discussion chapter.

- This chapter is specific and dedicated to the presentation of the findings of the research. Do not add personal comments or value judgments, and do not interpret the results.
- Provide all results in this section. The aim of the text is to disclose what the data show.
- When applicable, the findings should be presented logically, based on the order of inquiry. Be consistent by organizing the data in a structured way that reflects the data collection effort.
- All visual presentations such as tables and figures should be of high quality and easy to understand.
- Always describe and explain the data in the tables and figures in the narrative text.
- Set up the discussion chapter by providing appropriate comments that lead to it.

Chapter 5: Discussion

The **discussion** chapter is of particular importance because that is where the findings are interpreted. The researcher's primary task is to explain the data results. Issues regarding the usefulness and limitations of the research should be addressed. Typically, the chapter begins with a general statement of the results. Often, this statement reflects the most significant findings. Next, it is common to comment on whether the results were anticipated or unexpected and why. Much of the text should contain a discussion of the relationship between the findings and the aim of the research and indicate whether the findings can be generalized. Also, comparisons should be drawn with the results of previous studies. Finally, a conclusion should address the practical implications of the study and make recommendations and suggestions for further research.

Reference Section

This section lists all documents used as source materials in the report. The main purpose of the **reference list** is to give credit where credit is due and draw a clear line between your work and that of other scholars. The list should provide the information necessary for a reader to identify and retrieve each source. The specific format for documenting source on a reference list varies, depending on the academic field and your academic supervisor's preference.

Every academic discipline has specific rules about citing sources and the rules must be followed precisely. Style manuals such as the *Publication Manual of the American Psychological Association* explain how to properly cite periodicals, books, technical reports, doctoral dissertations, electronic media, and all other types of source materials. In social science, the most common style manuals are the *Publication Manual of the American Psychological Association*,[14] Goehlert's *Political Science Research Guide*,[15] the Sociology Writing Group's *A Guide to Writing Sociology Papers*,[16] and Sternberg's *Writing the Sociology Paper*.[17]

Abstract

The final segment is the **abstract**. Although this section is presented before the introduction, it is written last. The reason is that its purpose is to provide a brief, comprehensive synopsis of the full report. It allows readers to quickly understand the research problem, the methodological approach used to collect the data, the findings, and the conclusions and implications. The length of the abstract varies according to style manuals; it is typically no longer than 300 words.

Summary

- The writing task may be made easier if it is viewed as a process that begins with making notes about your research ideas. These notes provide an important foundation for what will be written in the formal document, especially pertaining to the research prospectus that encompasses the introduction, literature review, and methodology sections.
- The introduction sets up the rest of the report. It introduces readers to the study by explaining the research problem and why an investigation of the problem is important.
- The purpose of the literature review is to cite research that has been previously conducted in the area of study. In general, the review should include pertinent research published in journals, books, monographs, etc. It is important to stress that a review of the literature does not necessarily mean an exhaustive report of every study ever performed, but includes key studies that are directly related to the problem under investigation.
- The methodology chapter gives a clear and accurate explanation of the methods used to collect and analyze the data. Subheadings in the methods section include research environment, design, sample, procedures, and data analysis.
- The fourth section is the findings or results chapter that presents and describes the results of the data collection effort as they relate to the testing of the hypothesis. Tables and figures can be used to augment the narrative of results. Both descriptive and inferential statistical analysis test results are presented.
- The final chapter discusses the major findings. Comparisons may be drawn between the results of the study and the study findings from related research. Typically, a summary is provided that includes the researcher's recommendations for future research.
- A final component of the research report is the reference list that cites all documents used as source materials in the research report. The specific form for documenting a source on a reference list varies, depending on the academic field or the preference of the academic supervisor.

Endnotes

1   Adapted from P. E. Secret and J. B. Johnson. The effect of race on juvenile justice decision-making in Nebraska: detention, adjudication, and disposition, 1988–1993. *Justice Quarterly* 14: 445–478, 1997.

2   L. J. Moriarty. and J. E. Williams. Examining the relationship between routine activities theory and social disorganization: an analysis of property crime victimization. *American Journal of Criminal Justice* 21: 43–59, 1996.

3   Adapted from R. N. Haan and M. Morash. Gender, race, and strategies of coping with occupational stress in policing. *Justice Quarterly* 16: 303–336, 1999.

4   Adapted from S. T. Holmes, K. M. Reynolds, R. M. Holmes et al. Individual and situational determinants of police force: an examination of threat presentation. *American Journal of Criminal Justice* 23: 83–106, 1998.

5   L. Cao, S. Stack, and Y. Sun, Public attitudes toward the police: a comparative study between Japan and America. *Journal of Criminal Justice* 26: 279–289, 1998.

6   L. W. Sherman and D. P. Rogan. Effects of gun seizures on gun violence: hot spots patrol in Kansas City. *Justice Quarterly* 12: 679–693, 1995.

7   H. J. Brumm and D. O. Cloninger. Drug war and the homicide rate: a direct correlation? *Cato Journal* 14: 509–517, 1995.

8   D. A. Brent., J. A. Perper, C. J. Allman et al. Presence and accessibility of firearms in the homes of adolescent suicides: a case control study. *JAMA* 266: 2989–2995, 1991.

9   M. L. Birzer and D. E. Craig. Gender differences in police physical ability test performance. *American Journal of Police* 15: 93–108, 1993.

10   G. J. Bayens, J. J. Williams, and J. O. Smykla. Jail type makes a difference: evaluating the transition from a traditional to a podular, direct supervision jail across ten years. *American Jails* 11: 32–36, 1997.

11   Adapted from M. T. Britz. The police subculture and occupational socialization: exploring individual and demographic characteristics. *American Journal of Criminal Justice* 21: 127–146, 1997.

12   J. Van Wyk and M. L. Benson. Fraud victimization: risky business or just bad luck? *American Journal of Criminal Justice* 21: 163–179, 1997.

13   Adapted from T. D. Miethe and R. C. McCorkle. Gang membership and criminal processing: a test of the "master status" concept. *Justice Quarterly* 14: 407–427, 1997.

14   *Publication Manual of the American Psychological Association*, 6th ed. Washington: American Psychological Association, 2010.

15   R. U. Goehlert. *Political Science Research Guide*. Monticello, IL: Vance Bibliographies, 1982.

16   Sociology Writing Group. *A Guide to Writing Sociology Papers*. New York: St. Martin's Press, 1986.

17   R. J. Sternberg. *Writing the Psychology Paper*. Woodbury, NJ: Barron's, 1977.

Conclusion

This chapter provided guidance on how to assemble the final research proposal or report. The articles included in this book and the exercises at the end of each chapter were designed to encourage the reader to begin writing very early on in the research process. Readers who wish to complete a research proposal or prospectus should complete chapters 1–3 and include a references section. Those who execute this research should complete all chapters and include an abstract and references section in the final research report.

Chapter 9 Reflection Questions

1. Ideally, when should a researcher begin writing a research report?
2. What are the components of a research report? List and briefly describe the content that should be included in each.
3. What is an abstract? Should this be written first or last? Why?

Writing Your Research Proposal or Paper

Chapter 9 Exercise: Communicate the Findings; Ask Another Question

Using the subheadings presented in chapter 9, organize the work you have completed in the exercises at the end of each chapter. You may also refer to the helpful links provided to assist you with the process of writing your research. APA style is recommended for citing references.

https://libguides.usc.edu/writingguide

https://owl.purdue.edu/owl/general_writing/common_writing_assignments/research_papers/index.html

https://owl.purdue.edu/owl/research_and_citation/apa_style/apa_style_introduction.html

Required Subheadings:

Abstract*

Chapter 1: Introduction and Statement of Hypothesis or Research Question

Chapter 2: Literature Review

Chapter 3: Methodology

Chapter 4: Findings or Results*

Chapter 5: Discussion* (Be sure to ask another research question as you wrap this section up!)

References

Include only if you executed/carried out the research project.

CONCLUSION

This text provided carefully selected readings and introductory materials designed to illustrate the value of research, acquaint readers with understanding the research process, and assist with identifying an individual area of research interest within the fields of criminology and criminal justice (or related social science fields). Readers were invited to apply the information presented in each chapter to an area of individual professional interest, develop a research question or hypothesis, and design a comprehensive research proposal, which, if carried out, may produce data to answer the question and/or test the hypothesis posed. To achieve this purpose, each chapter provided an introduction to key terms and concepts, summary of key takeaways, postreading reflection questions, and exercises designed to encourage the application of materials to an individual area of research interest. These exercises were designed to collectively facilitate the completion of a research proposal (chapters 1–6), and depending on the goals and objectives for the use of this book, provide introductory guidance to support the execution of a research project (chapters 7–9). It is the author's hope that you were able to develop a research question and proposal that relates to a topic you are passionate about.

The primary areas of focus for this book are summarized in the Building Your Research Proposal/Project Checklist on page xii. It is important to remember that engaging in research is a step-by-step process that takes time and requires many considerations. No matter what your career goals may be, never forget the value of using data to inform decisions in your agency or organization. Collaborative partnerships are reciprocally beneficial for practitioners/agencies and researchers and are underexplored or underutilized in many jurisdictions. If you are a professional/practitioner do not be afraid to reach out to researchers at local universities to assist you with evaluating programmatic efforts within your organization. As an academic researcher, contact local agencies/organizations to ask if you can assist with evaluative efforts or discuss potential partnerships.

The future of research in many fields, including criminology, victimology, and criminal justice, will continue to explore the use and applications of various types of AI and related technologies. Although these advances hold promise for informing or assisting agency efforts and expediting the analysis of large amounts of data, many ethical issues and concerns abound. It is vital that individuals who work in these fields are familiar with and carefully consider the related ethical concerns before committing to the use of these platforms. Please do not forget these lessons as the agency you work for considers the use of new technologies.

It is my hope that this text helped to demystify the research process. I want to challenge you to use the information and skills you gained to inform decision making, personally and professionally. Each time you consider a new research question or project, be reminded that you should focus on the stairs (each individual part of the process) in front of you, not the entire staircase!

CPSIA information can be obtained
at www.ICGtesting.com
Printed in the USA
LVHW061509101122
732768LV00003B/6